It Was YOU, All Along

All Along

An easy to understand guide on how
to create the reality you desire!

Gary Spinell

Outskirts Press, Inc.
Denver, Colorado

ACKNOWLEDGEMENT

This book is for my Parents. For my Mother, whose inner strength is a model for us all. Her ability to deal with adversity, by believing something better was coming, was instilled in her children and sustained us even when we stumbled and fell. For my Dad, who, during his life, demonstrated a tireless effort and contribution to our family through his caring and taught me compassion and consideration for others. His strict belief in getting your work done before you play taught me discipline, which has kept me focused. I also want to thank my former boss and friend, Jim, who showed me how to move down the spiritual path of life and introduced me to Dr. Phil McGraw in a seminar in 1986.

Dr. Phil's teachings helped me continue on my path and journey. Thanks to Lori, a friend, who pushed me to examine myself from a different perspective. To Alma who provided a unique editing perspective. To Carol through her patience and persistence made me a better writer.

To my sons, Christopher and Joshua, who remind me every day how wonderful it is to be a father. Lastly, a special thanks to my wife, Michelle, who fills my life with love, happiness and joy more than she knows, and for her special gift to me of letting me be me.

TABLE OF CONTENTS

INTRODUCTION

"Success is neither magical nor mysterious. Success is the natural consequence of consistently applying the basic fundamentals."
— Jim Rohn, business philosopher

Have you ever wondered why some days everything you planned is executed smoothly, with flawless perfection, and yet on other days you encounter incredible resistance or delay? Why is it you experience some kind of interference no matter how carefully you planned to control the dynamic forces of life? Have you ever wondered why the project you were working on, the new challenge in your life or simply the drive to work, was experienced as if the planets aligned and all the pieces intertwined effortlessly together to accomplish your goal? Conversely, why do you experience days when despite your best efforts, you could swear that everyone and every Universal law conspires against you? Why do you feel these Universal laws prevent you from accomplishing even the first step of your goal?

Solving this riddle has fascinated me most of my life. For years it amazed me how some days I was on a roll, and on other days I should have just stayed in bed. Could it be coincidence that some days all of the events flowed magically in unison, as if I were conducting an orchestra? Was it just bad luck when nothing I managed came together, as if to suggest there is no connection to God or the Universe at all? Could it be that something I did or thought or believed somehow had an effect on what occurred in my life? Sometimes I felt so in sync with the flow of my life, and on other occasions I felt totally at the mercy of chance and those around me. It was as if I were barely hanging on for dear life on the roller coaster of life.

Over the course of my 50-plus years I have had the opportunity to not only do extensive self-examination of my actions, beliefs, feelings, and thoughts, but also to spend countless hours analyzing and evaluating how and why some people achieve success and how others struggle day after day. Deep down I believed there was more to success than working hard and being in the right place at the right time. Somehow I knew I had played a key role in the results I obtained and that I was not a mere puppet in the theater of my life. I intuitively knew that spiritual and Universal laws were also involved.

However, no matter how many books I read, no matter how many places I searched, the answers to these questions eluded me. At times I discovered partial answers, yet nowhere could I find how all of these pieces fit together. No one could provide me all of the key ingredients to create the life I desired, which included great success and an abundance of wealth, happiness and health. I was determined to find the answers.

My comprehensive journey began over twenty-five years ago; although, when looking back, I can see its roots in my childhood. I do not possess any special gifts or powers. At best, I felt the same hunger most all of us feel: the hunger to understand how life works, hoping to find internal peace and happiness, and be content with myself as a person, father and husband.

All of my life I believed there must be a roadmap or some guidelines on how all of these rules and laws, both in our society and the spiritual realm combine to allow us to experience the highest level of abundance in human form. I believed that if God created us and put us on this planet to encounter every life situation imaginable, God must be willing not only to give us the rules and laws of the Universe, but to clearly explain them now, instead of having to wait until passing on to understand the great mysteries of life. I wanted to know how each of us can tap into these dynamic forces and use these rules and laws to create the reality we so greatly desire.

As a child growing up in a Catholic Church, there were rules. (Definitely rules, just not the kind that I was looking for, and not all of them made sense.) There were also laws (it didn't always appear that these came from God, but, I suspected, from people). Something was missing, as the rules and laws of the Church left with me with too many questions, and any answers provided by those who were purported to be experts simply lacked depth. All I could see were millions of people going to church each week seeking answers and inner peace, yet struggling all week because the answers they were given weren't working for them. I also was not satisfied with the common refrain often heard when no one can explain life's mysteries: *"There are some things you won't understand in your life until you die and talk with God."* In other words, I asked, were we to stumble through life denied valuable information? Was it because it was unknown or because it was being withheld from people seeking answers? I couldn't help but ask, *"What were so many people missing?"*

I believed God was in my life, watching over me, yet I continually wondered exactly what role God played in my life. Quite evidently, there was a lot more to it than just being "good to your fellow man." I grew disappointed that being "good" and playing by the rules was not enough to succeed. When my plans didn't succeed I thought I must be doing something wrong or I was being punished. I wondered if the deciding factor in who obtained success was simply a matter of chance or something determined at birth. At times I considered that maybe it was not my destiny or fate to be successful.

The "logic" instilled in me by religion and my upbringing left me uncomfortable. Why would God allow others to succeed and let me fail miserably? I did not believe God favored one person over another. Most people believe we are all God's children. As a father I want both of my children to succeed. It makes sense then that God, as our spiritual Father, desires all of us to succeed. Any favoritism shown on God's part is inconsistent with our idea of a loving, caring God.

That old familiar line kept repeating in my head: *"God has reasons and you may never know them."* The more I heard that refrain, the more I believed I had been conned into accepting this reasoning because no one really had any rational answers.

My analytical nature drove me to seek answers. I was fascinated by successful people and read about them, not just those in business, but people in all aspects of life: politicians, world leaders, and sports figures. These successful people not only achieved wealth, but happiness as well.

In contrast, my success took the appearance of taking two steps forward and one backward on my life's journey.

Nothing frustrated me more than having a few days where I felt "on a roll" then, just as quickly, encountered events that took me further from my goals. My car would break down or I would get sick; something would always occur to interfere with my progress. We all experience those days, those times in our lives when we believe success is within reach, only to realize that we are no closer than when we started. Still, on some level I knew I had the ability to achieve my goals and find this elusive inner peace. I wanted answers, I wanted them now, and I wanted answers no one had provided me with before now.

Two main observations influenced my next steps. First, there is an abundance of evidence showing positive attitudes and feelings generate positive results. Rarely does one see someone with a negative attitude, depressed about life, receive some great prize or achieve some magnificent goal. Second, self-confidence, and self-esteem are also important to achieving success. In my mind, these two principles are closely connected.

Both observations may be rather obvious to most people. Yet, if we know that a positive attitude and high self-esteem generate positive results, why does a large percentage of our population suffer from low self-esteem and depression? A recent report stated anti-depressants were the most prescribed drug in the United States! What are we all missing? This is the key question I pondered for years.

I was no different than others who at times lacked self-confidence and self-esteem. I was not a negative person; in fact, I was generally optimistic about my future knowing I possessed some key strengths. As most people do, I had a tendency to focus more attention on my weaknesses and lack of success. Somehow I knew that creating the life I desired required me was to gain even more self-confidence.

The next question, then, was how to progress? Was there a way to accomplish this? What needed to change?

Interestingly enough, I quickly learned that improving my self-esteem was just the beginning. Creating the life I desired required not only acquiring new beliefs and traits. It was also necessary to understand the power my beliefs had on my results.

Most of us are aware that having a positive attitude in life makes a significant difference in what comes into our lives. Have you ever noticed days when you wake up in a bad mood and everything you experience during that day appears to mirror your bad mood too? For example, you hit all the red lights as you drive to work. No matter which line at the store you get in, your lane moves the slowest. Your wait for the elevator takes longer than usual. Just the opposite happens when you start the day off in a great mood. Almost everything around you seems to click into place, as if you got plugged into some magical connection or you slipped into the express lane of the Universe. How does that happen? More importantly, how do we make those events happen again?

How does a positive attitude create positive results? It is widely known and written that we are creatures of energy. If you look at cells under a strong microscope you will see atoms in motion. We produce energy and it runs through our nervous systems. Our bodies release and absorb energy. When the positive energy we project returns to us, we enjoy the helpful value of this energy. A few kind words we spoke days earlier returns when someone holds the door open for us today as we attempt to avoid the rain. Conversely, restricting the flow of positive energy can cause physical pain. Have you ever had a massage therapist reach a place on your body where there appears to be a knot, as if the muscles are tight? Scientists have long known this to be a collection of blocked energy. Restricting the flow of energy is unnatural both inside the body and all around us. We physically, mentally and spiritually feel happier and healthier when our energy is allowed to flow freely inward and outward.

Our bodies release and project energy all around us. Energy

fields around some individuals are so strong that others can "see" what is called an "aura" surrounding these individuals. At times we can feel the energy being projected from those nearby. Have you ever been around a person who is in a great mood? When you leave them you feel invigorated. She appears to enjoy projecting energy onto you. The reverse is true when you are near someone who is depressed, angry or in a bad mood. He seems to suck the life right out of you. In reality, your energy is stolen, which is why you feel exhausted after your encounter.

Energy is all around us. Everything living and inanimate is made of energy. Energy slowed down is matter, matter in the form of everything we see and touch in our world. In both the physical and in the spiritual world energies move around the Universe and attract similar types of energies. The energy you send out is then returned to you. For example, we have all heard that what we give comes back to us. If we project positive, loving, caring energy, it returns to us perhaps not always as we planned, but always well.

Thus, we are the creators of everything that occurs in our lives. Yet, we have been taught in school or church that we have no control or power to do so in our lives. Sometimes politicians, the news and entertainment media, even some religions and various churches reinforce this belief by telling us that what happens to us is out of our control and may even be someone else's fault. We hear stories how it is not someone's fault they are poor or that someone just had some bad luck resulting in losing his job. Maybe we read a story about a woman who no matter how hard she tries ends up in a bad relationship. The message delivered to us gave us the feeling it was someone else's fault for our situation. There were so many times I worked hard to achieve a goal and did not succeed. At that time my mind could only conclude other people were causing my lack of success.

People who are truly successful in life do not buy into the idea of their fates being tied to other's actions. People who have trouble creating a life they want tend to view successful people as somewhat lucky. Luck has very little to do with it. A positive attitude, on the other hand, has everything to do with it. Knowing one can create the life one desires is the key.

So, how can we be more creative in our lives? How can we get what we want? There appear to be so many obstacles to achieve this. Wouldn't my life be better if those around me just changed to suit me? After all, if my boss (or spouse or friends or parents) would just change, my life would be perfect, right? If the government would just give me more money to help put my kids through college, or lower my utility bills or reduce the interest on my mortgage, I could finally get ahead. If my spouse would just love me the way I need her to love me, then we'd be happy forever.

I asked all those same questions. Unfortunately, that thought process has brought us to where we are now: frustrated and disappointed. Some of us give up and use eating, smoking, drinking or shopping to keep our minds off of life's disappointments. We long for prosperity, love and happiness. We long to have some say in our destiny and influence the forces that impact our lives, so we no longer feel at the mercy of fate.

With determination, a keen sense of curiosity for answers and an unyielding persistence, I persevered through continual examination of my own behaviors, thoughts and actions. Consequently, I discovered how to create an exciting new reality around me.

This book will explain how our decisions, thoughts, beliefs, actions, and words put in motion many forces that take on substance and form to create the reality we live in. The chapters ahead provide insight and direction, as well as specific rules, laws and actions which explain how you create your reality and how you create what you experience. You will learn that the events and people we encounter every day do not occur by chance or by accident. Further, you will gain insight into how the dynamic forces of key Universal laws impact your daily life. Once you are aware of these laws, you will understand how you can use these laws to create the reality you desire. You will learn how each experience and person you encounter is created specifically to help you grow, learn, and achieve success. Finally, you will learn how you cannot help but bring these people and situations into your life. This is because your daily thoughts, beliefs, and actions created their occurrence.

This book is not simply about creating monetary wealth or

abundance. For many individuals, significant wealth may not be their driving force. Many people seek inner happiness, peace, and contentment, while others seek to be the best they can be, no matter the goal. Still others desire to push the self-imposed limit of their creative powers. My story includes how to reach these goals, and more.

You may ask what expertise I have to provide you with this knowledge. I do not consider myself a psychology guru, but rather a life scientist. A scientist examines what works and what does not work. He tests a variety of variables to determine what works and learns why other variables or approaches fail. In the end, isn't that what life is all about? Haven't we all been going through our daily lives with a trial-and-error approach hoping to find what works? Through the trial-and-error of my life experiences, and by constantly examining the experiences of countless others, I have arrived at the conclusions contained in this book. My conclusions came not just from observation, but from implementing in my own life everything you will read in this book. I tested each concept, each variable, and each approach. I watched as those close to me implemented these approaches, helping to make changes in their world. Most importantly, some were able, for the first time in their lives, to understand how their reality was created and how they could change it.

There are other authors whose writing claims to teach you how to secure a million dollar salary, or some claim-to-fame, based on their approach. My experiences more closely align with those of the average person, as I consider myself an average person. Once I was able to fully understand the depth of how all of us create our realities, I was able to make significant changes in my life. Over the past twenty years I experienced a divorce and endured unemployment on several occasions. I was laid off from three different companies and left another voluntarily for personal convictions. On one occasion I was unemployed for over two years. My experiences may be very similar to yours. For example, I watched as other employees and business acquaintances advanced quickly, while I less frequently landed a promotion. Through all of this I grew increasingly frustrated at the tremendously erratic path I traveled toward abundance and success.

Enduring the process of divorce is never easy for anyone, especially with two children involved. I experienced the full range of emotions, including guilt and remorse, and I questioned my self-worth. Once I discovered the key ingredients to creating abundance and finally understood the laws of the Universe, positive changes occurred in my life. None of these changes occurred overnight. However, once I journeyed down the path of fully understanding how and why I create my own reality, I discovered I could no longer go back to my old ways. Once I perceived the Universe from a whole new perspective, I no longer had any reason to go back. In fact, each day my excitement grew in anticipation of what new and exciting possibilities awaited me on my new path.

I no longer felt out of control, but rather more like an artist with a new canvas able to create a beautiful picture of the exact reality of my world to come. I met a beautiful woman, whom I married. She is not only my best friend, but truly a partner in our marriage. We support each other and do not look for the other to fill a void or need. When we have a disagreement we work through it with a focus on what is best for both of us and not a focus on who wins the argument.

I have achieved success in my career but most importantly, landed the exact position I desired at a great company. My life is filled with much more happiness than ever as I can see how I create each experience and draw each person into my life.

This book is here to help you navigate the jungle of emotions, experiences and people we encounter each day. This book is here to help you understand that by changing the way you perceive your self and your world, both you and your world will change. The amount of change and how open you are to change is up to you. Once you understand that you hold all the cards at the table of life, you will begin to have fun, enjoy your world, and appreciate each moment and experience, no matter if it takes you up or down. Each moment is special and is not only here to help you learn, but *you created it in the first place.* More importantly, the moment was created because of what you believe about yourself, about your world and about those around you.

You will come to understand that you couldn't help but create those moments to help you learn, and you keep creating them every day because of what you believe about everything in life. These teachings are here to provide not only hope and encouragement, but to show you that *you* hold the key. Learn how to use that key to unlock the creative power you already possess. There are no tricks here. Parts of the process might be hard work, and others will be easy. But as you move through it, your reward will be more than you hoped for or could ever have imagined.

How did I create a world in which I am truly happy and have achieved and experienced what I desire? To do so, I realized I first had to look at where we all have been, and how our society has evolved over the past one hundred years. How did this concept of blaming others for our lack of success come to be so widespread in our society? Where did we get this "I want it now" attitude, with no long-term view of life? How did I finally overcome the beliefs and actions that held me back and blocked me from moving forward in creating the life I desired? I persistently searched and discovered we all have the ability. I also discovered how we lost it along the way.

These first few chapters take a long, hard look at where we have been as a society and what has changed in our philosophy about life and about each other. Be prepared for an honest, open appraisal of how slowly and subtly our beliefs evolved into a different form today; setting up a major roadblock on our path to achieving our goals. Be prepared to look at yourself and all of us, including me, in the mirror, not in a judgmental way, but honestly and with a new perspective, free of bias.

I present what our society has been in the past and what it has become. No attempt is made here to make us feel disappointed, but rather to show us the admirable traits and values held by our parents and grandparents. Examine with me how these have changed and evolved into a different set of values and approaches, which we now consider our normal way of life. This look back is extremely important to understand how our society has evolved and fostered a completely new mindset for dealing with challenges, self-esteem and success.

It is most important to state here early on in this book that what I write here is not about a get rich quick concept. Whatever goals you have in life, whatever relationships you desire, whatever role you want to play in society is yours to have. You can create wealth, but so much more is available for you to create in your world. Nothing in life is completed or accomplished without effort on your part. The only change required is to consider a different perspective on your current beliefs and actions.

It is imperative that you read Part I of this book before moving on to Part II. If you are like me (who tries to assemble items before reading the instructions), this is one time when it is necessary to go step-by-step. In Part I, learning who we are and how we got here will help you implement the suggestions for change in Part II. Evidence tells us that when we desire to make a change in our lives we must first acknowledge who and what we are. We must acknowledge the path we have taken and appreciate its tremendous impact on our current decisions and beliefs. Over the last one hundred years we have changed our perspective on hard work, responsibility, long-term thinking, decision making and the definition of success. Each chapter examines these values and attributes to show the impact each has on our mental outlook today.

The second part of this book is about opening your eyes and minds and hearts to the true reality of where we are now and fully discover we have the power to create the world we desire. It won't be a world or reality without problems, but one in which you will gain amazing insight into yourself with every event, every person, and every place you encounter. How you view your world, your experiences, your personal and professional relationships, your work environment, your material wealth, and your definition of happiness will be changed. You will discover a reality you will enjoy, full of excitement and best of all, fun.

I have been able to create my world, the one I for so long have desired; not only the world of material wealth, but a world that provides me an ability to steer my way through the experiences in life. Understanding why and how things happen makes all the difference.

Much has changed in the U.S. in our philosophy, our belief

systems, and our approach to life in general these past one hundred years. We need to start by examining where we have been in order to determine how we can begin to make tomorrow everything we want it to be, and regain what we have lost in order to ***create a new reality***.

Part I
How We Got Here

CHAPTER 1

The Way It Used to Be

"The habit of saving is itself an education.
It fosters every virtue, teaches self-denial,
cultivates the sense of order, trains to forethought,
and so broadens the mind."

— Thornton T. Munger, American scientist

L ife was much different one hundred years ago. My grandparents came over on a boat from Italy in the early 1900's. Like thousands of others who came to the United States during those years, they sought an opportunity to create a better life for themselves and their family. For most, coming to America was a chance to have steady jobs and incomes, a home and three meals a day. Safety, shelter and food were the priorities.

Thousands of immigrants from many countries came here with little money in their pockets but a great deal of optimism and spirit. All they wanted was a chance at a better life. People who came to the United States from other countries back then came knowing the struggles would not be easy. They were prepared to work hard because the concept of hard work was deeply ingrained in them. The first instinct of survival dominated their actions, as their constant focus was solely on making enough money to buy food for their family. Slowly their focus turned to saving what little money they could for the potential to own their own home. Throughout the next decade, hard work continued to dominate their world.

Most families made small progress until the world's safety and economy were thrown into turmoil by the First World War. It was a time of worry and fear for what might lie ahead. Once the war ended, along came the decade known as the *Roaring Twenties,* which was as a time to celebrate the end of the war, and forget about their troubles and the long days of work they endured. Unfortunately, the good times did not last for long. The extensive economic destruction of the Great Depression provided a one-two punch straight to the gut of most Americans. Almost everyone's dreams of prosperity were crushed. Once again the daily concern was to earn a few cents, perhaps a few dollars to buy enough food for a few days. Once again, families met the daily challenges by relying on their work-hard mentality. Consider being twenty years old when you arrived in the U.S. in 1910, only to endure a World War and the Great Depression in your next twenty years. Survival surely would be your main goal, every day.

My parents often told me and my siblings the stories of how they had little more to eat than bread covered with olive oil for dinner when they were children during the years of the Depression. Their fight for survival was admirable, as well as their determination to make a better life somehow for themselves and eventually their children.

Countless times I heard the story of how my father went to high school during the day, and then worked until midnight riding his bicycle as a messenger around town, earning a few dollars. Those few dollars were enough to make a difference in having enough food on the table for him, his sisters and his parents. Later he lost the job and his family struggled for enough food to eat. My father quickly learned to take responsibility, work hard and muster up enough determination and will to survive. In his mind, there was no time to consider being depressed or angry about the state of the economy. He didn't have time and facing his obstacles was all he knew. He was not alone. There were millions of others just like him who responded in the same way.

My father was born in 1916, and was thirteen when the Great Depression hit in 1929. I can only imagine being a teenager faced with those excruciatingly hard economic times. It is not possible for my sons to relate, submerged as they are in a world of computers, video games, cable TV, and relative ease, by comparison. I am not sure anyone today can relate. I have been unemployed, with a family to feed, yet even that situation cannot compare to what my father's generation endured. There were no safety nets such as unemployment compensation. In the last twenty years many people lost jobs and suffered significant financial losses from the two recessions since the mid-1980s. Yet the economic impact of these relatively recent recessions pales in comparison to the financial calamity endured during the Great Depression. Americans saw and felt the unemployment rate climb to 12% and had many fewer options and no safeguards to total financial devastation.

Is there any wonder or doubt that this generation emerged from yet another World War to create the amazing economic growth of the 1950s? Faced with recent, real memories of personal and economic uncertainty, they grabbed hold of the opportunity. They worked hard to provide for their families and saved for the future. The goal was give their children a better life.

Along with millions of others, my own parents lived this goal. They worked hard. My dad gave his up his dream of attending college to make a living for my mother, my three siblings and me. They enjoyed life in moderation because they wanted to send their four children to college. I was the youngest of four, and it was not until I was in high school that I saw my mother and father really spend any money on each other.

We lived in a modest neighborhood in upstate New York, in a suburb of Rochester. Our house was larger than most, but it hadn't started out that way. My father learned the building trades — carpentry, painting, electrical and plumbing — from his father. Over time he expanded our one bedroom house into a comfortable home for the six of us, using borrowed tools and his own sweat and skill.

Dad was especially proud of our yard, and he worked constantly to keep it beautifully landscaped. Correction: My dad ensured that he, my brother and I kept it landscaped beautifully! While my brother and I worked every free day outside, my sisters worked inside, helping my mother prepare meals and clean. One of Dad's favorite rules: "If you don't work around the house, you don't eat." (I can't imagine where he learned that!) Everyone had his or her designated work assignments. Everyone was taught to do his or her share.

My father was a master craftsman, and he taught me some of his craft the way his father taught him. I learned how to build cement sidewalks, repair electrical switches and every skill in between. Some I learned easily. Most I learned after kicking and screaming, literally. I didn't exactly get excited about spending half of my Saturday helping my father. After a week of school, in my mind, Saturday was a time to go play with my friends. I wanted life to be easy. I wanted life to be fun and easy and I resented that I had to "work" so much. I believed life should be easier than working hard every day. I believed life should be fun. Maybe I obtained that belief early on already experiencing an easier life than my parents endured as children.

Somewhere along the way most of my father's approach to life rubbed off on me. (It was not easy. I resisted as much as possible. I understood the value of hard work, but was not excited about having to do it every day. I often resisted believing there simply needed to be more time to enjoy life.) In the end I learned to take responsibility for my actions. I learned to be honest. I acquired a strong work ethic. I experienced a sense of accomplishment for completing a task myself. My appreciation for the skills he taught me grew immensely once I had a house of my own. The values I learned served me well when facing real problems in my adult life. And most of all and through everything he endured, he taught me compassion for all living creatures.

But this story is not about my parents. I use them here only as an example of the times. Millions of others can recount similar stories of hard work, pride in a job well done, and patience to save for a new car, home or child's education. They demonstrated an unwavering sense of purpose as they pursued their goals with dedication and tenacity.

It is not hard to comprehend how this generation, united in its purpose and passionate about freedom, fought World War II to preserve the life they had begun building. Having survived their early years in America, and then the economic uncertainty of a depression, nothing could stop them from working to secure a better future for themselves and their families.

By the time of the late 1950s and early 1960s, most parents finally were beginning to taste some of the fruits of their labors. The economy flourished, new homes were being built, many families owned two cars, and something special: a color television. The world of electrical appliances made life easier. Our collective parents felt it was time to relax and enjoy. They had worked hard, took responsibility for their actions and saved for the future. They wanted everything to stay this way. After all, they had built a winning formula. It was a great formula for success. Nothing — no one — was going to make them change.

Well, almost no one. Changes were about to unfold which none of our parents could stop. The inevitable sea of transition loomed on the horizon.

Who created the changes about to unfold from 1960 until today?

Their children.

Their children determined it was time for a change.

CHAPTER 2

It Was Time for a Change

"Instant gratification takes too long."

— Carrie Fisher, actress, screenwriter and novelist

I grew up in the Sixties. As fast as I could grasp the meaning of how life, family, school, friendships, relationships, business and faith worked, I was bombarded with a new mentality in the U.S.: *Question authority.*

We were mired in a complex war as thousands of young men were dying in a land on the other side of the world. Most of America questioned whether we should be there, what we were fighting for, and when it would all end. Anti-war demonstrations were everywhere, while demonstrators identified the U.S. Military and Government as institutions to be mistrusted.

This war was different from the ones our parents and grandparents had fought. Previously wars were fought openly, as enemies were uniformed and identifiable. In Vietnam, our perceived "enemies" were not so easily seen through the dense foliage. Determining how best to fight this new war drove us to question everything — to question the way society, laws and prosperity had worked up until then.

No institution was left unscathed. The concept of Big Business was attacked, church-goers demanded more answers from their religions, colleges and universities were asked to provide different courses allowing more free thought, and the Supreme Court was pressed to address major social concerns such as abortion and civil rights.

Businesses were looked upon as untrustworthy, unfriendly to employees and as part of the "establishment" responsible for many of the woes afflicting our society. "Big Business" no longer represented the ideal company at which an employee could plan to spend his career, (yes, "his"; getting "her" into the workplace was another major change to our society). Now, a large company was deemed a polluter, accused of unfair labor practices and price fixing.

Some of those who were discriminated began to riot after trying every alternative they knew to get those in power to understand their plight. New laws were written to protect against discrimination of race, gender and religious preference. These were rights given by the Constitution, yet these rights had to be reinforced in our society by new laws and court decisions to eliminate historically acceptable bias and discrimination.

Colleges and universities were viewed as teaching old, worn out subjects, ideas, and courses. A new generation of students and scientists believed there were new economic forces at work requiring definition and review.

Our society, after fifty short years of growing economic expansion, asserting itself globally, and creating significant wealth and prosperity for so many, began to question itself. These children of a generation who had created businesses producing a record number of goods and services, employing millions of people, and enabling more individuals to afford a new home questioned if the new abundance had come at too high a price. The very core of who we were as a nation and society seemed under attack.

No doubt, our parents and grandparents had done a great job building this country. They had managed to harvest enough food to feed more people than ever. Supermarkets sprang up everywhere offering convenience and variety. Science had generated frozen meals, a long list of new products, faster and better cars and jobs for millions of people.

At the same time there were questions to be asked and answers to be found. Introspection is always a good virtue. Unfortunately, some of those in power did not want to listen to new thinking.

Among many other positive successes, our parents and grandparents had also been successful in polluting the air and water. This older generation was not so proud of other distinctions. They pushed America's righteous superiority by attempting to police the world. They also allowed discrimination against people of color and women.

By no means am I attempting to place blame or judgment or turn this into a commentary on our society. Our parents and grandparents built a great society, and at the same time there was much more work to be done. Although some problems, such as polio, had been erased, other problems had been created. My point here is to show how our daily lives changed due to the ongoing events around us. *Everyone* was affected in some manner by the forces attempting to transform our society. There was heightened focus on civil rights, religious dogma, new economic policies and a new appreciation and respect for the health and beauty of our planet.

As we moved into the Seventies, there appeared a new urgency to move change forward in all aspects of our lives. Daily on TV and in the newspapers we were told of new studies affecting our health, lifestyles and beliefs. Scientists first began stating that aerosol spray from cans could be depleting the ozone layer. There was growing concern that our lakes and rivers were being polluted. We learned about the effects of smoking, sedentary lifestyles, and smog.

We were bombarded — and it continues at an accelerated rate today — with advertising, news stories, press releases, medical findings, and books all telling us what foods to eat, and what not to eat, what to wear, do, say, and think; and where to live, all in the name of living a healthier life. Everything our parents had taught us — from how to interact, conduct business, have faith, and even eat — was being disputed. Remember the cartoon character carrying the sign that said the world was coming to an end? We laughed, yet it represented an inner fear we all had about where our society was and where our way of life was headed. It was like some bad memory in our life that we repressed not wanting to deal with it.

We had grown from a society that had worked hard for a living, had been patient in obtaining the material joys of life, and had taken responsibility for its actions into a nation where many of us questioned all beliefs and social norms. True, our parents and grandparents created a better life for us in many ways, and at the same time created or perpetuated problems that needed attention. Yet it was their hard work and creation of greater wealth that provided us the luxury of time to question our world.

So there we were, a new generation, throwing out the proverbial baby with the bath water. I was part of that generation and believed it was time for a change. My parent's philosophy of life seemed outdated and no longer appropriate. I began voting for candidates who wanted to entirely change the traditional establishment along with the rest of my generation. In our great urgency and desire to create and obtain change, we desired a clean slate. We had a brand new approach, or so we thought. In our haste to create change, we had no time to take the good from prior generations and build on it. My generation was not focused on the hard work and patience the older generation knew was required to obtain and appreciate the accomplishments they generated. Instead, our focus was on the ills of our society. We blamed the older generation and in doing so, decided most of the older generation's beliefs, ethics and approaches were of little value in this new world.

My purpose here is to show how our country has changed and evolved in social, philosophical and emotional terms. I pass no judgment on either generation. There are values, qualities and beliefs in each generation that are admirable. It is unfortunate many of us began to forget the key concepts our parents had taught us.

Hence was born a great urge to fix the woes of our society. It was a time when most of us worried if nuclear war would happen at any minute, if pollution was going to kill us in the next ten years if we did not make radical changes, and if social injustice would split our country apart. We were determined to change and fix our world as fast as possible. We concluded our vote for President was based on how quickly he might "push the button," sending us into nuclear war.

Further, with the apparent "doom" of war and the world coming to an end very soon, the younger generation made a radical change in their approach to life: live in the moment. Live right now, enjoy today to the fullest, worry about tomorrow when it comes. Marijuana became the drug of choice of a new generation. The goal was to find a way to feel good as fast as possible and stay there.

Looking back, it was a fun time. How could it not be? We were consumed with the idea of feeling good now, having fun now. Life was all about feeling good now, relax, mellow out, chill out, meditate, rock on and power to the people. It was a time to love your fellow man and love the one you're with. A sexual revolution helped by the medical advancement of "The Pill" was in full swing. No one was worried about AIDS, and rarely were other sexually transmitted diseases a deterrent to a new attitude. Free love, free sex and "get it on" were the new battle cries.

During the early Seventies, I discovered the second purpose of college was education. I wasn't worried with events on the other side of the world. I wasn't even concerned for events in other parts of our country. Instead, I joined my peers who were out for a good time. After all, the sexual revolution was well under way. Who had time to consider the long-term consequences of our actions? It was a time to party.

Our parents and grandparents' beliefs about working hard and saving for the future were quickly swept aside. And the "feel good" approach to life felt good for several years. Somewhere along the way, we slowly began to realize it took more drugs, even greater thrills, more living on the edge, more free sex, and more randomness to make us feel the good feeling. Each new "high" required a stronger dose of whatever it was we used to get us there.

Too many times some of my generation woke up with a hangover feeling their stomach ache, and a headache that made us pray for quiet. (Yes, I have been there before!) Too many times our bodies told us this path we were going down was not worth it. There is an old saying that if you can remember the Sixties then you weren't there! In college, it was fun to drink, have fun with the opposite sex and make sure your grades were good enough to graduate. Once out of college, this abuse to the mind and body got old really fast. The wear and tear became visible. For some of us, lost relationships, lost jobs, lost opportunities and even lost lives proved all too costly in the end.

At some point most of us woke up and wondered if this was all there was to life. We decided we wanted more than to just feel good in the moment. Feeling good only helped us feel good and not change the world we so desperately wanted to change. Some new ideas were implemented. Some changes were made. Yet, we wanted more.

Our mission was to feel good AND have every opportunity, experience and adventure and obtain prosperity *now*. The focus was on how to feel good through the unlimited possibilities the world offered, rather than through drugs or vices. Whether it was a new car, vacation to some exotic place, a nice house with all the amenities or all the perks of a great job, we wanted it all. Having all of these experiences and material objects helped us obtain the feel good feeling we could no longer get just with alcohol or drugs.

Something else happened to these children, people of my generation as we moved through the 1960's and into the 1970's: we got older. Many of us married and had children. Feeling good was great, but now there were mouths to feed and rent to pay so our children had someplace comfortable and warm to sleep.

Feeling good was still important, but living in the park, or under a tree, or with twenty other people in one house, and wearing tee shirts and torn jeans, was no longer satisfactory. Acquiring those nice cars and homes took center stage. Instead of the excesses of the Sixties and Seventies, we realized there were new ways to obtain a good feeling about ourselves: money and material things like fast cars, expensive jewelry, fine clothes and swimming pools.

The stampede was on. There was a clear difference between our parents, grandparents and us. In the pursuit of feeling good now, we lost our long-term perspective. We lost the knowledge and the ability to save for the future. There was no way were we going to wait fifteen to twenty years to move into the world of material goods which was clearly bringing us our new "high." No, we had to have it now. Our prosperity had to increase significantly, *now*.

It became our obsession. We needed to experience everything life could give us, now, quickly, and with abundance, as if each of us was a child in a candy store. The question wasn't when it would happen; it was how much I could get as soon as possible. Waiting and working hard? That was for losers. Working hard was possibly something we could buy into for a while, until retirement at forty or forty-five. Do anything to get that promotion, move anywhere in the company and country to move up the corporate ladder and taste the fruits of labor. But saving for the future or waiting to obtain all of life's pleasures? No, that was not going to happen.

It had to be now.

No lines, no waiting.

Now.

CHAPTER 3

Patience Was No Longer a Virtue

"The key to everything is patience. You get the chicken by hatching the egg, not by smashing it."

— Arnold H. Glasow, author

Our new lifestyle had shown us how to feel good now, to feel good whenever we wanted. There were many choices, options, and methods available to us to help us feel good immediately. But that wasn't enough. Feeling good today didn't get us that new car or house or latest electronic device we wanted.

We still had to get a job, and work to earn money to afford the material things we wanted. Yet, by the mid Seventies and in to the Eighties we had too many years of feeling good in the moment. We had lost our foundation given to us by the previous generation. The concept of working hard and saving for the future had slipped away from our standard approach to life. Advances in technology and science helped make it easier and faster to obtain material goods and success. New products such as the VCR (video tape recorder) made it possible to enjoy a part of TV we had never experienced. I remember rushing out and buying one for almost $1,000; a significant amount of money 25 years ago, but I did not want to wait until I could better afford it.

Armed with that mindset who wanted to work hard and save for so many years like our parents did? What advantage was there to that when there were so many new opportunities to make money fast? What advantage was there to saving for years when we needed exciting experiences now? Many of my friends stated how they wanted to retire by the age of 40. We had forgotten the reasons why working hard and saving for the future had any value.

The "You" decade was turning into the "Me" decade of the Eighties. We wanted it fast, we wanted it good and we wanted it now. After the economy took a hit in the 1970s and early 1980s, it took off and with it came a new "get rich quick" mentality. If we couldn't work for it, buy it. Try to hit the home run all at once. The stock market was flourishing and company mergers and takeovers became commonplace. Flocks of young professionals rushed to work in the financial world, as traders and brokers for companies were bent on acquiring other companies. Huge financial profits, large salaries and hefty bonuses were an every day occurrence.

The "Yuppie," or young upwardly-mobile professional, emerged on the scene. Countless articles were written about them. New designer clothes, expensive vacations, luxury cars, and houses no longer required years of saving. Patience was no longer a virtue. We could have it all now. We could have anything we wanted. We didn't ask ourselves if we were truly creating any value in the countless company takeovers, eliminating jobs to build a better bottom line for the winner. What about making better products or offering improved services? The end justified the means. Our only focus was to have it all now instead of waiting. We did not concern ourselves with the ethics of how we made our money. We knew it was legal but rationalized our business behavior as "eat or be eaten." Fairness often seemed like a forgotten value.

With women now common in the workplace (and long overdue) family incomes skyrocketed, producing a huge resource of wealth to purchase the cars, houses and vacations.

This generation of "baby boomers" was beginning to resemble the one group of people they had sought so hard to distance themselves from: their parents. This new generation began to address racial and sexual injustice and unfair labor practices. It pushed science forward. At the same time, this generation (of which I am part) became infatuated with money, to the point of greed. The plan was to block or stamp out your competition to prevent your company from having to change its way of doing business. The electric car has been around for decades, yet as the baby boomers demanded cleaner air, men in big business blocked the electric car at every turn. There was simply too much money to be had in oil and selling cars with planned obsolescence.

Let's stop again, for a moment. It was an interesting path we took over the prior seventy years. The amount of change in our perspective is significant when you step back and view it without emotion. There had already been a significant change in our approach to succeeding in life. There were many more changes to come in the next thirty years leading up to today.

The 1970s and 1980s saw technology help make our world smaller while producing the rise of a global economy. Our economy was increasingly affected by world events and the economies of other countries. Fear crept into daily thoughts. Our enemy was fear. We feared losing our wealth and prosperity, which we had obtained oh-so-quickly and taken for granted. Our enemy was ourselves.

Fear is one of the most compelling emotions and driving forces in the human race. It is amazing what we do and do not do out of fear. We block competition out of fear we will lose our jobs, or even worse be forced to change our habits, beliefs, our way of doing business. Intellectually, we know change makes us all better. But we do not like change. Change makes us uncomfortable. Change often makes us take a hard look at ourselves, and that is the last thing we want to do. We all believe that if the people around us would change, our problems would be solved. Change is ever constant; nothing is as permanent as change. We fight so hard to get to a certain point in our lives, to own a specific home or car and to enjoy a certain lifestyle. But then our human emotion takes hold and we fight in every conceivable manner to maintain the status quo. All sense of logic appears discarded as laws are created to prevent losing what we have. All of this keeps us from changing, when change is inevitable. (Is the steam engine still around?)

Take a look at how products have either gone away or evolved into something else. Should we keep making the pager or the typewriter? Of course not! But it required change, didn't it? Change is considered good if it is the other person doing it. Don't take my job away, even if the product I build is becoming obsolete, could be more energy efficient, is of lesser quality or more expensive than that which is produced from other countries. My job should be protected. Protected from what? Yes, protected so I can keep what I want, what I earned, and, now that I have it, I am focused on keeping my piece of the pie. It was as if few people cared what happened to the quality of the air and water. One might argue people lacked awareness of potential problems. Yet that required a long term perspective, something we were missing.

Examine how focused we are when businesses report their earning each quarter. The intense scrutiny on three month's of results can only be viewed as short-sighted. If a business reports slightly lower earnings the stock takes a beating. Mutual funds managers sell like the sky is falling. Talk about no long-term focus! But how can we expect money managers to invest in stocks with a long-term focus, when we as a society focus on what is in front of us today and seem to rarely consider the long-term implications? We took on this mentality when we threw out our parents' values and made feeling good our first priority.

There are countless examples of our lack of long-term focus. Our land fills are growing larger and larger because we toss everything. In our throw-away society, we forget to consider where to put all the garbage. As much as recycling is a system supported in most cities, it remains an expensive process. We continue to allow businesses, and the trucks and cars we drive to pollute the air. We continue to allow chemicals in our foods because the food tastes better and satisfies our cravings now, rather than considering the long-term effects on our body of these chemical preservatives and additives.

Presidents have talked for the past thirty years about reducing our demand for oil and investing in sources of alternative energy. Oil use, instead, is at an all-time high. The problem? There is just too much money to be made from oil in the short-term. Sadly, we may only move toward viable alternatives when forced by depleted resources or undisputable intensified evidence of global warming.

We lack political will or patience for long-term strategies and solutions to our problems. To do so might prevent some of us from enjoying our bounty now. We might have to wait.

So we hurried to acquire those material things in life that would help us feel good, and then did everything possible to prevent losing those experiences. We were scared of losing them, but just as important, we were afraid we could not re-create them again. We had already begun the process of losing our ability to create what we wanted in our lives. Somewhere underneath it all, are the pounding questions: why did we believe we needed to feel this good and feel it all of the time? Did our insecurity, did our lack of faith and lack of self-esteem, push us to feel good instead of examining ourselves, using introspection to see what made us run this fast?

Why am I making a big deal right at this point about fear? Because fear drives our actions, our feelings and our emotions. We create laws to save our jobs out of fear there won't be enough in the future. We perceive the world and everything in it as finite, and therefore, fear we won't get our share. We seek instant reward, instant gratification, instant success for fear it will forever be elusive. Amazingly, then once we have it, we fear we will lose it. Fear has a grip on us either way. I had fallen prey to this thinking many times in my life. Successful people, whether they achieve financial success or attain great achievements through following their dreams do not fall prey to fear. They believe in themselves, they believe in opportunity and they believe in viewing problems as opportunities, not roadblocks. We will discuss this more later.

Why am I spending so much time on the past? Examining how our society has changed is critical. This "have it all now" has stopped us from learning how to create the world we want, because many of us lack a long-term view and the desire to do the necessary work. But there is so much more than just work and patience to create your world. There are spiritual and Universal laws involved as well that no one ever taught us which I will explain later. For now, viewing our past with new perspective helps us understand how we block ourselves from achieving our goals.

Again, all of this is not here to depress you or make you feel bad. It is to give some perspective of what is here today. With the insight provided later in this book combined with your perspective of where we have been, you will create happiness and abundance.

You might question why I appear to suggest it is not wise to seek feeling good now or wanting prosperity as fast as possible. While there is nothing inherently wrong with it, be aware that the path we as a society have been traveling has formed a foundation for our thoughts and beliefs. Our generation has made great strides in creating prosperity for millions of people. In the U.S., more people can afford a home today than ever before. We spend millions of dollars on science and research to find relief for all diseases. Science has improved our lives in many ways. And yet we have paid a price for this progress. Can you see we shifted our focus, shifted our approach, shifted our belief system away from some of the values, qualities, and virtues of our parents and grand parents and replaced or perhaps refined these beliefs and virtues? And not always in positive ways.

In our push to obtain wealth quickly, we've made some strange choices and destructive decisions. Somewhere along the way, we shed an important brick in the foundation. We let go of a critical personality trait which could have kept us in check and balanced as we drove to obtain wealth at light speed.

We gave up being responsible.

CHAPTER 4

Responsibility Became a Foreign Concept

"The disappearance of a sense of responsibility is the most far-reaching consequence of submission to authority."

— *Stanley Milgram, social psychologist*

S omething happened on the way to the designer clothes, gourmet dining, expansive houses, foreign built cars, and exotic vacations. Some of us did not succeed in obtaining a great job or dream house. Many people felt left out as they watched others race up the corporate ladder, hit the jackpot on some hot stock, make millions starting a company, or make millions on a weird invention (remember the pet rock?), or be on the wining side of a corporate takeover.

So what happened? We learned there were two groups of people, those who had obtained wealth and success, and those who did not. There are many people who work hard, honestly and ethically, and are successful in building the life they desire. However, we in America tend to mistrust successful people, especially those who built their wealth quickly. As a society we tend to be suspicious of those with wealth as if they obtained it dishonestly.

Those who failed in their efforts were laid off in a merger, or simply couldn't keep up (or maybe felt they even were not as cut-throat as others who played the power-lunch game) and quickly became frustrated. Frustration quickly turns into resentment. Resentment fueled by frustration, leads to envy and anger. Eventually, all of the emotions lead to one reaction, one answer, and one way to rationalize all to help us feel better: It's not our fault. We did not deserve our fate. It was not MY fault that I got laid off; it was not MY fault that I didn't get the promotion; it was not My fault that I didn't think of that invention first. Someone beat me to it. Someone beat me unfairly in the contest for the promotion. Someone took my job.

In all sports, contests, job interviews, and vying for promotions, there are perceived winners and losers. And in our society, winning is everything.

Everyone has a choice in life to look at the outcome of a situation or event as success and failure, or learn what works and develop a new strategy. If we look at the world in the "either/or" terms of winning and losing, it leads us down one path. Either we win and others lose or the reverse is true, they win and we lose. This win-lose scenario creates a negative path that can lead to frustration, resentment, and anger. The negativity begins to dampen our self-esteem.

Conversely, when we look at losses or problems as opportunities, as if one door is closing and another door opens, it creates a different world for us.

How many times in your life were you passed over for a job, only to have a better opportunity open up for you? Or a relationship that you wanted to work out didn't, only to create the space for a new relationship to come into your life that far exceeded any expectations you had of the previous one? Many of us have experienced unfortunate events. Successful people do not view life in "either/or" terms. They examine what works and what does not work. They make adjustments and implement new tactics. Successful people don't take it personally. There is no impact to their self-esteem when they make an unsuccessful attempt to obtain their goal.

Yet we so often get "hooked" into going down the first path subconsciously thinking: "I didn't get that promotion, so I must be a loser. She broke off the relationship, so I must not be a good person and she's probably looking for someone better. If only I had been given another chance the result would have different this time."

These thoughts roll around in the subconscious, because at the same time we attempt to consciously compensate for our lack of success by rationalizing the events. We say to ourselves we deserved that job. Yet in the back of our minds, we know we may not have done our best. If we acknowledge we did not do our best, there goes our self-esteem. There goes our faith in ourselves. There goes our faith in God, if we believe one exists. There begins our resentment of others, who have won what we have lost. It is a vicious cycle. We then look to God for justice and hope God will make it all better, and when we don't receive a sign something new is on the way, we become further frustrated and seek compensation from those around us.

Since in our minds we deserved success as much as the next person, we then rationalized either the winner cheated, or by simply winning blocked us from succeeding in the future. We could have succeeded but we just didn't have the time to invest in more college courses or another program to improve or add new job skills.

Many individuals make up excuses about why they were unsuccessful and refuse to look at themselves in the mirror. Looking in the mirror means we may have to acknowledge we must change our belief systems or approaches to life. We can't do that. Doing so would force us to admit our approaches, our inaction, and our non-proactive/reactive approach was not working. If it wasn't working for us, we would have to admit to ourselves we needed to change or at least modify our habits, beliefs and approach. If we had to change, then logic follows that we must consider we've been going about life all "wrong". And we weren't wrong, were we? For most of us, our egos are so fragile we can't consider or comprehend the idea that we may have made a mistake. I reacted exactly in this manner. I had worked hard and was honest in my dealings and believed I was not the cause of the problem. To me, I was not going to change my ways; rather others needed to change.

True, some of us tried and worked really hard. We took the

right courses, we did some self-improvement. We cared about people. We looked both ways before crossing, but some of us still got hit. In the end, we did not achieve success. We did not reach our goal. Our reaction in these cases if often the same: if my teacher would have graded differently, if my boss had just given me a break this one time, everything would be different.

We are reminded every day that problems are not of our own doing. In all sorts of media — print, television, and movies — there are countless stories of someone depicted as dishonest taking advantage of people just like you. There are constant images of wealthy people treating others dishonestly to make their profit. Wealthy people are constantly portrayed as stepping on the little guy to get even richer. The wealthy businessman is always the one by the end of the show who is carted off to prison or has become a victim of his own foul transactions.

Politicians love to play this card to gather votes when running for office. Which candidate will you vote for, the one who says he will help you get your share of the pie, or the one who says you need to work harder? Too many of us will vote for the guy who will take from the rich and give to us because our needs are more important. This particular politician says he will help us be compensated for our losses, even if it was our own doing. If you look closely, you'll see this blame game, this idea of entitlement, is replicated in many forums and reinforced in our psyches daily.

Blaming others for our unfortunate circumstances in our lives is easy, and isn't "easy" exactly where we are today? We want it fast, we want it strong and we want it now. Changing ourselves or our strategies, learning new skills — in short, taking responsibility — means sustained hard work and patience, and many of us are not programmed for either. Yet for those of us who worked really hard no one could explain to us why the other guy got the promotion. We all ended up confused not knowing what to do. It was natural to blame our reality on others and even God. We figured God must not like us and most likely was punishing us even after working hard. Yet if we worked hard why were we being punished? We weren't and I will explain this in full detail later. Most of the time God provided no answers for us, so it is natural we turned to looking at those around us as the cause of our problems.

I can create an excuse for any unproductive, unhealthy, emotionally draining behavior by turning it around and blaming someone else. If I am fired from work for coming in late, I can blame it on traffic, rather than if I simply left for work earlier each day I would arrive on time. But I can't awake earlier, because that would take an effort on my part, as I would have to set my alarm each night, make better use of my time each morning and I might not be able to enjoy more of the evening. So we blame someone or something else.

Need examples? How many marriages have failed when a spouse determines that his/her partner can't provide what he/she needs to be happy? Somehow the rule was changed and my happiness is now based on my partner's ability to please me, instead of me finding my own internal peace and happiness, or even searching for that together as a couple.

How about blaming fast food companies for the obesity in the United States today? We believe they are making us eat food high in fat and calories. They even sell us hot coffee at drive-thru windows which can spill and scald us.

Having so many examples why others were to blame for our misfortune we rationalized the next step was to take action. In our minds, action needed to be taken now, because remember, we were not accustomed to waiting for our turn in life to be successful. We needed and demanded recourse and compensation now. Action needed to occur now in order for us to *feel good again.* NOW.

What has our society determined is the best course of action to take back what we believe is ours from those who took it from us or blocked our way to it? What is the quickest way for us to feel better fast when frustration turns to resentment? What do we believe is the most immediate way to right the wrongs that have been done to us?

A lawsuit.

After all, some of us believed someone had taken what was rightfully ours. Someone had taken our job, our promotion, our chance at success, or opportunity, our chance to prove ourselves. Again, frustration leads to resentment, which can move us to take action. We want compensation for the emotional toll the situation has inflicted upon us. Often we hurt so much, our thoughts turn to a need for quick resolution, swift justice and the immediate need to feel better. Yes, we want to feel better quick, because we have been programmed to pursue feeling better as fast as possible.

When events go against us our first tendency is to want compensation for the injustice and its emotional toll on us. If we suffer, we want others to suffer more. We want them to pay.

How can we expect others to be honest, hard working, ethical and disciplined in all ways when we are not? Simple. The system allows it. In fact, the system rewards it.

In the last twenty years or more, suing has become a way of life, an industry of its own. Suing someone or a corporation is the norm. Our courts are so backlogged with lawsuits, we don't have enough judges and we can't find enough jurors to work cases fast enough. Remember that we are now programmed to pursue feeling better as fast as possible, and a lawsuit is an attempt at immediate gratification.

I am not, of course speaking here of lawsuits with significant merit. Some injustices are real and a problem in our entire society. Take, for instance, discrimination of all kinds, whether it involves race, religion, gender or a myriad of other differences that divide our society. Here, the courts have stepped in to right some historical wrongs and are continuing to do so.

At the same time the frivolity of many of the suits we hear of in the news every day is apparent to just about everyone. It seems people eagerly sue over almost anything they determine to be an inconvenience, imposition or disagreement and hence are ready to place blame and seek damages. If a parent doesn't like the way a referee handled a sporting event at her daughter's game, she threatens a lawsuit. If a fan doesn't like the cost of a baseball game, he sues. The local bar is sued for serving too many drinks to a man who then drove his car and killed someone. A man tried to use a lawnmower as a hedge trimmer and cut his fingers, so he sued the manufacturer. If I stick my finger in the wall electrical socket and get a bad shock I should probably sue the builder for putting the electrical outlet right there where I could reach it, plus the electric company for making electricity. If it were possible, we would sue the sun for causing skin cancer, yet some people sunbathe all summer long!

We all know the risks involved in any choice we make. Nothing is guaranteed. Yet when an investor buys stock in a company and the stock drops for some reason, the investor is quick to bring a lawsuit demanding compensation.

The amazing thing is that somehow we as a society determined this behavior to be acceptable. Excuses legitimized even the most outrageous behavior. After all, he had a bad home life; she felt she wasn't being paid enough for all her hard work; his wife just left him: her father left when she was young; he was abused as a child; she didn't have a chance to finish high school. We allowed irresponsibility and grew more sympathetic to the problems and emotional traumas of life, thereby making the bad choices — and their consequences — no longer "our fault."

Lawsuits provided people not only swift recourse but a potential gold mine. Individuals, businesses and insurance companies were viewed as wallets with a lot of money inside. We began to sympathize with the "victim", the apparent "loser" who was wronged in some way. We could relate. Our pain was similar. Could the victim have prevented the mishap by his own actions? That was irrelevant and we didn't want to hear about it. When judgments favored the plaintiff, the larger the damages, the more of us felt better. If we couldn't have our pieces of success, maybe we could feel better about ourselves. Seeing others obtain compensation for their apparent losses helped us feel more deserving, too. Maybe some of these "rewards" would funnel down to us and help us feel better about the world. These people, businesses and companies have more than the need anyway.

Successful frivolous lawsuits have taken us down the path of irresponsibility, away from accepting responsibility for our actions and thus their consequences. So we now stand in a doorway, viewing a vastly different landscape than the ones seen by our parents. We have a choice. You have a choice. Successful people believe their own actions create their experiences. Successful people do not believe their world is created by the willful intent of others to prevent them from obtaining their goal.

Unfortunately, our society has supported us in believing other's neglect has caused our troubles. Parents who coddle their children, some laws, and even certain government "safety nets" can reinforce this blaming behavior.

If, every time I fall down, there is someone to help me get up, I never learn to get up on my own. Learning to get back up on my own two feet is one of the most valuable lessons a person can learn. However, if I learn there is always someone there to pick up after the messes I make, I become dependent on others continually for assistance and no longer take responsibility for my actions. If, instead of teaching me to take care of myself, to learn and grow from my mistakes, I am permitted to blame others and am handed everything I need, it actually "dis"-ables me. Finally, my clear thinking and problem solving capabilities become disoriented and my ability to take constructive action on my own behalf becomes disabled. I begin to approach the world wondering what can be done for me instead of what I can do for myself.

But there is a problem with this kind of thinking. The positive energy required to create positive results is missing when we expect help from others and blame others for our problems.

We give away our power to create the world we desire
when we blame others for our actions or our inactions.

Believing we are not responsible for our actions is denying
the power we have to influence our world and understand
how our choices, beliefs and actions draw people
and events into our lives which mirror our beliefs.

Too often we stopped looking at ourselves to take responsibility for our actions. Changes over the past decades changed the thinking and norms of our society declaring it good to want something now, to push for resolution now, and obtain compensation any way possible. What happened to us taking responsibility for our choices and our decisions? We see people who drink on the job and get fired, only to blame the company. How could that person not know he would be fired for drinking on the job, and coming to work drunk every other day, and missing a lot of work? Better yet, a person goes to a local bar, drinks excessively, drives home and crashes his car or worse and then blames the bar for serving him the drinks. Blaming someone else for our lack of discipline, restraint and control is the ultimate example giving up total responsibility for all of our actions.

But there is a problem with this kind of thinking.

We give away our power when we blame others for our actions or our inactions.

Don't we have free will to decide each choice we make? If events in our lives were only to happen "to us" then we would not have been given free will. God has given us free will to experience the impact of our decisions. Believing we are not responsible goes against the essence of who we are as beings having the free will to make choices.

As we stop being responsible for our actions, we forfeit our power to create the world we desire.

When we no longer take responsibility, we have given God permission to help us bring events and people into our lives which are irresponsible. We actually experience more of the behavior we are exhibiting. When we blame others for our misfortunes we give away our own power over our reality.

It is not easy to view ourselves this way. Examining our own actions, looking at ourselves with searing honesty may be painful, especially if we come to the conclusion that we have had a part in creating a world that most of us are unhappy about. Contemplating that we may need to change means we may have done something wrong.

But consider this: Do you like the same foods you liked as a child? Do you play with the same toys? Do you watch the same shows? Do you go to the same places for fun or entertainment? No, and since you don't, were your choices "wrong" as a child? Of course your choices were not wrong. Your choices served you well then, but they no longer serve you now. The same holds true for some of your long-held beliefs systems and the life choices and reactions they produce now. Some of them may no longer serve you as the once did.

There is nothing wrong with change. It is inevitable. Even if you attempted to do nothing for the remainder of your life, you would change. Your body would change, your eyesight, your hearing would change. EVERY new experience, EVERY new person in your life, EVERY new day at work, EVERY new day wherever you are, wherever you go, changes you. Today you have more information than you had the day before. You process this information into the data banks of your mind and compile with other past experiences.

Furthermore, the more we try to stay the same, to "keep" everything we have, to secure it some way, to control those around us so nothing changes, something strange happens: we lose it. Either we change and move forward or go backward. There is no standing still. The financial world is littered with businesses that failed because their management sat on past successes and didn't keep the company moving forward with new thinking and change. Remaining constant in a world that is ever changing can only result in a backward slide. Once we truly understand this, we will realize we MUST have a long-term approach to everything in our lives. We must understand there is long-term impact to our decisions...our own decisions. Decisions that we make everyday. Decisions about where to go, what to do, what to eat who we associate with, all of these have long-term implications.

I now understand how my decisions and actions affect *everything* in my life. Unfortunately, it took me 40 years to understand the power and the impact of my choices.

Change is good, new choices are good. Examine if your current choices serve you. If you set your alarm at the latest possible minute to get out of bed and get to work and you are always late to work, does that serve you? It is your choice to get up earlier. You may find yourself arriving at work less stressed from hurrying to get dressed and drive to work in traffic. You could easily find yourself more productive since you are not as stressed out from the morning rush. You DO have choices everyday.

Something happened as we gave up responsibility, resisted change and began to blame our unhappiness or lack of success on those around us.

We gave up our power to make choices.

CHAPTER 5

Too Many Choices Meant Fewer Choices

*"When you have to make a choice and don't make it,
that is in itself a choice."*

— *William James, American psychologist and philosopher*

Blaming those around us, suing for what we believe is due us, remains convenient, but we found other ways to extract our due share of satisfaction. We have found other ways to take out our frustration.

Unfortunately, some of us made the choices to hurt those around us that we love. Some of us made the choice to yell at our children. Sometimes we make the choice to argue with our spouses frequently over little things. When we discover our spouse can't give us the happiness we seek, we sue for divorce, and we've even created a tidy phrase for the problem: irreconcilable differences. The notion of irreconcilable differences perpetuates neither party taking responsibility.

I experienced divorce and am now remarried to a wonderful woman, with whom I feel extremely connected. I feel connected because of how I have changed and how I create what I want in my life. We do not blame each other if something unexpected occurs. We work together trusting each other to work through our issues, take on new skills, emotional and spiritual knowledge.

Everyone deals with the lack of success in different ways: some suffer through a divorce hoping a new relationship will be the key to success; others try get-rich-quick schemes only to lose more self-esteem.

Some of us chose a more positive approach by working even harder than we had before. I greatly respect those who put everything they have into their work, whether for someone else or in their own business. Many of us put in more hours at work hoping it would produce the promotion that eluded us for so long. For some working hard eventually resulted in the success they desired, while for others working many hours distracted them from thinking about their lack of success.

Along with working harder in their careers, some of us buried our little remaining time each day in hobbies, sports events, or our children's after school projects and sporting events. Our lives became filled with our children: taking them to soccer practice, art classes, ballet classes and martial arts classes. We worked very hard to fill our days trying to make our children happy and successful – all the things we were not, and what we so longed for. We believed that if we turned our attention to our children's pursuits, and hopefully their successes, we could relish in their accomplishments. Then perhaps some of our children's excitement and joy would rub off on us as we buried our own hopes and dreams, believing our dreams were unobtainable.

Our children became our new hope, our new path and our new chance at success. Wasn't that what our parents did? Our parents worked hard so their children could be more successful, achieve more, do more, obtain more and create more than they had done. With new opportunities, possibilities and options for our children to become involved, we as parents sometimes decided to go full throttle ahead involved in our children's activities. (And of course, if *we* didn't obtain satisfaction in the sport, then the coach, the system, the rules were not fair and there was always that lawsuit option.)

There are countless stories today of parents spending more and more money on their children to help them succeed in life. The money is not spent only for college education, but winning at sports or any other possible competition as an adolescent and teenager. At times some parents live through their kids. We adult parents, never having obtained the success we desired and more importantly never learned the formula for success have resorted to spending a significant amount of money on our children hoping they will succeed. With our children fully funded we are hoping our children might possibly succeed and we can share in their success knowing we possibly figured out the answer. This same logic is used why will do anything for our sports teams to win. Too many of us have not been able to create the life we desire so we latch on to our favorite sport team or hero to somehow feel connected and experience winning even if from a far distance.

As our children became our new focus and the consumers of all of our spare time, we found ourselves in a mad dash to hurry our children from one event to another. We hurried home from work to get our son to soccer practice, then onto guitar lessons before rushing home to do homework in what time was left before bedtime. The other parent hurried the daughter to art class and piano lessons, somewhere grabbing something for dinner, before rushing home to return a dozen work emails online as she prepared for the next day. We had so many opportunities available we don't want to miss out on any of them. And today, don't forget we all need time on the internet to read personal email, talk to friends and relatives and check out the best deals on purchases.

Fifteen years ago my world mirrored this scenario. Both my sons were playing baseball, with every night of the week filled with either a game or practice. Plus my older son often played in tournaments on the weekends, and played both outdoor and indoor soccer and basketball as well. Our focus was on winning games and at times lived through the successes of my sons at their sporting events. Physically and emotionally spent from the intensity of the games I had little time or energy left for anything else. I found there was little time left for any other interest or choices.

It is not difficult to see how busy our days have become. There is little time left for community projects, volunteering at school, being a juror, helping plant flowers in the neighborhood or giving assistance to those in need. How could we find time to do that?

There is barely time to plant flowers and care for our own yards, let alone take the dog for a walk. There isn't any more time left in the day to do anything else.

Instead of volunteering at the animal shelter, it is easier to make a financial donation. Instead of volunteering for our favorite charity or even a political cause, we found it easier to just send money. Church attendance is down. Even voter turnout is down.

I mentioned political involvement for a reason. We have no time to understand the issues surrounding world events, let alone the events in our neighborhood. Why get involved in a new highway project on the other side of town? If, on the other hand, that highway is being built two blocks from my house, well, yes, I might take notice and voice opinions. I just might even make a few phone calls. At the same time, who has time to attend rallies and neighborhood meetings on these issues? True, many people do find the time and take the initiative, and our communities are better off for their hard work. I commend them greatly and admire their efforts. Yet, don't we find it's always the same people involved in the neighborhood projects? These are of often the same people who help ensure the neighborhood is clean, and sit on the town or neighborhood council. You see these people helping out at the food drive, or volunteering at the voting polling place, (if we actually take the time to vote.) Hats off to those individuals who volunteer their time to their communities.

These volunteers are not better than others; they simply have chosen to help. We all lead important lives. Our families are important to each of us. At the same time, not enough of us find the time to get involved in our communities and volunteer for worthwhile projects.

When we do not believe we have enough time in the day for all of the important matters requiring our attention, we are left with only one choice: we make fewer choices. We make fewer decisions. We begin to let others make the choices for us. Other people can decide whether a liquor store should open near a residential neighborhood. Other people can decide on a recycling program for the city.

When we let others make choices for us that we are too busy to make ourselves, we give away our power. Giving our choices away by letting others make those choices for us weakens our ability to create what we desire in life.

Giving our power away reduces our capacity to create the world we desire. Giving our power away was caused by too many choices, forcing us to make fewer choices to keep control of our lives. When we give something away, it is not possible also to keep it. Making fewer choices pushes us farther away from our goal as we became less involved in our surroundings.

All of us make choices each day. We all are allotted twenty four hours each day to use as we choose. We all receive the same number of hours. By making fewer choices which will directly impact our growth and success, we begin to create a reality yielding fewer chances for success. The choices we make every day help create our world.

Watching sporting events on television or in person consumes some of our spare time. Cheering our team to victory makes us feel good and forget how we aren't achieving all that we want in life. Our country willingly pays athletes millions of dollars in hopes of securing victories on the field or the court or the ice so we can somehow taste a sliver of it. We wonder what it must feel like to score the touchdown, the basket, the goal. The need to feel like a winner is so powerful in us that we are willing to pay the athletes anything, do anything for them, forgive them for breaking the law, anything to get them back on the field so they can score and we can feel better.

There were many days when I felt miserable the next day after my team lost. I would let the disappointment of the loss negatively impact my thoughts and actions for a long time. I felt as if the world and God was working against me. Now I quickly remind myself it is just entertainment. My happiness in life does not depend on whether my team wins or losses (unless I say it does!!!) If my team loses and I get depressed and walk around in a bad mood, I created that feeling. The choice is there for me to realize my team did not play well, and to appreciate the skills of the athletes during better parts of the game. To let the game decide my feelings is a clear demonstration of how we give away our power to someone else or something else. When we do that, our ability to create leaves us along with it.

Over time we have resigned ourselves to believing we will only achieve a part of what we desire in life. Note, I do not define success as just wealth, possessions or power. Success is whatever you define success to be. However, we have become a society that does measure success on money, power and possessions.

Haven't we all had dreams of being someone unique or accomplishing something special? You may have wanted to write a song, build a bridge, travel the world, find a cure; the list is endless. Those dreams are still inside each of us, yet they are buried within us under the weight of our non-successes. Some of us resigned ourselves to live a life just getting by, with just enough to make it through another day. The more time went by, the deeper we buried our dreams and began leaving key choices to those around us. We hoped their choices would be better than ours and we could share in the wealth.

Notice I do not say we had failures. I do not believe in failures. The word failure implies we did something wrong and we often then infer there must be something wrong with us. It is said that when Edison was working on the light bulb filament, he tried thousands of components. Was he a failure when one did not work? Scientists more than anyone know the value in testing, examining what works and what does not work and CHANGING the strategy accordingly the next time. Success may come only after years of trying. Yet we never consider these people failures.

With all the years of trying and not getting as far as we dreamed and hoped, for many, our hopes of success turned to disillusion. With our perceived "failure", we added a burden from which some of us never recovered: guilt. Guilt is how we punish ourselves and lose our self-esteem. We will discuss this much further in later chapters.

In all this trying, we made fewer choices. The fewer choices only increased our loss of patience. With our patience lost we lost our perseverance to be the best we could be. We lost faith in ourselves and God.

In desperation we tried one last approach, one last option to make up for lost time and lost efforts, providing one glimmer of hope we could obtain our goals:
we tried to take shortcuts.

CHAPTER 6

Shortcuts Took Us Nowhere Fast

"All the so-called "secrets of success"
will not work unless you do."
— Author Unknown

"You cannot plough a field by turning it over in your mind."

— Author Unknown

For many, the solution became obvious. It was conveniently suggested by the daily bombardment of television, internet, magazine and newspaper advertisements providing the magic solution:

Shortcuts!

Killer abs in just 20 minutes 3 days a week.
Get rich in 30 days or your money back.
Learn to play the piano in 3 easy lessons.
Lose 10 pounds in 10 days or your money back.
Take 4 strokes off your golf game in 2 weeks.
Better yet, no money down!

We haven't even mentioned the proliferation of "how to" books for dummies promising a quick way to learn just about anything!

The proliferation of commercials and infomercials is mind-boggling. Day after day you can watch ads on TV showing "every-day people" who made fortunes in just a few short weeks in real estate or some other business venture. Buy the video or CD and you can do it too! A 30 day money back guarantee and you are supposedly on your way to instant wealth.

Every subject imaginable, everything relating to our health, finances, personal success and pleasure can be obtained in a short period of time if we believe all of the advertising we see. And most of it comes with little money involved, little effort involved and best of all, little time involved. How about the number of products advertised each day claiming to do the work for you? You can sit and watch TV while you effortlessly lose weight or develop great abs. Wouldn't it be great if achieving what we want were that easy?

Considering all of the approaches we tried that yielded little or no success, it is not surprising how many of us are so easily drawn in and hooked by these promotions. We were all willing to try that one last option which might provide our opportunity to "catch up"; thereby making up for lost time and effort from previous ventures. I agree it is easy to be drawn in hooked. Several times my curiosity and hope for a quick fix got the better of me and I made the purchase, only to be disappointed shortly afterward. I played tennis for almost twenty years. Playing 2-3 times a week was barely often enough to keep my skill level at the same consistency. There was not enough time in my week to play more often. I tried many products hoping to improve my game: better string, a better racket, the type of wrist bands for sweat, sticky stuff on my hands, different tennis balls and just about anything else there was available. But none of that substituted for not spending more time working on my game. The shortcuts just did not work.

Instant success is attractive, with our busy lives so full, working long hours, racing kids to soccer practice, choking down some dinner, checking email and watching TV for a couple of hours in order to relax before falling into bed. Furthermore, as a society we have long lost the ability to be patient, to persevere, to work our game plan and stay focused on our goal. In addition to all of that, the world around us, including politicians, church leaders and news media reinforced the quick fix concept by telling us what happens is not our fault. (At least nothing that couldn't be cured by a donation to their church, political campaign or cause). Our ailments, issues and problems in life were caused by those around us, and from whom we demand retribution. After all, we would not have made the mistakes we did if those around us had just done things the right way, "our" way.

We can learn so much if we would deviate from our busy schedule to spend time examining and analyzing the lives of those we consider "successful". We often do not learn of or recognize the number of years successful people have spent working on their crafts, perfecting their business plans and overcoming obstacles along the way. The media only shows us the fortunate outcome, which gives us the impression their success has been achieved overnight. These successful people seem lucky in their endeavors and it isn't fair if we cannot accomplish the same thing. These stories leave us thinking we should not have to spend years working to reach the same goals. Shortcuts to achieving success seem like viable options; the perfect method to "catch up".

So bring on the get-rich-quick ideas and show us how to make money in our spare time. Show us how to be anything we want in thirty days or our money back, guaranteed. In the end we tried these shortcuts and the result was a shortcut to frustration and even more resentment. We lost money and valuable time.

Indeed, our society has become accustomed to and after decades actually programmed to wanting and getting everything, fast. The grocery store has ten checkout lines with no waiting. Cook your microwave meal in four minutes. Get a degree online in just six months. Combine that with the speed of the internet and drive thru meals and we believe anything can be obtained instantly.

We are often surprised when we find someone very successful and marvel at how that individual is so talented, so great at what he or she does. Why is that concept so astonishing to many of us? Unfortunately, the concept is astonishing because the idea of working hard for many years perfecting a craft is as foreign to many of us as the dirt on Mars. Focusing on a goal, working at it and believing in ourselves have been lost along the way. Furthermore, these concepts themselves appear alien to many of us because we do not know how to incorporate these concepts back into our psyche.

Let's look at some of those whom our society considers "successful." Do you suppose Michael Jordan practiced 20 minutes a day, 3 times a week to become a basketball superstar? Do you believe Tiger Woods mastered his golf game by practicing for 20 minutes a day 3 times a week to become the dominate golfer he is today? And it must be so that Lance Armstrong, winner of seven Tour de France races must have been on his bicycle 20 minutes a day, 3 times a week. Why would we believe we can "be like Mike" if we only put in an effort of 20 minutes a day, 3 times a week? We can't.

We then rationalize these individuals were born with some special "God-given" talent that made it easier for them. We rationalize this "special" talent meant these individuals did not need to practice since they could automatically jump higher, drive the ball farther and pump their legs faster than the average person. Take a closer look at each of these athletes and anyone else you consider a success, in business or any other field. You will find the "special" gift each of these individuals acquired, and for many of them not at birth, was a strong belief in themselves and the willingness to work hard to be the best they can be.

We were led to believe that all we had to do to be successful was put a small amount of time, energy or money into the process. We had been taught from early on that anything could be accomplished quickly. We had not been reminded and no longer valued the idea that perfecting anything requires no short cuts. Long gone were the influences of our parents and grandparents who worked long and hard to provide for their families and create opportunities for their children to go farther than anyone in the family.

Even businesses attempt to take shortcuts. Hoping to catch up to competitors, they quickly acquire a company without conducting the proper research due diligence. When the acquisition fails, management lays off workers and never considers examining what

44

steps could have prevented the failure. Other companies take shortcuts in production, adding or deleting ingredients, resulting in a less reliable or unsafe product. The company loses more market share, confused about why their strategy did not work. Another company management enters into hand-shake deals attempting to drive a product or business venture to market to keep up with competitors. With proper business procedures and processes lacking, the company experiences mishaps and delays in implementation of the business venture.

So here we are. We have come to this point. Gone are the inner fortitude and mindset to work hard to achieve success. Gone is our patience, and in a world of so many choices, many of us retreated by staying focused on only a few choices, leaving other important choices and decisions to those around us. If, however, the decisions others made did not benefit us, we complain. Some of us demand compensation from anywhere we can attempt to obtain it, while deep inside our own self-esteem slowly slips away. Gone is our self-confidence, because we never learned how to pick our selves up off the ground when we fall. We were taught someone should be there to help us; in fact, someone owed us a hand up, even if they were not the cause of our fall.

We also believed if we went to church, were kind to those around us most of the time, and tried to do the right things, then we were entitled to some sort of shortcut. We have been sold an illusion, a concept that has impacted our decision making and penetrated our belief systems. We will discuss this concept in extensive detail because it is important in understanding how we can make our future be something that no longer resembles our past.

That is what I am here to tell you. You can change your future. You can achieve and create a wonderful reality for yourself. The world you create may have some obstacles, but you will learn how to address them head on and grow in happiness, wealth and abundance.

But before moving on, let's quickly review where we have been and how we got here.

CHAPTER 7

So Where Are We Now?

"You have to expect things of yourself before
you can do them."

— Michael Jordan

Before moving into the next part of our discussion, let's summarize where we have been as a society, and what we have discussed through the first six chapters.

As you spend time considering the change in your belief systems and attitudes over the course of decades you can begin to understand how deeply embedded are your belief systems. The deepness of our belief systems helps generate our potential strong resistance to change. But change and evolution of your belief systems is necessary in order to move forward. These past six chapters highlighted the belief systems you may find challenging to evolve and overcome. Knowledge is power, and this knowledge will help you create success.

Successful people demonstrate the ability to create the opportunities and experiences they wish to have present in their lives. In truth, we all have this ability and power. Somewhere in our quest to be successful, to obtain everything we want in our lives, we lost our power to create our realities. More specifically, we gave that power away. How did this happen? Slowly and systemically.

Whether you are twenty, eighty, or somewhere in between, you are affected by societal, economic and cultural forces which have changed and evolved over the last century and are now imbedded firmly in the psyche of the American culture and societal norms.

Our grandparents and immigrants in the early 1900s were forced to work hard to provide shelter and food for themselves and their families. They took responsibility for their actions, aware if they did not find work, they might not eat that day. And just in case they might have forgotten this hard truth after a great decade of the 1920s, the Great Depression came along in the 1930s reminding everyone how vital it was to work hard and save for the future, both for themselves and their children.

As the economy grew prosperous into the Forties and Fifties, the "baby boom" began. As this generation of "Boomers" grew from teenagers to young executives and are now facing retirement, they radically changed the face of our culture and society along the way. Rejecting their parents' and society's accepted institutions and methods of achieving success, these "Baby Boomers" promoted a more individually focused and relaxed culture. They wanted to feel good now, and soon had the means by which to accomplish this. Not everyone took part in this revolution, but the Baby Boomers had made their mark.

As the 1960s faded into the 1970s, and women came into the workforce in record numbers, another economic boom occurred. With average household incomes rising dramatically and memories rapidly fading of our grandparents worrying over their family's next meal, we discovered we had the power for instant gratification in many more ways. We decided waiting years to obtain success, to obtain financial wealth and obtain material pleasure was no longer acceptable. Instant gratification was our primary focal point as new homes, new cars, exotic vacations, expensive clothes and fine dining were all within reach. Instant gratification was not only possible, but was now our societal norm.

The 1980s ushered in a new age of technology, corporate growth, mergers and acquisitions, and a new optimism. Our new found wealth and self-focus led us to continue satisfying our grow-ing appetite for material goods. The economy roared onward fueled by the spending spree of millions of Baby Boomers, who had now reached their thirties.

As all this was happening, there were also millions of people who were not able to take part in this rapid rise in wealth. For some, doors were locked due to the same problems that have plagued our nation for generations, such as prejudice and its resultant — sometimes subtle and institutionalized — discrimination. For others, it was a matter of being unable to figure out how, or not having the skills, to enter the doors being opened. Many were left behind and became resentful and wary of the successes of others.

Many of us had become accustomed to "quick fixes" for our problems. Entire industries emerged to peddle instant gratification for every need, immediate solutions to every problem, everything one could desire in little time and with little effort.

As these "make-it-happen-quickly" ads bombarded us each day, our societal and cultural institutions began to preach that the upper class somehow had an advantage over the rest of us. They pointed out how it seemed unfair that those who had worked for many years (while some of us did, many of us did not) had so much while so many had less. Therefore, those who were successful in life needed to share with those of us who weren't as fortunate. After all, the pie was only so big in life and there was only so much to go around. The "pie" analogy was continually used and expressed by more and more people. Everyone's focus centered on getting a piece of the pie, because we all believed if someone else secured a piece of the pie, there was less pie to split among the rest of us.

According to this new cultural belief, none of what was holding us back was of our own doing. Others had done this to us. Others had an unfair advantage. Others were to blame for our lot in life and why we remained there. Armed with those thoughts and beliefs, constantly reinforced every day by our politicians and so many others, watching ourselves grow older without new results and feeling farther away from obtaining our goals, we looked for simple, quick ways to rectify the problem.

One process we got really good at was suing. This could give us some measure of instant satisfaction and help us obtain what was rightly ours from those who had more. Insurance companies, big business, even the little store down the street were all targets to pay out damages for real or perceived harm. There is no question certain businesses were unethical in their practices. Yet many good and responsible people have paid and continue to pay the price for angry plaintiffs' blatant irresponsibility. Like a feeding frenzy, lawyers swarmed the airwaves and media informing you how they could secure thousands of dollars for you. Lawyers were ready to ensure anyone, anywhere, was paid today for what would have been laughed out of court rooms a half century ago.

Forfeiting our willingness to be responsible for our own actions and their consequences have led us to believe that some who have achieved greatness must have had an inside avenue to success that we didn't know about. Thus, we have even demanded restitution for successful people hiding "the answer" from us!

The truth is "the answer" to a happy and fulfilled life has been present all along. We simply do not like "the answer". "The answer" takes too long. Being able to meet our every need and desire almost instantaneously has made us an impatient people. We lost our patience long ago.

When we finally realized we had to address some issues and make up for lost time, we tried to take shortcuts. Yet shortcuts have proved to take us nowhere fast. Living vicariously through others — actors, sports teams and figures, even our children — is a way of transferring someone else's success onto ourselves.

Our lives are further complicated by technology, specifically the world of the internet which lets us explore everything conceivable. Time has become an even less available commodity. We spend less and less time developing our talents and skills, helping to improve and "grow" ourselves. There are too many choices, which lead us to make only the choices that matter most. We let someone else worry about all that other "stuff".

Once we tried the shortcuts and failed, we lost faith in ourselves and God. We started to believe we were not worthy of success, happiness or achieving our goals. Most importantly, we lost our self-confidence, the key ingredient for anyone to succeed.

Why have I walked you through the changes of the last century? My purpose is to show our society lacks the "political will" to consider the long-term impact of our actions. We lack the mindset of patience to spend the time working towards our dreams or fixing those beliefs, bad habits, and any other undesirable traits we possess. Why? Because our society is now primarily based on what can be achieved in the short-term with short-sighted accomplishments. We make many mistakes along the way when we are hurrying toward success, and we must be willing to do what it takes to achieve true success.

Complicating the process is the need to feel good now which has deeply penetrated how we think, believe and act today. Almost everything we do revolves around how good it will make us feel, immediately. When something appears to go wrong in our lives, we seek an immediate remedy.

Yet, in the pursuit of feeling better, the actions we take often get us back to where we started. Why? Because to change the outcome you must change the process. To change the process you must change the biggest variable in the process: you. The change required is to change your belief systems — for some significantly, for others modestly — and change your perceptions of the world and to change your actions.

It is difficult to change, but the reward is more than worth it. When we do not or will not change us, then the outcome will not change. However, if we take a long hard look at ourselves and strive to learn from past road bumps and apparent setbacks, we have the opportunity to grow, to evolve, to become someone better, thereby increasing our self-esteem and with it, our success.

When we come upon someone who has worked hard, enhanced his craft to the maximum, whether it is Michael Jordan, or Steven Spielberg or Lance Armstrong or the late, great, Ray Charles, we have a tendency to view these people as unique and exceptional. We forget that people who truly succeed in life spent years working on their passion and perfecting it. For so many of us the time, effort and research necessary to obtain success are difficult commitments to make. In our eyes, these great people are superior human beings, very different from the rest of us.

And this is the point. We have come to believe these people are super human, when they had the same tools all of us have at our disposal: they believed in themselves, they did the work and they put in the time required to perfect their craft.

It is unfortunate so many of us have forgotten how valuable time and patience are, to the point that we have no patience for others, no patience for our dreams to be realized, no patience for the work required.

Successful people create their worlds out of successful mindsets. They succeed by going within and recognizing — sometimes not even consciously — that they have the ability within to succeed. They possess the ability to create their reality through goal setting, perseverance, determination and a deep faith in themselves. These successful people know they have the ability and the power within to create the world they desire. They seek out great teachers and are willing to learn, but only they can walk through the door of opportunity to success.

The ability to obtain the life you want is based on your ability to create what you want. How do you create what you want? By believing in your goal, by continuing onward while others say "no" or when your first attempts fail, but most importantly, believing in yourself. Believing in yourself, in your own ability in unison with higher powers, is the key *first* ingredient to the finished product.

There are many more ingredients. I will show you the road to success and abundance; as you travel this road successfully you will finally understand how the dynamic forces and laws of the Universe impact your reality. You will understand how you actually put these laws into motion with every thought, belief and action. Success and abundance will no longer be elusive if you are willing to take a different view of yourself, your world, your beliefs, actions, and the events in your life. You must be willing to consider there are avenues to success and abundance other than those methods you have tried and those you have been taught. The road is not necessarily easy, but along this road you will achieve levels of abundance and happiness you never thought were possible.

You have seen what has brought us to this point in time. You have begun to see some beliefs that are not working for you. You have begun to see beliefs you were not aware were deeply embedded in your daily psyche.

You must be willing to question many of your existing beliefs about the world and Universe.

There is, then, one course of action, one path we must decide to choose in order to create the world we desire. To do so involves changing ourselves by changing the way we view ourselves and our world. But in order for us to change who we are, we must change a belief strongly held by so many of us. This belief permeates our society and is the driving force behind most of our actions.

This one belief, this one concept, has been the root cause for millions of people, right here in our country, to be unsuccessful in their attempts to obtain — and be — all they desire. It is the most important reason we have become a society that blames everyone around us for our failures in life:

We believe in the zero sum game of life.

Part II

How to Create
The World You Desire

CHAPTER 8

The Zero Sum Game Idea is a Myth

"Expect your every need to be met.
Expect the answer to every problem.
Expect abundance on every level."

— *Eileen Caddy, American Spiritual Writer*

The zero sum game idea is a myth. I said that correctly. Most of us have been duped into believing in the zero sum game concept and philosophy. It has impacted our way of thinking, our belief system and how we view our own success as well as the success of others. It is an idea that has driven the political process in this country and caused us to create laws based on the perceived win/lose belief. It has cemented in us a belief that we are separate from one another. Believing in this concept has deeply affected our belief in ourselves, and even our view of life on a spiritual level. The concept of everything in life being a zero sum game has implications of enormous proportions. Upon closer examination you will discover a significant percentage of your actions were determined by your belief that everything, or almost everything, in life was a zero sum game.

What is the zero sum game? Simply put, it is the theory that if I am in competition with you for anything in life, only one of us can win. If I win, then you lose. If you win, I lose. Nowhere in the concept is there room for the possibility of us both winning. This belief is held fast by many of us today and has been integrated into our culture.

If you were using math, you would consider giving a point for a win and subtracting a point for a loss. Hence, a plus-1 added to a minus-1 equals zero. This theory assumes a finite, or limited amount of outcomes. To imply that when someone wins, therefore someone else must lose, assumes that there was only one outcome or possibility.

Believing in this "limited" thinking is contrary to the real events we watch unfold daily. Applying this to our daily lives, it means if there is a job opening we both apply for and you get the job, then I must lose since I did not get it. Did I lose? Of course, I didn't. We all have experiences in which we thought we "lost" in an attempt to achieve or obtain something, only to turn in another direction ending up somewhere even better than we originally expected. Recently an old friend was telling me how thirty years ago he was about to join a small company, promised a potential ownership share of the business, but just before he was to start, the company decided to rescind their offer. Instead of feeling angry that he lost, he went on to start his own business, that he stills owns today with great success.

Believing you've lost when you do not land a job is a myth. This implies there is only one job that exists for you. Applied broadly, there are far more people who are searching for jobs than there are available jobs. These are both myths. There are always more jobs available, some that haven't been created yet.

Over eighty percent of the jobs created each year are generated from small businesses, not the industry giants as you might first assume. You might have to learn an extra skill, or even take on a position in a different industry, but consider the long-term benefits. If you aren't adding to your job knowledge and skill base each year, chances are you are barely staying even with the rest of the workforce, and most likely are falling behind. As discussed earlier, once we have reached a comfortable position in life, we have a tendency to do anything to stay just where we are. It doesn't matter if you are a CEO of a company or you are a worker in a factory. If you feel comfortable in the life you have, chances are you don't want it to change. However, if you view life as a constant opportunity to learn, you will benefit greatly. Trying to maintain the status quo is very difficult and in the end we end up falling behind. Will Rogers said, "Even if you're on the right track, you'll get run over if you just sit there."

I know many of us wish everything will remain as it is. However, life is an ever continuous flow of energy and change. There are some things we hope will improve, but once we seem to have our piece of the pie and life in balance, we work hard to keep it as it is. Staying within our "comfort zones", or daily routines, is important to us: Driving to work each day to the same company, taking the identical route each day, doing the same tasks at work, coming home to our families and lives outside of work. We find comfort and security in the "sameness" and find discomfort in change. Consistency helps us feel as if we have some control of our outer world. Too often, changes to our "comfort zone" create fear and anxiety within us.

The truth is you, and the world around you, keep changing. Look at the advancements in technology, medicine and even social awareness. There is so much truth in the old saying, "Nothing is as permanent as change." We only believe there are no more jobs because we want the same job we had for the last twenty years, but just as the world changes, and we change, those jobs change. If you have been in the same position or doing the same job for over five years, take a close look at your specific tasks. Although the product or result may be the same, the individual tasks will have changed due to technology, productivity gains, and additional job training.

Where did this idea come from if you win, then I lost, or vice versa? How did it become so deeply rooted in our consciousness and our way of life? One only has to turn on the TV or pick up the newspaper to see the latest results in sporting events, where we clearly establish that there is always a winner and always a loser. We have made it quite clear that only a pure winner, only the last standing, is worthy of anything, is worthy of a prize, our attention, our adoration and respect. Though you may be the second best pro tennis player (or insert your favorite sport here) in the world, you are considered a loser. Who remembers who lost in the Super Bowl or who lost in the World Series 3 years ago? We have come to believe in "all or nothing."

But is that all there is? Of course not! How can we ever equate being named second (or third, or fourth…) best *in the world* in anything is losing? Those "losers" have often gone on to further success and did not perceive they had "lost" something, but in fact had gained something valuable. These successful individuals were determined to push onward, not giving up, while they continued their belief in themselves and their ability and their dreams. Our sports lore and records are filled with players who came back from injuries, defeats, being traded, forgotten or given up on, to unimagined levels of success.

If you win a soccer game are you a winner, and of what? Aren't there other teams in your state, your nation and the world? And when you win the game today, isn't tomorrow another day, another game, with different teams and different players? And isn't there another season next year? Then there is no zero sum game. There are always more mountains to climb, more challenges and more opportunities to "win". Winning is really succeeding at being the best you are and creating the life you want.

Too often we view the world in the here and now. Our reality is based only on what we can feel, see and touch. We view our world in finite, exact terms. For example, many of us would like to win the lottery. Lottery jackpots have escalated in the last several years to over one hundred million dollars. When I was a child I could not "imagine" the significance of one million dollars. I could not understand fully the magnitude of that much money. If the amount was all in one dollar bills, I wondered how high the pile would reach if each dollar was stacked upon the next. Today, I can conceptualize one million dollars or one million people in my mind, although it is still difficult. If we have difficulty imagining the magnitude of one million, or maybe one hundred million dollars, imagine the reality of one billion dollars or one trillion dollars, or stars in the universe. Some numbers are just too big for us to get our minds around.

The mind has a tendency to ONLY hold on to that which it can rationalize and make sense of. Since it is very difficult to understand and comprehend such large amounts, our minds reduce it to amounts to which we can relate. Our minds reduce the amount to something we can understand. This concept is so important in our understanding of how this belief and so many other beliefs impact our actions. We take so many things we don't fully understand and wrap them in some known rationale or logic in order to file these concepts away in our minds to be used later.

> *The problem occurs when we believe the amount*
> *we can relate to is all there is!*

Any amounts beyond those we can comprehend are eliminated in our minds as unachievable and not part of our realities. It is critical we understand the "limit" our minds force onto our imaginations and thought processes. We can only achieve that which we can first visualize. Walt Disney was able to visualize Disneyland, imagining in great detail the wonders of the place eventually to bear his name. He was able to create this amazing "world" by pushing his mind to accept the vastness of something unheard of before that time. Many of us only achieve limited results because our minds have constrained us and limited our thinking. If you have difficulty visualizing in specific detail your goal or outcome, then the end result will be far less than you had hoped for.

Here is another example, closer to your own life. You may want a new job, and you take some time to write down many of the attributes of the job you seek. Most people would stop at four or five items. This short list would most likely include: more money, more responsibility, better benefits, friendly atmosphere and a supportive boss. I probably have just listed the top five most people would write down, and leave it at that. Yet, it is imperative that you examine and explore in greater detail the depth of each one of these goals. What does it look like to you to have "better" benefits? Does that mean your health benefits are flexible, more comprehensive, cover more conditions and provide excellent customer service, all at a lower cost? Or, does obtaining greater benefits for you include more days off at holidays, a greater number of days awarded for vacation, paid leave and sickness time off? You may reply, "I want all of that". I am not surprised you do! However, if you do not visualize all of that is possible, it will be difficult for your mind to believe finding employment with all of those great benefits is possible. If you do not give your mind a clear picture of the many possibilities, your mind will "limit" your thinking to only those you believe are achievable. Many companies do not provide every benefit you desire or to the depth you desire. Visualizing all of the benefits clearly helps you spiritually connect to those specific companies that meet your requirements.

Unfortunately, we get hooked into this limited thinking mentality because we have been so focused on a win-lose thought process. Politicians, media, schools and even some religions have promoted these concepts. These institutions reinforce the concept of working hard to get your share or someone else will get it. Some even go further, insisting if you didn't get your share then you should be given your share from those who obtained it! Many wars in history were about defending what belonged to one country as another country tried to take it from them.

We live in a world in which we can touch and feel everything. We mistakenly believe we can see everything that exists. Our issue arises when we don't look past what we see, or touch or feel. When we view the number of jobs available in the world, or the amount of money the entire population can have at their disposal, we tend to think in terms of a finite amount. Everybody talks about getting a "piece of the pie" as if the pie size is constant and never changes. Many believe this "pie" never gets any bigger, and if you believe the pie is a finite amount, you will do anything possible to get your share of the pie.

Examine the actions of those around you every day and take a close look at how many actions are implemented to help one group keep "their share" of the pie. Oil companies don't want electric or hydrogen cars in use because they would lose "their share" of the pie. Manufacturers of children's cereal continue to use sugar and artificial colors instead of healthy alternative ingredients because these cheap additives produce greater profits. These companies are afraid of losing profit by offering the healthy alternatives. Mass merchandise stores continue to sell products with artificial colors, flavors, and various other chemicals in order to generate higher sales through competitive low prices, fearing offering higher quality merchandise would threaten their business profitability. Many of us in companies whose profits are dwindling due to mature markets and competition from abroad want the government to step in an protect our jobs so we don't lose our piece of the pie. The list goes on and on.

Many politicians have convinced us that not all of us can achieve what we want in life and therefore must seek restitution from those who have succeeded. Each time a bill or law is debated in Congress, politicians enjoy touting how the less fortunate will benefit from taking from the rich. Look at the class warfare some are so eager to extenuate. Why have they done so? To protect their share of the pie they are sure is finite. If a politician gives more money to you via benefits or tax cuts, you will vote for him and he retains his job.

Some politicians make irrational decisions that do not have long-term value for you or the country, but they do it anyway in an attempt to preserve their share of the pie. The last four Presidents have requested the line item veto and Congress refuses to approve the law. The line item veto would allow a President to approve certain pieces of legislation but not all of it. For example, there may be an important piece of legislation on healthcare passed by Congress waiting the President's approval. But included in the legislation is requested funding for a museum in one city, a library in another city, tax credits for certain companies, and many other unrelated spending projects. The President wants the power to eliminate those unrelated spending requests, but Congress will not approve a law granting that authority! Politicians are protecting their pet project and their piece of the pie.

Some of us will cheat others just to protect our piece of the pie.

Numerous laws and watchdog agencies in our government exist simply to protect us from each other. Many companies take short-cuts to earn quick profits at the expense of others and only do so out of fear they will lose what they believe is their piece of the pie.

Let's take a closer look at the "pie". There are more people working today than ten years ago, and more than compared to twenty years ago. According to the U.S. Government Department of Labor Statistics, in July, 2007 the number of civilians employed in the U.S. was 146.1 million compared to 129.4 million in July, 1997. In that ten year period, the number of civilians employed in the U.S. grew by 16.7 million, a thirteen percent increase.

The truth is, the "pie" actually got significantly bigger. The economy had to grow dramatically to create almost seventeen million more jobs. The "pie" is not constant in size, but continually grows, yet we have been taught to believe there is only a limited amount to go around.

Universal Law #1: The concept of a zero sum game is a myth. Rather, the Universe is expanding and with it everything expands, including the potential for abundance for everyone.

Fact: There is enough for everyone. Where did the jobs come from? Most jobs are created by small business owners, people just like you, who had an idea, took the risk, believed in themselves, and persevered. I worked for such a company started by two men with an idea to sell hotel rooms to the world on behalf of the hotels in this country. These men believed they could find more "buyers" for these rooms than the hotels could find on their own. They were right. They were right to the point of building a $1.5 billion dollar company with over 1,200 employees.

The pie is only so big? There are only so many jobs to go around? All companies started out as a simple idea in the minds of a few people who then believed in the concept and turned it into a business.

Once you see and understand that the pie is increasingly expanding, your actions and results will be different. You will no longer be scared of the person next to you. You will no longer be scared when someone else lands the job you applied for, nor will you believe you have "lost" as a result. You will no longer take short cuts out of fear. You will no longer believe there is less to go around when someone else succeeds.

The same conclusion is true for the amount of wealth and abundance in the world. It is continually growing and is NOT finite. Yet continually we are led to believe that somehow if someone gets rich, there is less abundance to go around for the rest of us. This is not only a huge myth and extreme deception, but if you believe this concept, you have been hurt by it extensively.

In 1996 there were 4.8 million millionaires in the United States. This number almost doubled to 8.2 million in 2005. Merrill Lynch and Cap Gemini issued a report in June of 2007 stating there were 9.5 million millionaires in the world in 2006, a more than eight percent increase compared to 2005. How was this increase possible? Considering the huge increase in U.S. and worldwide population in the last 10 years, this is a significant increase in total wealth for the world. If the "pie" was constant, the increase in millionaires would have been far fewer.

If you believe the amount of abundance is finite, then your actions, beliefs and thoughts will have been focused and impacted by the belief someone won and others lost wealth. In reality, there is greater wealth all over the planet than ever before, and it continues to grow. There is enough for everyone. Yes, *everyone*.

Once you truly understand there is enough abundance for everyone you will then cheer on the success of others, realizing their success is your success. Wishing them goodwill is positive energy you send into the Universe and it returns helping you in your endeavors. Most importantly, you will not attempt to cheat someone else out of his or her money for your own gain, for you truly do reap what you sow. What goes around does, in fact, come around.

Herein lays the core of our inability to succeed. When we believe the size of the pie is constant, and does not increase, we are left to believe and work under the philosophy that one person's success is achieved at the expense of another. Often, if you believe there is not enough to go around you may react with jealousy. Jealousy is an emotion created from fear. The fear that the pie is finite is driving your jealousy and your actions. Start today eliminating your jealousy and your fear by believing there is enough for everyone.

While money is not always the measure of success, it is clearly used as the biggest measuring stick in our culture. Most of us, if asked, admit we would like to be wealthy. In addition to providing us with material comfort and a certain degree of security, wealth permits us to pursue our interests, hobbies and passions. Yet, (as discussed in Chapter 4), wealthy people are often viewed with suspicion.

Have you noticed how we view the people in our country who have obtained great wealth? They are often viewed as having cheated or lucked their way into fortune and are often portrayed as dishonest in movies and on TV. True, some inherited their wealth and others may be "lucky" lottery winners. But those make up an extremely small percentage of people who have abundance. There are thousands — actually millions — of people who have worked hard and persevered while demonstrating honesty and high ethics.

While we all secretly wish we could achieve the wealth and success these others have achieved, many of us resent these achievers because of their success. A word of caution: if you resent someone else's success, then you are building and reinforcing a belief system that you can not achieve the same success! And if you have come to believe you can not achieve success because the pie is only one size then when someone else achieves monetary success, there must, therefore, be less to go around for everyone else. Can you see how this thinking fills most everyone with envy, anger and jealousy?

You will only resent someone else for having something you desire if you believe you can't have it!

By demonstrating the feeling of resentment you are telling God you believe you can not obtain success and it becomes a self-fulfilling prophesy. You create what you believe.

We have an issue in this country regarding entitlement programs, both domestic and foreign. I am all in favor of using tax dollars to help those less fortunate. At times we all can use a helping hand to get back on our feet again. Unfortunately, for some, the "receiving" has occurred for so long that they begin to believe it is their right and the "receiving" should go on indefinitely.

When we demand compensation for our lack of success, we send a message to the Universe and God that we believe we can not achieve success on our own. We send a powerful message to God that we believe we are not worthy of success, that we shouldn't have to work hard and that we doubt God will provide for us even if we do. In doing so we create a cycle, staying where we are and continuing the pattern. Only when we stop this cycle, believe in ourselves and create our own experience and happiness do we achieve and receive all of God's blessings.

Much of what we do is based in fear. We are worried there is not enough to go around. Fear limits our view to what we see. Fear will not let us conceive of what is beyond our purview. What is not seen is not understood, and what we do not understand we fear. Fear has us believe jobs are a limited commodity evidenced by the major debate about companies "shipping" jobs overseas to countries and people who are paid less than workers in the U.S., to cite just one example. If a company ships jobs overseas to reduce costs, then the company has an opportunity to make more money. What does a company do with more money? The company can invest its extra profits both in its people and its business. Yes, the company could pocket it and pay upper management bonuses and we know some companies have done that. At the same time many other companies invest in their people and new products. If money is not reinvested in research and development, none of the technology you see today would exist.

As I sit and write this book I ponder how many years ago someone writing a book would use a typewriter. My college age sons have never used a typewriter and would be appalled at its slowness, messy ink and inability to type over mistakes. What if we had kept alive the industries that make the typewriter and not advanced to the computer? Perhaps if we had created laws to protect the typewriter industry and its workers the typewriter today would cost extensively more and the computer may not exist. Typewriter workers might believe the government should protect their jobs by passing laws to ensure the industry's continued existence. Fearful that if displaced they would not find other jobs — certainly not one that pays as much as making typewriters — they also try to ensure that the computer industry is thwarted from developing into a viable competitor that can steal their slice of the pie. These workers may have feared they would not find another job, nor would they find one similar to the ones they had. Yet as we can see today, the tech industry has created millions of jobs. The tech industry created millions more than would ever have been created by the typewriter industry further evidencing the fact the pie is not finite.

People fear having to change, grow, add new skills and adapt in order to compete in the marketplace. All of these actions are born in fear. Most of us agree that we are more productive and have more fun on a computer. Today, not only my sons, but my wife and I as well, spend a significant number of hours using a computer both at work and at home. The computer industry not only continues to create millions of jobs, but is actually creating other, new industries by the advancement in technology, also employing millions of people. New industries are being created such as the 3-D world of animation, and now the animation and science is used in criminal DNA testing. Jobs will continue to be created as long as human beings desire and pursue growth in all areas of our lives.

What happens when fear rules your beliefs and your beliefs rule your mentality of obtaining success? Fear warps our beliefs and our perspective. Consider the numerous new political, social and economic issues causing fear and heated debate in our country and world. Emerging issues, some not conceived of thirty to forty years ago are directly impacting our belief systems. Issues such global warming, AIDS, bird flu, same sex marriages, cloning, stem cell research and terrorism are greatly affecting our lives. A natural human defense mechanism when we feel threatened is to lean significantly on our most trusted and deep-seated beliefs. Hence we read and hear constantly about the far left and far right political and social views in our country. Why? Because when people feel threatened they go to their respective belief "corners" of the ring. These strong beliefs are greatly influencing political and economic policy as people fear their piece of the pie will be impacted or lost.

Sadly, there are countless other examples of people willing to cause others pain in order to secure their own jobs. Look at the cigarette industry. They were willing to look away from overwhelming evidence indicating the health hazards of smoking, yet continued to sell cigarettes because of the numerous people dependent on smoking for a livelihood. Other jobs were out there, and their talents could have been used for more productive ventures, but for the fear of change.

Unfortunately, many believe in the zero sum game of life. Pharmaceutical companies create drugs to be consumed each day and do not appear as concerned about finding cures. If people were cured of diseases, pharmaceutical companies fear their profits would plummet. This is another example of not only fear based thinking, but short-sighted thinking. They fear once they cure the known diseases they will be out of business. Yet as we live longer, we are finding there are new diseases to combat. My father passed away from Alzheimer's disease, and his mother, my grandmother, may well have suffered the same condition. However, when my grandmother was alive, scientists had not fully understood and concluded such symptoms to be what we now call Alzheimer's. These companies could put their income dollars to work in other areas of science for the body, where so much is still unexplored, still a mystery.

People are living longer today than ever before. As we age new health issues are affecting people's health. The reduced air quality, chemicals and preservatives in our foods and diminishing nutrient value in our foods are all creating more health challenges. There are plenty of opportunities for research dollars to impact the long-term implications of our life styles. Scientists acknowledge they are only just beginning to understand how parts of our complicated physiology works to prevent disease and coordinate the thousands of functions required in keeping us alive each day. Vitamin C was discovered almost one hundred years ago and scientists today are still examining its value and affect on the body.

Over twenty years ago when the first computers began to make their way into the mainstream of the business world, early critics were concerned with the high speed capability of computers. These critics feared there would be less work remaining for workers and consequently millions would be out of work. Imagine that! Do I have to ask you if your work load has decreased? There is always more work, more opportunities, more challenges and more horizons to explore.

There are countless examples of how we not only take a short-term view of problems but also have become a reactionary society instead of a more proactive one. We wait until an unfortunate event occurs before resolving problems, and then often with a knee-jerk overdone, quick fix reaction.

Take for example the chaos today at our airports. Consider that the technology today exists for more airplanes to be routed on shorter routes to destinations with greater safety. Yet the major airlines, small commuter planes, union workers and even Congress won't make changes because they all have a fear and short-sighted mentality that they have something to lose if changes are made. We can only hope that it does not require a major tragedy to spur the parties involved to take action and make air travel safer for everyone.

Unfortunately, we often trade a long-term view for a short-term view, for short-term satisfaction, for short-term reward. Sound familiar? Believing in the zero sum game we determine there is not enough to go around, creating fear within each of us. Fear motivates us to do everything possible to save our piece of the pie from being lost or taken from us.

Look closely and you can see many people view God in the

same manner. They believe that there is only so much of God to go around, so they have created religions that have strict rules and beliefs and do not tolerate different thinking and viewpoints. In doing so, the people who created these religions and those who follow them, have been able to prevent everyone from being included. Those who are part of this religion then feel more secure, safer, and closer to God because they feel they get a bigger "slice" of God. The more others are included, the less of God there is to go around. No wonder we have wars in the name of God.

Scientists today will tell you that the Universe is expanding and has been for millions of years. Everything in our lives and our world, including God, is expanding. There will always be enough of God and food and wealth to go around for everyone because we all are made from God, and in essence our souls are God. If you take a glass and fill it with water from the ocean, is the water in the glass still not the ocean? Our souls are God, and therefore we are all part of God. Call God in terms of what ever your faith may be, but we are all part of the same divine energy, no matter what we call it, him or her. God created us and everything around us. Similar to the glass of water from the ocean having the same propensity of the ocean, we also have the ability to create everything in our lives.

Let me expand on this concept further. God loves all of us as most all of us agree he/she made us. Our souls are from the essence of God. As a father I want my sons to be happy, healthy, obtain wisdom, enjoy prosperity, and experience all they want to experience in their lifetimes. My sons have free will to do so in any way they choose. As a parent it is difficult at times to watch them struggle, yet I know I must let them pursue their goals and ambitions and desires in their own manner. However, whatever it is they desire, I want them to have it, assuming they mean no harm to anyone else. As a parent I want to do whatever I can if they want my help, but, more importantly, I want them to succeed. As parents we view our children similar to how God feels toward every one of us. If that is the case, then wouldn't God want all of us to succeed? If we are all God's children wouldn't God want ALL of us to learn and grow, have prosperity and happiness and peace? Of course God does. God wants everyone, including you, to have abundance in *every,* aspect of your life.

The Universe has enough for everyone to have abundance. You have the power to create abundance and the reality you desire, because the pie is ever expanding. God gives you the ability to create abundance on your own. God is not selective about who achieves abundance. Only you decide if you will achieve abundance because there is no limitation to the pie.

Religions and churches have had trouble with the idea that we create our own world. Some of them have not understood we have it within us to create the world we desire. Therefore, church leaders had to come up with a rationale about why we don't always succeed. They would say "God has a plan, and you just don't know it". Somehow this rationale was supposed to make us feel better and console us for not achieving success in our lives.

If God wants us to succeed, like I want my sons to succeed, wouldn't God tell us HOW to succeed? Of course, and it is simple. You create success by what you believe about yourself, others and your world. And if you believe there is not enough success to go around, then you believe in limitation and you will experience the lack you believe in. Or you can move forward, believing all of us can achieve and obtain wealth, happiness and joy in our lives.

The problem is that we have been taught the zero sum game. We have been taught there is only so much to go around for everyone, whether it is love, money, or success. Some religions teach that God has reasons that some of us fail. They teach that if we do not adhere to God's rules then we suffer the consequences. When you are all you can be you have the ability to give more of yourself and what you have to others, thereby creating an even more wonderful Universe. Some religions, or religious leaders attempt to show they are better than people who attend their service to keep the worshippers coming back to donate more money, because some leaders fear once you understand you create your own world and can find your connection to God yourself and achieve success, you might no longer need these religious leaders. Their shortsightedness makes us all pay in the long run.

God wants everyone to succeed, learn and grow. There is no value for God if you are not being successful and achieving your dreams and heart's desires. To believe that being poor but having a good heart is somehow going to make us more worthy or deserving is a myth. There is great value — for God and all of us — in being all we can be, in having all God can provide, if we are willing to accept it. If God is "saddened" by anything, it is each of us not being all we can be. The only true "sin" is not being the best we can be.

When you have abundance, knowledge, emotional and spiritual balance, you have the ability to help others, teach others and impact the world. Just as I want my sons to be all they can be, so God wants us to be all we can be, all we can create and experience.

Now that you know the zero sum game is a myth and there is enough abundance in the world for everyone, you are ready to take the next step down the path to success.

We will realize the amount of love, joy and wealth is always within our grasp and understand it is infinite in its abundance when we come to know:

We each create the world we experience based on what we believe. We acknowledge we can not change our experience by changing those around us. Instead we must change ourselves. No one ever told us we create everything in our lives and create everything that happens to us, but we do.

We create our world. We create our experiences. I explained how we lost this insight a long time ago.

To regain our ability to create our experiences, we first need to understand we never lost it. To become aware of how we never lost it:

We have to change how we perceive our lives.

CHAPTER 9

Perceive Your World Differently and Your World Will Change

"It is one of the commonest of mistakes to consider that the limit of our power of perception is also the limit of all there is to perceive."

— *C.W. Leadbeater, English clergyman and theosophical author*

You didn't lose it or really give it away. You just stopped recognizing your own ability and power to create your world. You rationalized the events in your world you "perceived" as unfortunate were caused by something else, someone else or other, outside forces.

You believed these forces were not connected to you. You questioned how you could create these happenings in your life and why you would create these happenings in your life.

You can understand this concept better if you step away from defining the experience as "wrong" or "bad" or "good" or "successful", and instead simply recognize everything occurring in your life was created by you. It is all you.

You might be saying to yourself "Why would I want to create the situation in which I was laid off?" or "How could I have created the experience that put me in a car accident when it was the other person's fault for running a stop sign?" Examining the process and answering these questions require us to take a long, hard look at how we perceive the world and each other.

You probably have heard it said that *"there are no accidents in life."* Many people believe in this concept. You probably have experienced situations in which the apparent coincidence of an event was so amazing that it felt like divine intervention: Running into an old friend in the grocery store whom you had just been thinking about; sitting next to someone on an airplane who just happens to be in a business you are interested in learning about; taking a different path to work one day, seeing your old heartthrob and rekindling the romance; deciding to wear a special suit to work one day when the president of the company visits unexpectedly and notices your professional look. We chalk all of these incidents up to "coincidence," yet most of us actually believe *there are no accidents in life*.

In these situations where there are positive results we are quick to believe it was not an accident. We are beings inherently filled with and created out of love and want to believe in God and God's love so much that we take a leap of faith, believing there must be a connection to events which appear "meant to be".

Often we only view specific events were "meant to be" when they create a positive experience. Yet, are there not unfortunate events that from a different perspective would also be considered as "meant to be"? To only consider there are no accidents in life when the events appear favorable can get rather confusing. It is often difficult to determine if the event was fortunate or unfortunate. And yet, if we believe that it is "no accident" only when the events were fortunate, wouldn't that suggest outside forces are at work in your life? Who determines what events are fortunate and unfortunate? And most importantly, who is driving these "meant to be" events? Your answer most likely is "God".

Let's examine the scenario if that these events that are "no accidents" and "meant to be" are originated from God. It gets a little more complicated, however, when we make the mistake of projecting our belief system of right and wrong onto God. We assume God views us, our experience, and the world in a judgmental way, handing out rewards or punishment. Upon closer examination, this concept is not practical. Do you see God *always* providing abundance to those whom you believe deserve it and *always* punishing everyone who appears to have earned it? It is confusing and frustrating to see bad things happen to good people and bad people reaping rewards. If we believe God rewards and punishes, God seems pretty inconsistent sometimes.

Confusion arises when we attempt to establish the specific actions which deserve credit and those which deserve punishment. If we ask 10 people for those rules, we will get 10 different answers. Your view of justice and punishment for a particular situation can be much different than mine. With that said, how can anyone ever know which is the correct action that will receive punishment or reward? Many people would say it is very difficult to ascertain when justice prevails or not.

Consequently, to say God is only involved on the positive "no accidents", who drives the negative "no accidents"? If God drives both we constantly have difficulty understanding the system of "justice" we believe God uses.

We have a difficult time connecting the dots when events work against us, or harm comes to us. In those situations we don't want to believe there was spiritual intervention in unfortunate events because we don't want to believe God would allow — or worse, *cause* — something bad to happen to us.

We were taught that God has it all figured out. Many of us were taught we may not know when events will occur, and probably will not ever be able to determine the reason for the events, but don't worry, it all made sense to God. If God is directing all of these "no accidents" and "meant to be" situations, then God is doing a lot of controlling. If that is the case, that process seems in direct contradiction to us having free will to make our own choices, and hence create our own cause and effect.

If we step back and do not attempt to project our belief system of right and wrong on to God, the answer becomes much clearer. We have believed we are at the mercy of God because we have projected the system of punishment and reward onto God.

The reality is God does neither.

Change your perspective to understand God gave us this world to create anything we want and provides us the opportunities to experience all sides of every emotion, gaining wisdom and enlightenment in the process.

Everything in life is comprised of two sides. Nothing can have only one side. A coin has two sides. The same is true with emotions. Love does not exist without hate. Happiness does not exist without sadness. Success does not exist without failure. You may have been fortunate enough to have several loving experiences. Yet you can not fully appreciate nor measure the total value of these loving experiences if you had not encountered the other side or unloving experience. I am not suggesting you must experience an unfortunate event to appreciate any value of a positive event. However, I am saying it is imperative to understand that once we understand we create our reality, we then manifest how much of one side or the other we experience. The depth of each experience is created by our beliefs and actions, not by God controlling our lives.

Once we realize and accept that God is not controlling our lives or destiny, we are led to the next conclusion:

We create our entire world by ourselves, with God's help.

Let's examine this concept further. If we believe there are no accidents in life, meaning we believe there is order in the Universe and in God's world, then can't we also assume *there is consistency in the Universe at all times?* If there are truly no accidents in life, we can not say that one event was "meant to be" but another was simply coincidence or chance. Either the concept is and always is valid, or it is not valid at all. There is no in between, no middle ground.

But wait, you are thinking "How can there possibly be order in God's world when I see so much chaos every day?" As strange as it may appear, there is order in chaos. Furthermore, what appears as chaos to you may appear to be total order to the next person! So in fact, there is no chaos.

This is why it remains true that:

To change your life you must change your perception
of the world and everything around you

If there are no accidents in life, there must be another driving force involved. If these events did not occur randomly and if we are not at the total mercy of God and those around us, the true driving force is you. You create everything in your life.

Change your perception to understand
you create the "no accidents" in your life.

It's not so hard to understand everything happens for a reason, or that we create the events in our lives, when things are going well. It is much more difficult to hold onto this belief when events don't turn out the way we planned. If I am constantly fatigued because I fail to get enough exercise or eat right and being tired causes me to fall sleep at the wheel of my car, I **did** create the situation. If I had a bad attitude at my job ultimately forgetting an important task resulting in missing out on an opportunity for advancement, I created this event. However, I did not create those situations for the purpose you might consider on first examination. Most everyone can see the connection of cause and effect in these examples and accept in these cases I was responsible for the outcome. All events and experiences in our lives follow the same cause and effect. Remember, Universal laws apply always and consistently, not just sometimes.

Universal Law #2: Universal laws are totally consistent.

No Universal law applies only part of the time.
A Universal law either applies always or
none of the time. There is no in-between scenario.

At this time you may still be having a difficult time seeing the connection to the more complicated and powerful events in your life.

I can answer your questions by providing an example of something that happened to me many years ago. Wait, were you paying attention? What is wrong with what I just wrote? The events and people I encountered many years ago did NOT happen *to me*. The events I experienced did NOT "happen to me". Instead, I created them. The belief, and illusion, that outside events *happen to us* is a major misperception we must change immediately.

To continue with my story, I was working at a well-known company and held a good paying job with considerable responsibility in my field of work. At that time, my divorce from my ex-wife had been final for about a year following a long separation. Similar to many people, moving through the divorce process, I experienced feelings of inadequacy and a hit to my self-confidence. I have never been a person who gets depressed, but at certain times, as many of us do, simply doubted my own abilities. This was a difficult time for me. Sometimes certain events can cause us to have self-doubts and for me, this was one of those times.

At the same time, I yearned for a new life with a partner who was working to grow spiritually, mentally and emotionally. We never stop growing and I had done a lot of hard work on myself over the previous fifteen years, and although I know that the learning never stops I believed I was ready for a new journey.

I had been dating a woman, "Susan", for about a year who I thought I could potentially marry, yet the relationship was going nowhere. As much as I tried, Susan did not feel the spark we all need to make a relationship work. As we continued to see each other, I began to feel I wasn't good enough for her. (Note, I was the one feeling this inadequacy and I do not blame her for the situation.) As I look back, I am grateful to her for putting me in a position where one might ask "Why am I with a person who makes me feel inadequate and unsure of myself?" I bet most of you can guess why. I created the situation for me to deal with my own issues. The only way to deal with feelings of inadequacy or self-doubt is to put you in those situations that trigger those feelings and face them. Hoping the feelings go away to never return does nothing, except cause you to hope and wish even more. And, isn't it interesting that the same situation continues to present itself in your life until you address it and resolve the underlying issues? If you look closely at the problem areas in your life you will recognize old themes resurfacing until you face them, break through them and grow from them.

We often ask God in prayer to help us through a difficult situation. What God will give us is strength and love. We must do the work. He can lead us to the door, but we must walk through the door, break through the wall, go up and over it, or tunnel underneath it! God gives us courage, but we have free will and power of belief to push through our personal emotional and spiritual boundaries and become a new person.

At the same time I was struggling with self-doubt in my personal relationship with Susan, it became quite apparent that my supervisor at work no longer considered me as effective in my job as in previous years. There was no rational basis for this as I had continued to meet or exceed all goals set for me each year. In addition, my boss hired someone into the department who was fifteen years younger than me and over time was giving this younger guy more work and responsibility, taking some of it away from me. This was particularly troubling to me because I believed I was ready for more responsibility, not less.

For months I was dismayed, trying to understand what was going on. I was not asking God "Why is this happening to me", but instead said to myself "Why have I created this experience?" and I wanted to know what I was supposed to learn and experience in order for me to grow.

What were my thoughts, beliefs and actions which put in motion the energy resulting in these events? There was no doubt in my mind I created the experience as an opportunity to address something significant in me. From the outside you might be able to quickly see why all of it was happening, but in the middle of the experience it is much more difficult to see clearly. Painful as it may be, we have to stay determined to work through the issue.

Finally, during the last stages of my personal relationship with Susan, I took a step back and took a long hard look at what was occurring. To do this, I had to pay close attention when I "felt" certain emotions, then look for the cause. I began to notice my own feelings of inadequacy when Susan made certain statements or acted in a particular way. Shortly afterward, the relationship ended and I quickly understood how I had allowed myself to be treated poorly and the experience generated feelings of inadequacy. I created the experience and it provided me not only the opportunity to manage or eliminate my self-doubt, but also to realize I could have stopped the relationship at any time, and yet I allowed it to continue. I had stayed far too long in the relationship unsure of why the events were occurring, and hoping somehow the relationship would improve.

Once the relationship ended, it didn't take long for me to remind myself that down deep I believed in myself, believed I had value, was smart, had come along way after my divorce, had a lot to offer another woman and was not going to look back. My self-confidence was re-energized by remembering how on numerous occasions I had persevered by facing my fears and reaping amazing results. Once I started my search again for someone to share my life with, the quality of the women I encountered was even more wonderful than before, as these women matched my self-confidence with so much to offer. I learned just how powerful my beliefs, actions and emotions are in creating my experience and world.

On the work front, the situation continued to deteriorate. Once I had reviewed with my bosses the extensive accomplishments for which I did not receive credit, I wanted out. I was unsure where I would go, and had not begun a job search. But for once I was not afraid. Having an employment contract, I was willing to take my time job searching because if they laid me off, I had previously signed a contract providing a severance package. However, after several months passed I was ready for a change no matter what it involved. With full faith in myself and realizing I can create my future to be anything I want it to be, one day I woke up and said to God "Let's do it." Either they keep me or get rid of me, but I am not afraid. I have a lot to offer another company. So I want movement now".

I was laid off that afternoon.

God had helped open the door for me once I requested it by believing I could move on successfully. Now was the time for me to step through it. I worked hard networking and landed a job in less than three months while the economy was in a major downturn! The job was with an excellent company, I had a supportive boss, greater responsibility and a promotion in title. Remember earlier I believed I was ready for more responsibility? Was being laid off fortunate or unfortunate? Some might consider being laid off as unfortunate, yet I landed a position in a very short period of time with greater responsibility. Remember from chapter 8 that losing a job does not mean failure? Remember the pie is ever expanding and there are other opportunities to win?

Was it no accident? It was no accident. Did I create it? Of course I created it. I believed in myself and when I changed my perception of what was going on around me, and changed my belief in my self, my life changed.

Now you have an example of how what clearly appeared to be "chaos" or a "bad" experience in my life was in fact, one of the best things that could happen in my life.

In my new job my confidence grew and my new boss complimented me constantly on how much work I accomplished and the positive impact I was having on my new company. I went from a situation where my work and opinions were disregarded to one in which respect for me was shown every day. And isn't it fascinating how I received little respect at my old job which precisely mirrored the way I felt about myself? Once I truly began to value my skills and experience I came into a situation in which I was greatly valued.

Most importantly, this event did not "happen to me." Instead, I *"happened it"* to myself, if there is such a way as to describe it. I could easily have blamed my situation on my boss, his boss or on my relationship with Susan. I could have gotten depressed and blamed God for letting this happen to me. But I did not.

I will say it again:

I happened it to myself.

The change only happened when I made the change. No one, not even God, was going to make the change for me. I had to walk through the door. It was difficult. Looking at ourselves and deciding to change something about ourselves can be quite emotional and intimidating. And yet, when we look inward and recognize what can be changed, it proves we are all strong and deserving. Looking inward requires time, patience and consistent effort. The reward is priceless.

There is another significant concept here which must be understood: Not only did I create what I experienced, but

it happened because it was a reflection of what I believed about myself.

I created the experience providing me an opportunity to resolve my issues and grow, plus I created the experience because it reflected what I felt about myself. Some people may suggest this experience was only created because I needed to address my self-confidence. Yet, the key lesson here is this experience was inevitable because I created it out of my beliefs.

My belief in my self doubt created an experience filled with people and events that "mirrored" my strongest beliefs: a boss and a dating partner lacking confidence in me.

Universal Law #3: You create the experience.

The experience provides an opportunity to

learn and grow from the challenges. At the
same time, the experience is inevitable
because you create it in the first place.

We create our own "catch 22" cycle:
- We create our experience based on our beliefs;
- Our experience causes us to reinforce the same belief;
- Unless we change our beliefs and actions;
- We create the same experience all over again.

Take note: our beliefs have a significant impact in creating our reality, whether we like it or not. Have you ever repeated the same experience in your life, maybe in your romantic relationships or career? Have you found no matter whom you meet, the same relationship issues rise up each time? Do you experience the same job related issues even when changing jobs and companies?

No one is *doing* anything to you. There is no "negative force" out there somewhere causing bad things to happen to you. No life force is *making* these events happen to you. You create them, all on your own.

Due to my feelings of inadequacy and self-doubt, my world around me, my reality, mirrored what I believed. Please understand this concept because once you do, you will fully grasp and understand that you create everything, drawn every person and experience to yourself and into your world.

The fact is, you can't help but create these experiences.
They automatically happen because they represent
what you believe to be true!

Once you realize this truth, the world becomes a different place in which to live and grow. Gone is the thought of blaming others around you. Gone is the desire to project negative thoughts onto others. Gone is the desire to get even or have vengeance or be compensated from others for what appeared to be what "happened to you." We then know it is about us, what we think, what we believe and how we feel about ourselves and how we view the world.

This is a huge concept that you must understand and incorporate into your being if you are to achieve all that you desire in your world. Not only do you create your world and have the ability to do so, you create *ALL* of it by what you believe to be true. Notice I did not say what *is* true, but what you *believe* to be true.

I once knew a man who did not trust most people. Because of his automatic distrust of people, "Fred" believed that the workers he employed were always trying to cheat the system. Many workers were paid on an hourly basis to prevent him having to pay added benefits. Once Fred realized he was paying a lot of overtime, he changed his employees to salaried so they would have to work many hours and he would not have to compensate them with overtime pay. I watched as he attracted people into his life in business dealing who at first attempted to work with him ethically, but once they saw how he tried to shortchange them, they quickly reacted by taking shortcuts in return. The result? Fred brought the very people into his life who represented his own beliefs of the world and other people. Any new vendor Fred negotiated with automatically tried to find a shortcut in a pricing deal. Any workers he hired soon learned how to call in "sick" periodically to be compensated under the salary arrangement for the excessive hours they were working. Fred brought the very people into his life who represented his own beliefs of the world and other people. Since he believed he needed to be tricky in his dealings with everyone, all of these people in-turn were tricky in their dealings with him. His world was a mirror of what he believed. Each person then further reinforced his own distorted view and perception of the world.

The entire time I knew Fred he never understood why his business dealings created further mistrust for him. He never learned why he needed to change his beliefs and actions.

Each experience you encounter is a gift from you
giving you the opportunity to break through
old patterns and beliefs to help you grow.

This concept is one of the most compelling ideas I hope you absorb from this book. Many times, after experiencing some life changing event, we look back and are amazed and feel blessed that something so wonderful came into our lives. This specific experience gave us the opportunity to change direction. Yet the experience automatically was going to happen because it was created out of your beliefs. There is a little bit of the egg and the chicken concept. You may find it difficult to figure out which came first.

Sometimes, unsuspectingly, we may have an experience and from this we draw a conclusion that we believe is true. Let's say your first serious dating relationship turns out badly, because the person betrayed your trust and lied to you. Your tendency will be to approach each new person and relationship cautiously, believing he or she will lie to you. Sure enough, every person you date lies to you. You then deduct that your belief is correct, since it happens every time. However, as long as you continue to radiate the belief into the Universe that each person you date will lie to you, this belief becomes reality.

Once you change your belief
you will no longer have the old experience.

Therefore:
changing your belief – changes your experience.

Working through this thought process requires further examination. You may ask "How do I simply turn off this belief that every person is a liar, when in fact, I have been lied to over and over again?" To change your experience, you must examine what you gain by retaining this belief. Does it somehow protect you from potential liars in the future? Does this belief allow you to treat someone rudely early in a relationship knowing that if the relationship fails, you have a built in excuse? Examine deeply what you gain by this belief and then you will know how to change your future experiences.

Take a look at what you are experiencing today. What do you

see going on around you? Do you "believe" you are being treated unfairly in some way? Do you "believe" or "feel" your boss does not treat your fairly or your spouse is unfaithful or you wonder why you get ripped off when you hire a repair man? Examine what you believe about these situations deep within you. If your boss treats you with disrespect, is it because you treat yourself with disrespect possibly by not taking care of your health properly? Is it because you lack confidence and thus do not take on responsibility for new projects? The people and places in your world are a mirror of your own beliefs.

Next, step away from your emotion. View the experience in a non-judgmental way. Examine the experience from a distance knowing that everything in the experience mirrors your beliefs. What are the specific actions of the experience?

Now proceed to determine which emotions surfaced during and after the experience. As we stated earlier, if an emotion such as jealousy occurred, consider you created the experience from your jealousy. Further, if this experience occurs again, is there a way you can react differently? Is there a way you can change your belief about jealousy to longer experience feeling jealous?

Several years ago, after my father passed away, my mother was determined to ensure everything in the house was in good working condition. Small repairs were needed on a leaky toilet, the fence in the back yard, and so forth. After repairing several items, my mother grew frustrated when something new required repair. She would say, somewhat exasperated, "Now what else will need fixing?" Her tone was filled with the belief something else would soon require repair. Sure enough, in a short time another repair was required. Once that repair was completed she would ask the same question until finally I recommended she delete that question from her belief system! Oddly enough — or perhaps not — the need for further bothersome repairs stopped! Her beliefs were mirrored in her world.

As I think back on my own story, I recognized I *did* create everything in my life. Not just some things, *everything*. It may be difficult to comprehend that we each possess this ability. Whether you like it or not, whether you believe it or not, *you have this power and ability*. The best part is you were born with it, and it's not something you have to spend years learning how to use. However, you may spend years un-learning the misconceptions deeply imbedded in your mind and belief systems.

But how did we come to have this inherent skill and power naturally? We all are a part of God, not separate from God. We all contain the essence of God. I doubt this is a totally new idea for you. I am sure you can look at all the experiences in your life and see how your beliefs at that time helped determine the power of the event on your life. You can look back remembering how one morning before playing a round of golf, you woke believing in your ability to hit the ball flawlessly, then went out to the course with your buddies and proceeded to have the best game of your life. Another day you may have had the feeling that life was out to get you and soon discovered your day was filled with one mishap after another, hitting every red light on your way to an important appointment, ending up behind the guy in the bank whose transaction takes twenty minutes.

We do create our world, and we do it every day. We simply forgot that we do. We often don't recognize the power we have.

Once we understand and begin to perceive the world around us differently, we can take the next step to create the world around us that we desire. You create the world around you by knowing,

It was you, all along.

CHAPTER 10

It Was You, All Along

"Within each storm of life is hidden a key that will unlock another door that you were meant to walk through."

— *Steve Brunkhorst, motivational author*

Yes, it was you all along.

You are the one who creates your world. You are the one who has the ability to shape your destiny, to produce the experiences and environment you choose to live in.

For too long we have been told by too many people that we lack the power and only a chosen few can lead the way. Too many people have viewed us to be no more than sheep following in line to give these leaders our power. (And don't forget the large donations they make you believe are required to prevent bad things from happening to you!)

Be excited by the potential and magnitude of the possibilities and power you have within you. When you begin to embrace the possibilities, you realize there is a whole world of options for you to experience.

Not all experiences may be pleasurable. I have not said you can create a world free of problems and struggles. The fact we are here on earth substantiates that we are here to learn. Learning can be fun. It can also be painful, if we let it be.

How many of us have found ourselves playing the fool in a relationship, or have been the one making someone else play the fool? In either case, we learn something about ourselves. Even though it may hurt emotionally, we often go into subsequent relationships with a new appreciation of what we do and do not want. When we don't learn the lesson, we do not graduate to the next level and consequently, we create for ourselves another, similar situation with another chance to get it right.

Does the idea of you creating your world and reality make you uncomfortable or go against what you have been taught? I am not surprised if it does make you feel uncomfortable or question if this concept can really be the answer you have been seeking for so long. The fact you are reading this book indicates you are looking for answers which your upbringing and current or prior religious beliefs could not provide. Now the results are up to you. Although this concept may be scary to some, for most and eventually even you will enjoy the freedom and excitement of possibilities that await you.

It was you all along. You have the power. You have the ability to make your life be whatever you want it to be. You have already created some pretty amazing experiences in your life and may not realize it. You also may have created a few experiences you would rather forget. But creating the world around you, and drawing to you the people, places and events is not magical at all. Your world is comprised, created and built by the energy of your thoughts, words and actions. Energy is the powerful component of which we are made. It is a part of the very essence of every human being.

When I look back on my life I can see many times when I created both really fun, rewarding experiences and some not so pleasant. During my first year of marriage with my ex-wife over thirty years ago, we were in search of a home in the city where we lived. There was one particular homeowner development which I thought would be a great place to live, but all of the houses under construction had been sold. I remember driving past the development rather often, telling myself that I would live there someday. Now, these were not million dollar homes. These were comfortable homes in middle class neighborhood, ideal for a couple planning on having a family.

We drove through the streets of the development every weekend hoping to find one of the few remaining houses under construction for sale. The various builders in this neighborhood confirmed to us that all the parcels had been sold, but they were planning another development nearby in about six to nine months. After viewing the sites and blueprints for the houses in the new development we were discouraged. Not only were these proposed homes smaller, but also the yards were as well. We were ready to give up and look elsewhere, yet I remained positive believing we would live in this neighborhood.

On a whim one weekend, I took a drive through the development where I wanted to live and happened to see one of the builders out working. When I stopped to say hello, he surprised me by inquiring if I was still interested in purchasing a house in this development. He informed me that through a strange twist of events, the people who were expected to purchase the house he was finishing no longer qualified for the loan. The house was partly built and because he wanted the house sold, he offered me a deal on the price to which I quickly agreed!

It took several years for me to realize the process behind the event and feel the magnitude of the lesson it taught me. In retrospect, I was determined to live in that neighborhood, knew somehow I would, and *created the outcome*.

I am sure you, too, have several stories of your own once you think about it. Some experiences will be significant and others seemingly minor. We all have some memorable experiences because we created everything — yes, every situation — in our lives. The people who have come into our lives were drawn to us by our thoughts and beliefs. These people came into our lives to help us learn, give us information about ourselves and guide us along our journeys.

I have seen these same scenarios play out in my children's lives. My older son, Chris, developed a keen interest in the stock market in his teenage years. All money he could accumulate he invested in the market and had a rather sizeable portfolio for his age. During these same years, Chris also obtained a substantial interest in computers. While working at a computer store one summer he quickly learned the capacity and complexity of every computer's internal components. Upon entering college, although enjoying the world of computers, he decided to pursue a degree in finance.

On one occasion Chris and his buddies attended a computer convention and as "no accident" he was selected from an audience of hundreds to participate in a competition on stage. His vast computer knowledge and savvy ruled the day as he succeeded in building a computer faster than his competitors. His reward was a check for $2,500. It was not long afterward that he changed his major to the world of computers. From a distance it is easy to see he created an opportunity to demonstrate his fascination with computers.

Today, everything in my world, my wife, my house, my job, my pets, people around me and daily events all reflect my beliefs of how I view myself and my world. All of the people who enter my world and the events I experience provide me an opportunity to see and examine the results of my beliefs while at the same time provide me an opportunity to make different choices and change my world to the better. I respect myself and believe I am worthy of sharing my life with someone who possesses these same traits, and now share my life with a wonderful woman who is my best friend and partner. I do not attempt to control her, nor she try to control me. We find no value in that. Neither of us is a pushover, as we both possess a strong self-esteem and firm sets of beliefs. We are both working hard to grow and in doing so we challenge each other, while providing encouragement to take the necessary steps which at times can be scary. But that is the fun part. We know often the door is open for us, and it can take all the courage in the world to walk through it into a new world.

Back then, in the early years of my first marriage, I slowly became aware of the connection to the concepts I was thinking and the events happening in my world. I read every book I could find related to personal development and spiritual growth. Through this extensive reading, my mind began to open to other possibilities, different approaches and new ways of viewing myself and how I viewed my world.

I began to pay attention to what happened around me when I was in a good mood, and as well as when I was moody or upset. Over the course of fifteen years, one event kept repeating itself. Every time it happened, I was startled at the connection. A few days after I had expressed some negative behavior — expressing frustration over failed attempts to make progress personally or professionally, or giving up on some project rather than working to make it a success — my car would break down. Each time it would require a repair costing me several hundred dollars.

First, this clearly showed me my negative energy was going out into the Universe and coming back to me with a negative impact. Second, because I was in a bad mood and unproductive, the energy affected my car — a perfect representation of my inability to move forward in life. I was amazed at how many times this happened.

I also began to notice the particular people in my life. There were many individuals over the years that assisted my growth in various ways. Although reading was helpful, I recognized I needed someone who could help me down the path of spiritual learning and enlightenment.

At about this time in my career I realized I had gone about as far as I could in one section of corporate finance, specifically financial analysis, and began to search for other jobs. I was drawn to corporate treasury, yet the company I was working for was too small to have its own treasury department. However, I wasn't sure if a job was available in which I could transition from financial analysis to treasury. I remained determined to make the jump to treasury. Soon a search firm called that I had previously contacted and told me about a unique position. It wasn't long before I accepted this new position that involved both financial analysis and some modest treasury tasks. Looking back, once again I can see how I created my new opportunity.

Managing the cash required that I call the bank each day to determine our balance, (yes, this was before there was an internet to access information online!) estimate what monies would be deposited into our account that day, and estimate what checks would clear thereby estimating our ending balance for the day. If we projected to end the day with extra money we would wire it to our parent company; conversely if we projected to need funds our parent company would wire funds into our account.

This wasn't exactly the fast paced, highly complex world of treasury, but for me, it was a start. I wanted this to happen and I was determined to be a Treasurer some day. After only eight short months of working at this company, the parent company spun us off (a finance term meaning they offered us to common stockholders who would now own shares of our stock). Suddenly, we were an independent, public company, which meant the company needed an experienced Treasurer who in turn would be my boss.

Jim was soon hired for the job, a man with extensive experience and considerable expertise in corporate treasury. As it turns out, Jim and I became good friends. Jim taught me about treasury, but more than that, he was one of the best teachers about life I have ever encountered. Just as I was waking up to myself and my surroundings and attempting to embark on my own spiritual growth, Jim offered unique guidance, perspective and support for several years for which I am forever grateful.

Did Jim come into my life by accident or did the environment I created invite a teacher into my world? You may believe God orchestrated all of this and I was just a puppet on strings pulled and pushed in various directions. Instead, I created the situation in which a teacher arrived. Remember, God loves like a Father and Mother by suggesting, but never pushing. A loving God helps manifest what you put in motion by your beliefs. The energy of my thoughts, belief and attitude projected into the Universe, like a light bulb giving off light and heat, and this energy returned to me manifested by Jim entering my world to help me along the path. I was searching for answers and needed someone to help give me some direction. I created the situation into which a teacher arrived.

When you believe in yourself and believe you can accomplish something, God will help lead you to the door. You must recognize the signs along the way to get yourself to the door. Then, your actions and beliefs create the opportunity to walk through the door.

Are you possibly wondering how and why my boss simultaneously created the experience of bringing me into his life? If so, congratulations, you are catching on. Yes, he created the experience to learn from me how to be a good teacher and communicator, as I was not always the best pupil! To teach me required his communication be clear and concise; hence doing so reinforced these beliefs in him. There are likely many other reasons I came into his life. Later, we will discuss how the true magic of creating experiences happens when both parties created the environment which allows them to meet and develop a relationship.

To continue the story: I enjoyed a successful tenure with that company for over eleven years, including two promotions. Unfortunately in my last few years of employment, the company began to struggle financially. At the same time, unfortunately, severe cracks appeared in my marriage. I was unhappy and so was my ex-wife, and we didn't know how to fix it. Born with a sensitive, caring nature, watching my marriage unravel, I felt like a failure. As many people do, any time I perceived I had failed, I beat myself up pretty good.

My friend and boss, Jim, had left the company a couple of years earlier, and I was struggling on my own to deal with problems I encountered personally and professionally. There is nothing more frustrating than knowing something is wrong and not knowing how to fix it. I knew I had to change the way I viewed the world and what I believed. My self-esteem was slipping.

In another clear demonstration of my reality being created out of what I believed about myself, it wasn't long before I was laid off. The psychological impact hit me like a ton of bricks. Being unemployed with two children under the age of eleven forced me to focus all energy on finding a job, but I was emotionally bruised. The economy was in a downturn and although I had excellent skills and a positive employment record, I was not able to find work for over six months. My self-confidence continued to go the way of the economy. Not one job interview came my way. The work I did find was not in my field and I was forced to try something new.

The continuation of the story provides further examples of creating our world. Over the next two years my wife and I dug into our savings, borrowing a few thousand dollars from my parents while I worked a few different jobs. Yet, I was determined to learn how to succeed and was not giving up. Someway, somehow, I was determined to learn how to create the reality I desired.

Strangely, having had so much time to be introspective, to examine who I was, noting in great detail my strengths and weaknesses, I finally was convinced I had a lot to offer a company. I began to believe in myself knowing my work experience was extensive in my field with some rather significant business accomplishments to my credit. Although no interviews had occurred, each person seeing my resume of experience was greatly impressed. My self-confidence began to grow, although nothing in my reality was supporting my newfound optimism. At that time I was working for a magazine publisher selling advertising space, something which made me very uncomfortable as I did not consider myself the kind of extrovert who thrives on that type of personal contact. In fact, this job moved me way out of my "comfort zone" of financial analysis because I had to make cold calls to total strangers. Self-confidence is a requirement for this type of work......Amazing what we create, isn't it?

After only three months on the job, and only a handful of modest sales to my credit, I managed to land an appointment with someone showing a considerable interest in purchasing some ad space. When I met this man, I had a strange feeling about him, although I did not really know what to make of him. We spent a couple of hours talking and he asked me numerous questions about my background. He showed genuine interest in my experience, knowledge and skills. Finally after two hours he stated he was not interested in purchasing any advertisements. Of course, I was extremely disappointed. Oddly, he told me how he knew I was not supposed to be in this job selling advertising space, but rather told me he knew I had great talent and experience, to keep the faith, and informed me I would soon be very successful, landing a good job relatively soon.

I walked out of his office quite bewildered. I was struggling to get by on a commission-only job, so at first his words seemed empty and certainly didn't pay the bills. However, less than three months later I landed a promising job with a well-known company back in my field of finance and treasury! I do not remember this man's name, nor had I ever encountered or even considered someone I meet could be an angel, but this experience might have made me a believer. I know this may sound strange, but his words were so pointed at me and comforting to me. There is no doubt I drew him into my life due to my growing optimism at the time, helping validate my self-confidence. Landing a great job shortly afterward proved I created my reality.

So, let's take our first step into our new world.

Let's talk about a fundamental truth that we all must come to understand, believe and work with in our lives. This fundamental truth involves the impact of what we decide to be our own truths.

I often tell people if they believe something to be true, then for them, it is true, regardless of whether in reality it is true. In their reality, it is true. What we "perceive" to be real quite often is not exactly the same for many other people.

Let's walk through an example of how we create our world and the implications of continuing old beliefs compared to the change in our world different or new beliefs will create for us.

For example, if you are a woman seeking a good relationship, but believe all men only desire to have power over a woman in a relationship to the point of controlling her, taking and never giving back, then for you, that will be true. You will draw men to you who exhibit these traits. You created your reality, and since we have the power to create our world based on our beliefs — especially those deeply embedded beliefs in our consciousness — our beliefs manifest into reality the exact thing we believe. People will fight with all their might, perhaps even to death, to retain their beliefs. Look no further than our world today where you see many examples of wars fought based on different "beliefs" about God. Both sides are willing to die rather than consider a slight modification or evolution of their beliefs. Rarely, will one reverse course, "see the light" and change his view of the world.

Closely examine your own beliefs and be honest with yourself if the beliefs are biased or skewed in any way. Very often we let our minds string thoughts together, adding a string of fears building upon each other until we have a belief in our heads wrapped in fear, preventing us from action or distorting our view of the world. Some people might believe if they wear nice clothes to work co-workers will give them compliments. Others might believe they can only date someone in their race or their religion. Some religions have taught us we must do certain things, and not do others, in order to find our way into heaven. Watch closely and examine the reality you create each day based on these beliefs.

We all have hundreds of beliefs, some small ones and many powerful ones, that drive our every action and thought each day. Each belief and action sends energy into the Universe until there is sufficient energy to manifest into the experience mirroring your belief.

This action occurs because of a Universal law:

Universal Law #4 of what we weren't taught in school or church:

The Universe works on the law of attraction.

This is a fundamental and extremely significant law to understand. You attract to you which you believe. You create it by thinking, believing and acting out.

The Universe works on the law of attraction; more specifically, equals attract. We have often been taught opposites attract. However, they do not. When we send out energy to the Universe very profoundly stating what we believe, that energy attracts other similar energy until one day, in its strength, it manifests in our lives.

Energy accumulating in the Universe is a natural process. Why? Because everything in the Universe is made up of energy: our bodies, plants, clouds, air and even rocks and the earth. If you were to examine a piece of a rock under a powerful microscope you would discover atoms and electrons in movement. How can there be movement when there is an appearance of the rock being solid? Energy slowed down is matter; however all matter is constantly in motion. Consequently, similar energy attracts and builds to manifest the appearance of matter — in reality — your experience. I was able to meet my wife because the energies we both projected were very similar, hence there was an attraction!

A woman who is seeking a new relationship and believes all men are controlling meets a new man and soon discovers he is, indeed, controlling. This new man confirms exactly her beliefs! And then she will ask "Why do I always attract a man to me that is controlling and uncaring?" It is because she believes men to be that way, so she creates her reality.

Wouldn't it have been nice if someone had told us these things a long time ago?

She may have had the belief she was not totally capable of making all of her own decisions and someone would take care of her. The result will be the same. In either case she attracts men into her life who are controlling as she holds firmly the belief she should not have to make decisions, so someone else makes them for her.

Through examining your beliefs and experiences, you can quickly see the connection, or cause and effect.

Back to our example, our female friend could have a different deep-seated belief and still attract controlling men: she believes she does not deserve a better man than those who have come into her life already.

It is important to understand that the same experience — attracting controlling men into her life — could be created by a variety of deep-seated beliefs. In this example two different women could have attracted controlling men into their lives created by different deep-seated beliefs: one woman believed all men were controlling, another woman believed she was not worthy enough to find a true partner. However, the result is the same. Hence, many people can have the same experience, but a different belief was behind why they created it and what they are to learn from it. Therefore, examine your beliefs closely to determine which ones are manifesting key events in your life today.

Let's examine more closely the woman who believed she was unworthy of a genuine relationship. If she believed she was more deserving and worthy, why would she tolerate being with a man who is uncaring and controlling? To stay with someone who treats his partner with disrespect means that the person has one or more of four beliefs: 1) She can, in time, control him and turn him into what she wants (which is not going to happen; in fact controlling is exactly what she doesn't want him to do to her!); 2) She believes she can not find someone better, and therefore out of fear, stays with this man; 3) She is afraid of going on by herself, alone for a while, so she stays with this man, convinced that a poor relationship is better than always being lonely and alone; or 4) she believes she is unworthy or undeserving and by never looking for someone better reinforces her belief.

For all four potential reasons, the result is the same. Take notice how the underlying driving beliefs in her actions were out of fear of being controlled or fear of the unknown. Her beliefs generated strong emotions of fear which projected significant energy to the Universe manifested in bringing to her people and experiences mirroring her fears.

From a different perspective, look at it this way: Each of us deserves better and is worthy of much more in our lives. We are worthy of a partner who treats us kindly and lovingly and we are worthy of living a life that contains excitement and meaning. However, the key is you must first begin treating yourself the way you desire to be treated, and treat others in the same manner.

In order to forge a new path, you must first begin to change your beliefs about God, yourself and life itself. When you do, you will create what your heart has sought for so long.

If I walked up to you and started criticizing you, saying you were lazy, stupid, irresponsible and uncaring, what would you do? You certainly know those statements are not correct. So, what would your reaction be? If you were smart you would smack me across the jaw. But more importantly, did I hurt your feelings by striking a nerve in you suspecting I might be correct? Or was I totally wrong and you were putting me in my place? I would hope I was wrong and you were standing up for yourself. You are smart and caring, right? Of course you are. So why then would you tolerate being with a man who is not caring? You can only do so if you also believe it is correct to be uncaring, otherwise why would you tolerate this partner?

If for some reason, and you might have plenty of them from a difficult childhood, prior relationships or other unfortunate events in your life, you may actually believe you are not deserving enough or worthy enough. If you are at a place in your life where you do not believe you are worthy, the important thing is to acknowledge your belief and understand the relationships coming into your life resemble your belief about yourself. If you do not believe you are worthy, you will attract people into your life who are not worthy enough, or make you feel unworthy, in either case matching your belief.

When you allow someone to act in an undesirable way around you, and furthermore, you tolerate the behavior, you are encouraging more of the same behavior from that person. By tolerating and encouraging more of this intolerable behavior, **you are disrespecting yourself.** Think about that. This whole process is not about the other person. It's about you. You are disrespecting yourself when you allow someone to have an impact on your life inconsistent with the way you want to live your life. I am not saying the resulting experience for you is the fault of the other person. Rather, **it is you** who is deciding to continue these events in your life, and continue to perpetuate them every time they occur.

It is imperative you break through your old belief patterns and view your beliefs from a different perspective. If you have low self-esteem and are seeking a partner who will sweep you off your feet and care for you, you will not find him or her. More im-

103

portantly you will only find a person who matches the way you perceive yourself. You will attract to you a person who is also dependent, the exact opposite of what you want.

Try this exercise. Go in your closet and only look for a particular blue shirt. As your eyes focus on the many blue shirts you have, what happens? You selectively train your eyes and mind to filter out all of the other color shirts and only let the blue shirts register in your view. Now suppose a friend walks into your closet searching for a particular red shirt. Your friend does not see any of the blue shirts as those are filtered from view and only scans for a particular red shirt.

The same filtering process is in operation when you are armed with your set of beliefs, and are looking for a relationship. You may want someone who is special, confident, compassionate, and caring, but if you do not possess these same qualities, then you attract to you someone who matches your view of yourself. Your dating partner's filters are also on, looking for someone who is confident, caring and respects herself. Therefore, if you lack self-esteem and want someone who is very confident, your paths will not cross because the Universe works on the law of attraction. As is the fundamental principal of the Law of Attraction, similar energy attracts similar energy. You can not be radiating low self-esteem energy and expect to draw to you a person with high self-esteem energy. It is not possible.

On a cosmic, spiritual level, you won't register on his energy "radar screen" and he won't register on yours. You could be attending a sporting event with thousands of people, and the right man could walk right past you, but he will not register on your energy radar, nor will you register on his because you are creating a reality juxtaposed from each other.

The same applies for any other goal you have. You can not "attract" it to you; it can not appear on your radar if you do not project the same energy the goal can provide to you.

If you are in a difficult relationship and desire to move toward one involving mutual respect then take action. When, knowing he will not change, you tell the person who was treating you wrong to leave because you will no longer tolerate that behavior; you have generated the first small amount of energy into the Universe to manifest a different world for you. Now you have started to break the cycle of bad relationships in your life and can start on a path toward greater happiness.

Now take notice, I didn't state all is well, and your work is done. It is just starting. You didn't think you were going to get off that easy, did you? Remember, the beliefs systems you possess were created over many, many years. These beliefs won't be undone in one quick action. Some beliefs will be modified or eliminated more quickly than others. However, don't despair, because you can undo what has been done, unless you fall back into your old patterns again.

Take a long look at your life and what you do and where you go and what you believe and what you eat and what you say about others and how you view yourself. Examine everything you do and examine the underlying beliefs you have that cause you to take those actions. You might be someone who puts three dead-bolts on every door in your house out of fear of being robbed or worse. How did this fear come about? If under closer inspection, no one in your neighborhood has been robbed, no one in all the streets around has been robbed, when and where did this fear develop? Perhaps you read somewhere that crime was on the rise and you began to fear it might happen to you. *(Remember, it doesn't "happen to you", you "happen it to yourself.")*

Taking this a step further, maybe you stopped going out with friends because you were afraid of being out too late and you sleep with many lights in all rooms of your house. Each day you take particular notice of all of the break-ins and robberies reported in the newspaper or on the television news. This information adds fuel to your fears. And you may actually experience a robbery. Can you see you created it, not only your fear but also by your extremely strong belief you would incur a robbery? Your beliefs created a self-fulfilling prophecy.

You may see where I am leading you with this thought process. I am not saying the belief you have is not valid or incorrect.

Rather, I am showing you that your actions, and consequently your experiences, are dictated by your beliefs. In order to create a different reality, you must change your beliefs, and you can understand how deep down in your consciousness and subconsciousness these beliefs are entrenched. Removing or changing these beliefs will take some effort.

To add one last note to this example, I have occasionally noticed a story in the newspaper about homeowners being trapped in a burning house, unable to get out because they had bars on the windows and multiple locks on the doors — for protection. We create our own realities. We create the world we live in. These people so deeply feared being robbed and were so concerned about preventing others from having easy access to their home, in doing so they prevented not only easy escape but firemen easier access into the house to free them from the fire. Beware what you belief deeply, because you bring exactly that to you every day.

One last thought for now regarding disrespecting ourselves. There are many ways we disrespect ourselves and this behavior must stop if we are to create the abundant and successful world we desire. You can't just tell this one person in your life to leave and believe your work is done, thinking you now have respect, when in many other ways you disrespect yourself. We disrespect ourselves with no help from others. Some examples: smoking, over eating, talking bad about others, resisting change, unwilling to learn and grow, or only focusing on your mistakes and faults and never acknowledging your attributes. Can you relate to any of these or do you put yourself down in other ways? Any action you take, any thought you have that is not done with your highest good in mind is an act of disrespect to yourself.

We all have special and wonderful abilities. You may be a caring and compassionate individual. You may have the ability to teach. You may be skilled at building. We are all special in some way. There is some special talent, some special gifts, we each uniquely possess. Therefore, be good to yourself, be kind to yourself. Give yourself a hug or a word of encouragement. You are special.

If you do not believe in yourself, or do not respect yourself, why should you expect everyone else around you to believe in you and respect you? Your beliefs tell God how you feel about yourself, and your actions inform those around you how you feel about yourself.

Although your beliefs about your self and others must change, that is only the first step.

The next step is to change your actions.

CHAPTER 11

Your Actions Speak Volumes

*"Good judgment comes from experience and
experience comes from bad judgment."*

-- The Old Farmer's Almanac

You now understand you create the events and experiences which happen in your world. You now understand your beliefs create your reality. Now, how do you create the world you want to live in?

Before we begin examining our actions and beliefs and how to create our world, step back and view the Universe on a grander scale. For many years most everyone believed we are human beings having a spiritual experience, when in fact, we are actually spiritual beings having a "human" experience. Our souls one day decide to incarnate into a human bodies and here we are experiencing life from unique perspectives. The second a soul enters the human body, by its mere existence the body consumes space and a place in time. Space and time are inseparable and we are all aware of the limitations we encounter each day due to these Universal forces. We can only occupy the space our body controls and we can not be in two places at the same time. Being bound by the Universal laws of space and time *automatically* creates an environment and reality in which we must make choices.

We have choices such as reading this book or watching TV or working or riding a bicycle. Although most of us may have mastered the art of multi-tasking, our true focus can only be on choice per moment. Therefore, to exist in human form inherently requires we make choices; hundreds of them every day. We decide when to eat, what to eat, where to eat or not to eat at all.

Further, the dynamics of time and space force us to make choices concerning everything around us. For example, everyone wants to own a home which of course takes up physical space on land. At the same time, we want to give room for animals to run freely in their native habitats. In some places due to the increasing human and animal population, we are already competing for the same space. This is not meant to be a commentary on how we treat animals. The finite amount of space on earth creates an issue we must address and consequently we are forced to make choices regarding the diminishing space.

If you solicit opinions and ideas on how to solve the problem, you will receive a wide variety of suggestions. Which solution is the "right" solution? One amazing aspect to the reality in which we live, is there are many working solutions. Unfortunately, getting everyone to agree on one solution is highly unlikely, yet many of the solutions will resolve the problem. There are numerous possible solutions and each solution may require with it many more choices. *No matter which road is taken, the choice of solution becomes the experience.*

If you decide to journey from California to New York, your mode of travel could be by car, air, bicycle or your own two feet. Further, your path and choices may not lead you in a straight line from the point of origination to your destination. Your choices and path may take you north into Canada or south to Mexico, before you reach your destination of New York. The choices you make create experiences for you to enjoy and use for learning. With all of these thoughts in mind, examine the dynamics of making your choices. Your choices are made based on your thoughts and beliefs.

First, let's take a look at your actions and beliefs. Better yet, pretend you are standing in God's presence and God says, "Show me what you want in your life. Demonstrate to me how you desire your world to be, whether it includes success, abundance, love or inner joy. Show me through your beliefs and your actions what this looks like".

If I were to demonstrate my desire to have an abundance of money in my life, would my action be to cheat my customers or business partners in order for me to make more money? Would I create scams on the internet or take short cuts when providing service while over charging in order to make more money? Would I promise service or products of superior quality and then replace them with knock-offs when the products were shipped? Would I lie about my abilities to my friends in order to obtain a job?

If I desired more love would I criticize those around me to make myself feel better? In my desire to make myself feel better, would I harm my spouse physically, mentally or emotionally? Would I work to control my spouse in order to always have the upper hand, giving me the feeling of power? In an effort to shirk responsibility for my own actions would I blame my spouse for everything that goes wrong in my life?

If I wanted more inner peace would I lie to those around me in order to make myself look better? Would I blame those around me for my own failings as an excuse for what I was not able to accomplish? In order for me to maintain my self-esteem and attempt to overcome my inadequacies would I talk bad about those around me?

I don't believe I would. Certainly not right there in front of God! None of these examples are representative of how I would best demonstrate abundance, happiness, love and health in my life. The same is true for you. Yet, some of us do all of these things, or have done some of them at some point in our lives.

So what would God think of seeing me using any of these approaches in my life? Would God think I really believed I could accomplish my desires in this way? Or would God realize that I really want my life to be abundant but I believe the opposite behavior is completely appropriate?

You might answer "But you don't understand that I **had** to cheat those people because that is the only way I could make money." Really? Sorry, but you are telling me this because your deep-seated beliefs are getting in the way of your potential, and you have rationalized your actions.

However, God makes no judgments. God only helps us create what we ask for, and the way we ask is demonstrated by our actions. Consequently, God does not attempt to force us into specific choices, as we have free will. If God did force us into specific choices, then we would be no more than a puppet in this world. Yet, we make thousands of choices every day on our own. We create the world around us by what we believe.

Our actions are our beliefs put into motion.

God will help you create your world based on your choices, which, in turn, are based on your beliefs. Through life you experience the full breath of emotions and acquire spiritual knowledge.

Your actions are produced based on your choices, and you're your choices are dictated by your beliefs. Consequently, your actions are directly linked to your beliefs. Your actions can not and will not contradict your beliefs. You can't believe in being honest when your actions are demonstrated by cheating others or acting insincerely. You can't believe in loyal, monogamous love if your actions are continually to seek out sexual companionships with other people. You can't believe in the value of a healthy mind and body when you make the wrong food choices, smoke or don't try to learn and grow. Your actions convey your true beliefs about yourself and your world. You can tell me all day long you believe a certain way, but your actions demonstrate your true beliefs.

God will take a cue from your actions and allow the energy of the Universe to manifest itself to prove your beliefs are correct! If you profess love to one person, but continually seek out sexual relationships, you will have a great abundance of events in your life showing you can only have a relationship in which you cheat on your partner and your partner cheats. If your actions demonstrate you cheat people believing that is the only way you can make money, then your experiences will demonstrate you can only make money by cheating someone. Your actions indicate your beliefs, and if your choices are inappropriate, the result is a reality filled with inappropriate experiences.

Consider someone who is part of the ever-increasing world of deceiving unwitting people, either through telephone or internet scams. I read recently in the newspaper how someone scammed 50-100 people out of their hard earned money. Some were immigrants, who came to this country with very little money, but had worked hard for many years saving as much as possible to make a down payment on homes. Imagine learning that the payments you had been making to the real estate company had never been delivered to the bank which owned the mortgage on the home you thought you were buying. The banks, with mortgages in default, were now going to re-possess the houses, with the "real estate" people no where to be found. How sad for the people who were swindled.

The people who perpetrated this dishonesty and theft perhaps believed they had every right to obtain income in this manner. They likely had little remorse for those from whom they stole the money. Would these crooks continue this approach if they believed they could make money honestly? No, they believe this method is the only way to make money, and make it fast.

Earlier we examined how we have been conditioned to require full abundance immediately in any shape or form, with no concept of patience. This demonstrates another perfect example.

I can hear these people saying "but I can make more money this way and faster than I can make it honestly". And you know what? They are correct. Their actions and results every day prove they can only earn money by being dishonest. What you believe to be true is, in your reality, true. It doesn't matter that it is, in fact, false.

If someone believes cheating is the only way he can make money, or believes he can make more money faster this way, then for him it is true. In reality, it most likely is not true. He can earn it honestly, but chooses not to use this approach. And because his belief is so strong, his world will reflect this belief. He will only make money by cheating people. Every time he tries to earn money honesty, it will not work, only reinforcing his belief that cheating others is all that works.

Actions like connecting your cable TV differently by-passing the box in an attempt to obtain service without paying for it, taking home a variety of office supplies from your work, fudging on your income and deductions on your tax return, not only demonstrate to God and the Universe your belief that cheating is appropriate, but also send the message you do not have enough income to pay for these services or taxes. You rationalize your behavior in some manner to convince yourself the actions are appropriate, and yet you manifest the exact opposite of what you desire. Attempting to avoid paying what you honestly owe says you want to live in a world where you will continue to not afford what you desire.

However, there is a second side to all actions. Those who cheat others will find they draw to them those who reflect their beliefs. In their experiences, the world is full of cheaters, so this justifies their cheating behavior!

Notice the two facets of the belief occur. One believes he can only make money by cheating, and that truly is the only way he obtains money. The reverse is also true: He believes he cannot earn money honestly. Most people are not aware of this reverse thinking, and it is a subconscious process.

Universal Law #5: The reverse is always true.

Whatever you believe to be true,
you also believe the reverse to be true.

Whatever you believe to be true,
your experiences will substantiate
the reverse is also true.

Take your time and re-read these sentences. Their truth is extremely far reaching in our lives. Their truth has a tremendous impact on our actions, and consequently what abundance, love or lack thereof is created in our lives.

Let's look at this concept more closely. If you believe you can only make money by stealing or cheating people, then you also believe the opposite to be true, which is you can NOT earn money honestly. If you believe in being honest, always telling the truth, treating others fairly, then your actions will reflect this belief. In addition, you will also NOT do the opposite as you believe it to be of no value, without merit, or unjust. Therefore, you will not lie, cheat or be dishonest in any way to others.

In your business dealings you would always be honest and ethical. In your personal affairs, you will treat your spouse with caring and honesty.

It is impossible to believe one side of the truth, and not believe the other side of the truth. You cannot believe honesty is the worthwhile way to live your life, and at the same time believe it is reasonable to cheat others. If you think you can do both, then you really **don't** believe in being honest. You actually believe it is rational to be dishonest. Your attempts to be honest will only be used when you are working to actually use it to your advantage, which is another way of being dishonest. Your reality will be filled with times when you encounter dishonest individuals and even the honest individuals will quickly turn dishonest in dealing with you.

God helps you create what you believe and what is demonstrated through your actions. God does not go against your free will. God only works to give you what you ask God for, which is demonstrated by your beliefs and your actions. If we act dishonestly in relationships, we will draw to us people who also believe that dishonesty is legitimate. Ironically, believing this course of action will somehow gain us leverage in the relationship only results in a pain as the other person brings dishonesty to the relationship as well.

Why is this concept so important? Consider that if you believe something to be true, and you create what you believe, and your actions are a direct result of your beliefs, then your actions dictate your reality and your happiness. Further, by your actions you are telling God what you want, and if your actions are not showing your efforts to move positively forward toward abundance, love and spiritual inner peace, then you are moving in the opposite direction.

Your actions either move you toward your goals or away from

them based on what you believe. God helps you create fortunate or unfortunate events in your life based on what your beliefs and actions.

Remember, God is here, always with us, helping us create everything we desire. Our strong desire for happiness, no matter what shape or form it will take, is seen through our actions. If I want to have a good job, I prepare a good resume, network effectively and am prepared to answer key questions in an interview. I believe in myself and put forth positive actions while trusting God and the process that my efforts will be rewarded. My actions — positively presenting myself via my resume, phone contact and interviews — are the result of my beliefs that these actions will generate positive results. I move forward with confidence that these actions will lead me to the results I desire, because I believe them to be true. I believe these actions are correct and appropriate.

However, what if I did the opposite? What if I was unemployed and longed for a rewarding job, but believed that I was unemployed due to the fault of my ex-boss, my spouse or the company for which I had worked? What type of results would I produce in my life? If I believed someone should compensate me for being unemployed, from letting me go from my last job, then what signal am I sending to the Universe? If I send letters and e-mails to my ex-boss and to the company telling them they must compensate me in some manner, examine the world I am creating.

It is important to understand something fundamental here. God only helps provide you what you ask for. If I believe my unemployment is someone else's fault God will bring people into my life that reinforce that belief. God does not bring me compensation from anyone. Instead, God helps manifest what I believe and is demonstrated through my actions. If I believe that my misery is someone else's fault, then I will meet people, and encounter more situations which will permit me to blame others.

Suppose you are a jealous person and envious of people with whom you work. You continually feel others get the better deal and greater opportunities at work. Someone else always gets chosen for a promotion. What message are you sending to God and the

Universe? You believe in jealousy and instead of removing it from your life you actually invite more of it into your life, because you believe jealousy is real and has value. In addition, you will continue to experience events in which you will find yourself jealous.

The beauty of this situation is that you can create the experience which provides you an opportunity to understand why you are jealous and remove this negative influence from your life. However, again understand you automatically create the experience for you to learn from because you believe it in the first place! First, your beliefs manifest the experience, and only then — if you are aware — have the opportunity to react differently, change the outcome and ultimately change your beliefs. Once your beliefs are changed, you will no longer create this experience.

Let's examine this concept of jealousy further. Jealousy is a segment of fear. You can only be jealous of someone if you do not believe you can obtain the same thing. Wishing and hoping you will not experience jealousy only keeps you entrenched in feeling the emotion. You can only grow out of it when you choose to feel and act differently when the next opportunity occurs. The result will be your creation of a different world for yourself. When you ask *"Why does that person get to have a good marriage?"* you are really asking *"Why can't I have a good marriage?"* By that simple question you are stating a belief that you are not worthy, or deserving or believe it can not happen for you. Simply stating the first question implies you believe you can not achieve a good marriage, abundance, or any other goal you seek.

If you believed it could happen for you, you would not begin by asking the question. In fact, the question would not enter your mind. Why? Because if you believe you can obtain a good marriage, then you believe it possible for everyone to have a good marriage. If everyone can have a good marriage, questioning why someone else gets to have a good marriage is irrelevant. Understand this concept clearly, because it is present in our lives quite frequently. If you believe something exists, then you believe it is possible you could experience what you believe. Acknowledging the possibility someone can not have a good marriage puts that thought in your mind. Once the thought is in your mind, under the right circumstances it can grow into fear. Once it has grown to a large enough fear you will manifest it in your life.

As I stated in chapter 8, if you believe the pie is only a specific size and someone else's fortune leaves less for you, you have created a belief that is dangerous and often self-destructive. If you believe there is enough in the Universe for everyone to have abundance, as we all should have if we are all God's children, then there is always abundance available for you. Consequently, you will never need to be jealous or envious of another person, rather you will hope for everyone's success. Believing everyone should have success reinforces your belief that success is available for everyone, and helps speed up manifesting success for you!

Let's examine another example of God only providing specifically what we ask for through our actions and beliefs. Consider someone you know who continually experiences one problem after another. It seems like we all know someone who fits this description. His life is one crazy event after another. He hurts himself or is sick frequently, or often gets the low end of the deal, or is always late for some reason. He never seems to have enough money and is always borrowing money, then spending it frivolously. Interestingly though, someone is always there to help him out, either lending him money or giving him a ride when his car is broken down — as it is regularly. It's always something.

You probably know someone who exhibits this behavior. Besides always looking for and expecting a helping hand, our friend never even suspects he is creating his world of continual problems because he demonstrates he can not take care of himself. Believing there should always be someone there to assist him creates a reality for him where problems continually occur which make him expect assistance. He receives the assistance, never suspecting he could change his reality, nor does he ever have the desire to change, hence his reality is one continuous repetitive cycle.

Our friend is often the first to be looking for government assistance, whether through hand outs, job fairs, training or other programs. Government assistance programs are valuable, yet intended as temporary help. The government and our politicians have made it too easy for us to turn this temporary assistance in to a permanent right. Unfortunately, with others' good intention to help a person in need, it is very easy for our friend to begin believing help from others is necessary for his survival. Expecting help from others can become an addiction.

People entrenched in this pattern soon begin to believe receiving help from others, including the government, is their right. And most of all, our unfortunate friend, has built and put in motion the ultimate reverse belief. He believes he is entitled to all of this help, and now believes he can not survive without it. Yes, he believes he has a right to entitlement, but whether it is conscious or subconscious he does not believe he can make it on his own.

Look at the power this belief has created in his life. His belief has paralyzed him. He is frozen in place, with no way of ever changing his world until he changes his belief and actions.

If you believe you should receive constant help from others,
then you are putting in motion the reverse as well,
believing you can't succeed without the help.
Therefore, your world will mirror your inability to
succeed unless others help you constantly.

Successful, achieving people are not dependent on others
for their mental and emotional strength and wealth.

I am not stating that successful people do not "need" other people; personal and business relationships are the strongest experiences from which we can learn and grow. Successful people do not "need" other people to fill them emotionally. They find their strength from within, not from the outside. Certainly, we all appreciate encouragement, support, and coaching along the way. These are all valuable functions. In the end, ultimately we have to find and grow the strength from within.

When emotionally balanced, we will look for someone who works as a partner with us and does not fill a need within us. Expecting someone to fill a need within us is an unfair demand to place on another person. Expecting someone to fill a need within us reinforces our belief we are missing something valuable; hence we are unworthy or inadequate. In addition, we will attract people into our lives that who will reinforce our belief we are missing something.

It is up to you — it is up to each of us — to break the cycle and stop blaming and depending on others. Unfortunately, we have a tendency to repeat the same actions day after day. You must change your actions to stop the process from continuing.

Almost every one wants to be rich, or at least accumulate greater wealth than they currently experience. Yet, how do feel about people who you see with a lot of money? Wealthy people are often portrayed on TV as being dishonest or ruthless. We watch these TV shows and find ourselves agreeing with the way these rich people are portrayed. We demonstrate our agreement with these TV programs by making sure to watch them each week, especially if there is a chance we might see the rich person get taken in some way, or beat at his/her own game.

Even our real world mirrors the same view towards those who have abundance. Politicians are wonderful about accusing the rich of not shouldering their fair share of the tax burden. Surely the rich should pay more and you (the less fortunate) should pay less. More importantly, maybe you should be given some of the rich people's money. History shows many people jump right in and vote for these politicians agreeing with that view of the rich.

What are our actions really saying about us? Our actions are only put in motion by what our beliefs are. What are our beliefs in this situation? Our beliefs are really saying rich people are dishonest and we like to see them get beat at their own game.

At the same time you are walking around telling everyone how you don't have enough money and abundance in your life. Can you understand that if deep down you really believe rich people demonstrate qualities and traits you do not want to be associated with, then God is helping ensure you won't be a rich person? You are stating by your beliefs and actions you really don't desire to be rich!

When I was young, I had a slightly similar belief. If I saw a person driving a Jaguar, or other expensive car, or drove past a home that I knew was extremely expensive, part of me was very envious and jealous (being jealous at times caused me a lack of abundance not knowing then the "pie" was not limited in size). The other part of me rationalized to myself that the owners were probably snobs or shallow people and out of touch with reality. What message do you think I was sending to God about how I really felt about being rich? God was just sitting there stating, 'Ok, Gary, if you believe being rich will make you a snob and out of touch and you don't want to be like them, then you can stay right where you are." The amazing truth was every time I started to make some progress towards saving a sizeable sum of money, I would incur some additional expense, mainly in the form of a major repair, which would quickly absorb most of the extra money I saved! My car would need a new compressor for the air conditioning, or on one occasion, a new timing chain (a pricey item costing over $1,500!). Or my house would need a new air conditioning unit, a new roof or a new fence. Something would always halt my progress.

I was creating not only what I believed to be true, but the opposite of what I believed to be true. Since I believed that being rich was not good, I was able to create not being rich. Just as important, I was creating the opposite of my desire to be rich because deep down I believed having just enough money was better than being rich. Remember, the opposite in my belief was also creating itself.
In order to stop the old thinking, remember the process here is similar to realizing what we don't say is as important as what we do say. As I have shown, believing and demonstrating we truly believe that the rich are not people we want to associate with, then God helps us not be rich. First, if we are envious, jealousy demonstrates we believe we can not have what someone else has. Second, by expecting those who are rich to share their wealth with us, we are stating we believe the pie is not big enough for us to get our "piece." Third, when we enjoy watching the rich outsmarted, humiliated or losing a lot of their money, we are demonstrating our

distaste for wealth. In all of these situations we put energy in motion creating a barrier for us to obtain wealth. The result? We get hit from both sides. We can't obtain wealth because we do not want to be part of it, and we also believe being wealthy is not better, and so additional energy is drawn to us keeping us where we are. No wonder we get depressed, frustrated, confused and angry about our lack of success.

Here is another way to view this concept. Use an example in which you do not honor and fully respect yourself and demonstrate this by over eating, smoking, spending beyond your budget, drinking excessively or doing drugs. We know these vices are extremely harmful to the body. Yet we do these things anyway, to provide us with immediate pleasure. No one would purposely do any of these things if he or she did not have a feeling of disappointment with himself or herself. We may think that one indulges in these activities due to unpleasant events in his or her life. However, we have discussed how we cause those events in our lives that we interpret to be unfortunate.

We feel upset by our lack of success, abundance, or love. We turn to vices to help us feel better or forget about our troubles. Medicating myself may help me forget — for a time — that I am a failure. It may help me forget about something I don't like about myself. It may help me forget — for awhile — a traumatic event from my past. But I am not a failure and neither are you. At times we may doubt and "get down on" ourselves. Hence, the belief we are not worthy slowly creeps into our consciousness. The next step is over-eating, drinking excessively, taking drugs, smoking, or even over-spending. Doing this supports the feeling and belief that we are not worthy or deserving of success. We are, thus, disrespecting ourselves. It is unfortunate because we are worthy, although sometimes we no longer believe it.

When we have low self-esteem and our actions
give evidence of not respecting ourselves,
we create an outer world mirroring those beliefs.

These beliefs attract people to us who do not
respect us, and we attract experiences to us
through which we incur stress to our ego and self-esteem.

So now we have put into action something which supports the belief we are unworthy and undeserving. These actions create our reality by continuing to manifest experiences in which we continue to be unsuccessful, supporting our belief that we are unworthy. Unfortunately, the reverse of our belief is also true. The reverse belief is that you believe other people should not treat you respectfully. Other people should not treat you as someone who is deserving and worthy.

You may now have jumped up out of your chair proclaiming "What? I believe other people should treat me disrespectfully? I would not want that! Why would I believe that to be true?"

You believe it because you are willing to disrespect yourself, and your actions reinforce to the Universe that disrespecting yourself is rational and valid. Therefore, if you are disrespecting yourself by treating your body or your emotional and mental self poorly, then how can you expect someone else to treat you respectfully? You can't. You can only demonstrate to God and everyone else to treat you respectfully by first treating yourself with dignity and pride. Therefore, if you treat yourself poorly, then you must also believe it is valid for someone else to treat you poorly, which is the why this concept is so important and yet, so often missed as applicable in our lives.

Treating any other being or living creature with disrespect is also a sign to the Universe you believe in disrespecting others and thereby attract disrespect to you. People hurt animals often as a way to express their anger and frustration in their own reality. Being an animal lover it pains me deeply when I hear of an animal mistreated in any way. If everybody would understand their own actions and beliefs have created their own feelings of inferiority or frustration in their world, they would not take out their anger on defenseless animals. Further, the action of hurting another animal implies they believe it is acceptable to harm another living thing, so they bring it upon themselves since they believe it is appropriate behavior. Purposely and knowingly hurting another living creature is demonstrating a belief of one's own inadequacy. Anyone who is emotionally in balance, believing she is worthy and loved, will treat all other living creatures with respect. Consequently, these people then attract respect to them. The Universal laws of attraction do not apply only to one's actions towards people, but to all living entities.

There are many other examples of how we disrespect ourselves. In fact, we practice it so much that we are really pretty good at it. We show up late for an appointment, making the other person wait. We are inconsiderate of others or their time, which demonstrates our laziness and lack of commitment. Or we beat ourselves up for past mistakes and bury ourselves in our past, never allowing ourselves to move forward. We do not realize today is the only day, and now is the only moment, in which we have an opportunity to do something different. We can't change the past, but so many of us go through life as if we are driving a car by looking in the rear view mirror. We have all made mistakes, although when we step back and look there really are no mistakes. We have all made choices in which we would like the opportunity to "do over." If indeed such a thing were possible, we would proceed through the "doing over" experience with added knowledge, learned from the experience the first time. Yet the first experience was *exactly* the reason you experienced it in the first place! Hopefully you will have learned from the first experience so you do not repeat it again!

The negative beliefs you have not only create unfortunate events but also manifest in your body. Remember, energy runs through your body and is projected into the Universe. Consequently, the energy of your beliefs and thoughts manifests in the body since mind and body are connected. For example, if you are afraid to move forward on a new project or leave a bad relationship, you may begin having physical ailments in your legs, knees or ankles. Your legs are symbolic of your ability to move forward, and your mind creates both events in your outer world showing nothing new as well in your body, both mirroring your belief of staying where you are. In *"You can heal your life"* by Louise Hay, she lists numerous ailments and illnesses and how they are created by matching them to our specific beliefs and thoughts.

I was fascinated by the number of speeches and sound bytes both candidates spewed before the 2004 Presidential election regarding the rising cost of health care. Each candidate stated his own views regarding the reasons we are faced with rising health care costs. Each candidate explained how his plan would reduce or slow the rising costs. Yet, both refrained from mentioning the one simple fact that drives up the cost of health care. Neither candidate was willing to talk about it because it is sensitive to most people. We are the cause of rising health care costs. I am not making a political statement or a political commentary here. What I am saying is candidates from both sides were either unaware or mistaken as to the major cause of higher health care costs.

The simple fact is health care, like any other service or product provided, is priced based on supply and demand. A recent article on MSNBC online reported a study by John Hopkins University stating that 65% of Americans were overweight or obese in 2003 and the percentage is expected to reach 75% by 2015. The article went on to point out that over 16% of children are considered obese or overweight and 34% are at risk of becoming overweight. Those numbers are significant. We are a society comprised of playing hard and working hard individuals who demand fast relief for all of our aliments. We get stressed out at work and run for the fast acting medicine to take away the headache. We eat fried foods and run for the acid indigestion. Yet, do we try to get at the cause of the pain? We are encouraged to eat the fried food again. We eat the fried food again. After all, the commercials tell us to eat those foods. The commercials tell you to go ahead and eat, and know your medicine will be there to help relieve your pain. We are a country that at times takes no responsibility for our actions causing pain to ourselves and then expect medicine to cure the pain instantly, so we can go out and do it again. Does this situation sound familiar?

If we simply begin respecting ourselves, by not abusing our bodies, we will live longer and happier lives, and most of all, dramatically reduce the demand for health care. Do you think doctor and hospital charges would continue to rise if very few people needed their services? We would find doctors and hospitals competing for our service. Wouldn't that be nice for a change? Prices would go down and you could be selective about the doctor you use. Can you imagine a scenario in which doctors would be giving incentives for you to choose them? Why is that so strange to us? It's because we have been led to believe the demand is high and can go nowhere but higher. Yet, it is very possible we can reduce the demand for health care.

The message here is not simply about eating better, exercising, and respecting ourselves. The message is if you demonstrate these beliefs and actions you will no longer *attract* health problems to you. Having a healthy mind and body while believing you are treating yourself with healthy respect attracts positive healthy energy to you.

I am amazed at the extensive number of medicine ads on TV and in magazines. There are numerous medicines to help ease the pain or discomfort of every imaginable problem we have. Further, the side effects of the medicines cause more problems. A former business acquaintance of mine has to take cholesterol medicine, yet eats meat and other high fat foods when we are at lunch. Let's change the way we perceive the world, change our actions, and we will change our world.

The message here is for us to realize we create our world by how we feel about ourselves inside. Our outer world mirrors our inner thoughts in so many ways. When we respect ourselves, we no longer look to any other person to give us what we can give ourselves. We no longer blame others. And most importantly, we do not have to demand that doctors give us what we need to survive another day. Certainly, doctors and scientists perform an important service and research should continue in every way. At the same time our demand for over-the-counter medicines, antibiotics and many out-patient services can be reduced if we treat ourselves better. It's time we stop hurting ourselves by expecting the world around us to fix our problems, when we have the power within us at any time to do it ourselves.

This leads me to one of the biggest ways we disrespect ourselves: our choice to either miss or "get" the lesson. When we "get" the lesson, we gain valuable insights from the experiences. Sometimes, even though we understand the lesson, we refuse to change our behaviors or belief systems. Refusing to change our behaviors or belief systems causes most of the headaches we have in our lives because when we miss the point or get the point but follow the same route again, we only set ourselves up — again — to experience the same situation. It's like repeating the fourth grade. How many times do we want to experience the same unfortunate event? We are all extremely stubborn when we want to be. Events must unfold our way or we are determined to mold the situation or people involved into the shape we demand or we will die trying. Take a close look at most of the people you know and many will be attempting to force a process somehow or force a person to bend towards his or her point of view. The value of the experience is your opportunity to react differently and learn thereby helping you to move onward to new levels of spiritual knowledge.

I have demonstrated this unfortunate behavior as well. There are many times when I repeated the same experiences because I did not learn if fully the first time. We spend so much time doing our lessons over and over again. The amazing part is we actually know the experience when we see it, we wonder why we are there again, and yet our behavior is no different from the first time. Why did we believe our outcome would be any different this time? We hope it will be because we do not want to change our approach.

Changing our approach might make us consider we were wrong, and we never want to tell ourselves we were wrong. Again, we did nothing "wrong", we simply keep choosing not to see there is benefit to a new approach. If we change our approach we are forced to examine our prior actions and beliefs, and for many this process can be painful. Yet the pain we continue to live with every day takes a much greater toll over many years. We don't want to change our approach because it is easier to blame someone else. We don't want to admit to ourselves the approach we have taken has not only been unsuccessful, but we have been using the same approach for a long, long time.

It is very tough emotionally for many of us to look ourselves in the mirror and face up to the fact that we need to adjust our approach, our beliefs and our actions to get the results we desire. Our fears tell us we will have wasted all of those years and we don't want to change now. How many of you are stuck in relationships going nowhere? How many of you have stayed far too long, giving the relationship a chance? Certainly, you need to do your part to learn, change and grow. But if you can honestly tell yourself the other person is not growing with you, then wish them well, and move on. If you stay, you are disrespecting yourself.

Too many of us are comfortable running the marathon of life with slippers on when our feet would do much better having a pair of sneakers made for the pounding of the pavement. We also would use a lot less energy in the process if we do the work. The amount of energy we spend each day maintaining our old approaches and the same old actions far outweighs the energy used to make changes.

Take a close look at your relationships, especially the men or women you have dated. I have met so many people who have said "I can't believe I wound up with the same type of person as my last relationship". It is no mystery that if you fish with the same bait you catch the same type of fish. If you hit golf ball with the same swing the ball will always travel in the same direction. Different results require you making changes in yourself. Different results require making changes in your beliefs and your actions.

Its time to implement several new steps to create the reality you desire.

CHAPTER 12

What Must I Do Differently to Create the Reality I Desire?

"I find the harder I work, the luckier I get."

-- Thomas Jefferson

*"Not everything that can be counted counts,
and not everything that counts can be counted."*

-- Albert Einstein

Many years ago a former boss once asked me *"Which is more important: Doing things right or doing the right things?"* I sat there puzzled for a long time, until he explained it's all about doing the right things. You could, after all, be doing some things very well, but these things may produce little value to obtain your goal. If in planning a road trip spending an extensive amount of time focusing on all the places we will stop is fun, but if we neglect to ensure our car is fully maintained, we were not doing the right things. It is imperative we do **the right things**.

What are the right things? There is an old saying, "Do first things, first." If you already have sketched out a broad goal, start by making a list of short-term and long-term **actions** or **steps** you believe necessary to take to meet your goal.

If you are interested in finding a new job, do you send out resumes, network with business acquaintances and seek out classes to enhance your skills, or do you sit at home waiting for someone to contact you? Although the answer may appear obvious, believe it or not, there are those who choose to wait for someone to knock on their door. When looking for a job, we may get away with only doing the few steps mentioned, but to land the job you desire, we must do them all.

Many years ago, after being laid off, I became a student of how to find a new position and I sought out people who were fantastic at networking, communicating their skills and landing interviews. Believe me, the process stretched me and put me out of my comfort zone. Along the way I met many fascinating people possessing a wealth of knowledge to share. The input they provided helped me land a job quickly during a slow economy. Doing the right things matter.

A clarification may be needed here, to help you understand how this approach is different from thousands of other self-help books: In doing the right things, **you must also believe** they will work, and you must believe in yourself. You must believe you are worthy and deserving to receive more in your life than you currently possess.

How do I become a person of high self-esteem when for years I have been told I was not as smart or as good as those around me? How do I begin to believe success for me is possible, when I have repeatedly tried to set and reach goals and failed? Have patience…..the answer is coming.

Step 1: Make a list of the *rights things* you must do. If you only put a half effort into the right things, you will get inferior results. Solicit input from other knowledgeable people if you require help preparing the list. Seek out others who have experienced the same issues you are experiencing. The key is to examine your current actions and strategy and evaluate if you are simply doing something right, or if you are doing the right thing.

Why is this process so important? Keep in mind that *you have the power to create the world you desire.* Believing you are doing the right things *automatically* puts you into an important mindset of believing positive results will come from your actions. It is imperative that you must believe in the process. You can't simply go through the motions. Put your passion, your heart, your faith and confidence in yourself into the process.

Have you noticed how often people just go through the motions in their lives? We go to work, we come home, spend time with the children, maybe exercise a little, watch some TV and then we get up and go through the same routine the next day. Many go through the day with little emotion, thinking as little as possible, feeling hopeless about their future. Too many have given up or resigned themselves to believing where they are now is as good as it gets in life.

Having passion for what you do, having faith of expectation that a much better life awaits is critical in this process. We will discuss this later in more depth. For now, understand what you see around you in your world and the world you are at work creating is made manifest through a connection with the Universe and the force many of us choose to call God.

Remember, it is not the specific "thing" we desire, but we desire the experience and opportunities to grow generated by reaching the goal. We desire to be wealthy, but it is what we can accomplish with the money that we seek, not the money itself that matters.

My desire for additional wealth is to use it to provide financial assistance for animal shelters everywhere in the U.S. Caring for animals financially and through volunteer work is a part of who I am. It is how I have determined I will give to my world, as well as through volunteering my time. My passion is to teach how we all can create a better world. At the same time, my desire is to use my wealth and abundance to help animals.

Every day I see so many people trying very hard to move forward and create the life they desire, yet are frustrated and resentful and do not understand why they can not achieve their dreams. Doing this work defines who I am — it is my journey too — and through helping people understand their own ability to create their own paradise, I feel connected to the world and God. The expression of my love for animals is also a way I feel connected to the world and God. Michelle and I both have compassion and love for animals and are determined to help reduce the abuse of animals everywhere. So the wealth I achieve and the greater freedom provided by success permits me to carry out my life's purposes and bring me closer to inner peace. The experience of counting money and making deposits is not what I desire, but it's the end use of it that means so much to me.

Therefore, make sure your actions point you to your desired end result and do not sidetrack you into directions that waste your time. This process will help you stay focused, increasing your desire and determination and hence, create the world you desire.

Step 2: **Balance your focus between the desired outcome (your goal) and doing the right things (your action steps). Don't let anything distract you from your goal.**

To start, remember your goal must be humanly and personally achievable. Losing twenty pounds in one day, or building a successful business in a week or a month is not only personally but also humanly impossible. Such goals only set you up for failure, and we all know the effects of failure upon us. Reach for the stars and follow your dreams, and at the same time, give yourself and God reasonable time to accomplish your dreams. Consider, too, that the time schedule you have for your dreams may not be the same as what is best for you. (Remember those shortcuts many of us like to take?) There may be much more you need to discover and learn; more than you originally planned when you began your journey. We all encounter some experiences we had not anticipated during our journeys, yet when looking back the experience provided keen insight and helped to accomplish our goals.

If you daydream all the time about what it will be like when you reach your goal, but are not taking steps towards your goal, your dreams will turn to disappointment and frustration and ultimately you will quit. While giving time and attention to the steps you take have faith you will obtain your desire. It is important to be **in the moment**, living in the reality of each day and taking notice of your daily results. Like a scientist, each day, examine what is working and what is not working. With this information, make adjustments and change your approach the next day. The "results" showing up in your world come from your beliefs and actions, so examine what is causing these results, both positive (moving you toward your goal) and negative (moving you away from your goal). You will then understand which of your actions move you forward and which stall or limit your progress.

You may already feel you have been working your plan for years without much success. Examine your experiences. Have you truly not had any success, or are you making progress, but because you have not obtained your goal you can only focus on what you do not have? Understand you are on the right path no matter which path you take. It is up to you to learn from your choices.

Wherever you are today is where you need to be to learn what is required of you to move you farther down the path. As an infant, we must first learn to crawl before we walk, and walk before we run. Soon we are eager to drive a car. Besides needing the physical skills required to drive a car, we also need to be old enough to possess the mental skills involved in driving. We must be able to anticipate actions of other drivers, as well as have an appreciation for the power of a vehicle and its ability to damage property and even kill someone.

If you are not in possession of the mental skills required, then even though you believe you are "ready" to drive a car, your efforts to obtain a drivers license will fail. Simply because you "want" or desire something, does not mean you will create or manifest it in your life. Have you ever purchased something on impulse then later regretted the purchase because it did not perform or provide the value you anticipated? The same is true for being ready. To secure what you desire you must have a complete understanding of its full value.

In the midst of these learning experiences, you may not believe you are making any progress toward your goal. Only later when you obtain the skill and understand its value are you able to look back and appreciate the present you gave yourself. The challenge for all of us is to dive into each experience and explore the possibilities of what we can learn from it. Using this approach provides us an upbeat, positive feeling as we go about our day. My wife and I constantly ask ourselves what we can learn from each situation we experience as well as how we created the experience. You will see life so differently when you take this approach. Life becomes a fun adventure instead of a boring, dull process that wears you down over time.

Step 3: Stop doing things which disrespect who you are and who you want to be. When we don't eat the right foods, do not exercise, and do not spend some time to meditate to understand the quiet in our minds, we are telling everyone that we don't care about our bodies. Furthermore, such behavior reinforces the message to ourselves that we are undeserving and unworthy of better things in life. While smoking and overeating may medicate us and help us feel better for a while, we know that the feeling is only temporary. In fact, we look for these temporary good feelings because we are not creating the true "feel good" feeling we want so much.

Step 4: Go *do!* Take actions, which demonstrate the person you want to be. After I was divorced, I was living in an apartment by myself, with no pets, for a few years. All of my life I talked about how I loved dogs (I had four at different times, one when growing up and three at times when married) and talked about how I would like to care for dogs if I ever had enough money. One day the light went on in my head and I decided I should put my love of animals to use, instead of just talking about it and attempting to feel good about it. So I went to the local animal shelter and inquired about becoming a volunteer. Management at the animal shelter provided a list of various tasks for which they needed assistance. To my excitement, they needed someone to walk the dogs twice a day, and I jumped at the opportunity. The organization was a non-kill shelter and greatly appreciated the help. During the week I was eager for the weekend to approach when I could meet the new arrivals and walk with them. As I walked the dogs through the park nearby, I often sat with them and hugged them, letting them know they were truly loved. What a wonderful experience it was for me. In the end, I am not sure who enjoyed the time more, the dogs or me! To give a few dogs some love, and see them respond, meant so much to me. I was no longer someone that just talked about wishing to help animals; I went out and did it. And my self-esteem grew, knowing I was making a difference, although a small one, in the world.

This small act set the stage for additional successes and accomplishments in the next few years. By putting beliefs into motion, I demonstrated I could help others, make a small difference in the world while reinforcing my values. Enhancing my feeling of self worth ignited the potential for greater goodness to come through me powered by the Law of Attraction.

Step 5: Remember your actions and beliefs create your reality. Therefore, as you try to create your new world, any attempts to manipulate the results will disappoint you.

If you try to create a world in which you can control others, or have obtained significant wealth in hopes of using your wealth to harm others, you will draw to you exactly what you have put into motion. True, you are very likely to produce the wealth or power you desire, but at the same time you will continue to draw people into your world or potentially events that will exert influence over you and work to take your power away. You will be in a constant fight for control, taking a great toll on you mentally, physically and emotionally. You could find that what you sought — a person or your business — may end up controlling you, instead of you controlling him/her/it as you first desired. In either case, you will experience control and power, which you desired. However, the results may not be exactly what you anticipated and you pay a price you had not anticipated, but truly created out of your actions.

Don't get wrapped up in control, as control is an illusion. You can't make me love you or respect you. The amount of time you have to spend attempting to control everyone and everything in your world inflicts a tremendous drain on your energy and overall health. After all, the need to control is based out of fear. Fear occurs when you do not have faith in yourself and God. In addition, the need to control your environment most likely mirrors your belief that you lack control of yourself or believe others are trying to control you. The more you try to control your environment and your world, both inside and out, the more you will invite issues of power and control.

If you are taking the rights steps as I have shown in this book, you have nothing to fear. I did not say, and have never said, you will not encounter challenges in your life. In fact you could experience some tough issues. The issues are there for you to experience and learn from in order to get you to move to the next level of knowledge and most of all happiness.

Step 6: Stop resisting change. The more you resist change, and the more you resist learning and growing, the more you invite the same results you see every day. Everything in the world changes continually. Nothing remains the same. Neither do you. The greater your resistance and stubbornness remains, the longer your goal remains out of reach. In fact, the greatest obstacle to securing your goal in a timely manner is your resistance to change.

Step 7: Always think, believe, and eventually take action toward the highest good for yourself and others. When you seek to be the best you can be and do what is in the highest good for yourself, you will find yourself opening up to many options, choices, and alternatives you had never thought of or contemplated before.

God wants you to be prosperous. God wants you to have abundance and happiness in your life. However, many times our experience of abundance does not come in the exact form we had envisioned, yet often our reality is better than we had hoped for. If you are uncertain of which actions you should take or which direction you should turn to help ensure you are proceeding in your highest good, turn inward and use your intuition. God attempts to connect with you not just once or twice a day, but hundreds of times. Your job is to open your mind to allow this information in. Most of the time our minds are busy blocking and filtering out the thousands of messages coming our way every day. The more your beliefs and actions are focused on helping you and those around you, the more rapidly positive results will occur.

Step 8: One by one, examine the cause of old beliefs and either discard or evolve them into something more reflective of where you are heading. You may be wondering where to start, considering you may have hundreds of beliefs and "programming" routines running through your head. Look at your current daily experiences, the people in them and how you feel about all of it. Select a particular situation in which you are frustrated, confused, angry, sad, or jealous and remember it, as we'll come back to it shortly.

Keep in mind your world mirrors what you believe, similar to programming running constantly in your subconscious. Most beliefs we have are buried in our subconscious, as we do not consciously consider each one and make decisions based on it each day. Instead, this programming is deep, imbedded into the very core or essence of who we are. If I have a natural distrust of people, upon meeting someone new, I will automatically go into a defensive, skeptical and protected mode. This mode automatically influences the words I use, my body language and thoughts as I experience the encounter with this new person. I don't say to myself "This is a new person and I don't trust people, so I need to start acting in a defensive manner." Instead, it's automatic, so automatic it's like breathing. I will do it without noticing my responses.

Because these beliefs are buried within us in our subconscious, they are hard to detect. Once detected and given voice, they can often surprise to us. If confronted, we may even become defensive and provide a rationale explaining the perfect validation for this belief! Sometimes, these buried beliefs cause us unpleasant experiences. In many cases, our beliefs may just need tweaking or adjustment in order to become helpful and help us grow. None of us stay in high school all of our lives. We graduate on to higher levels of learning. The information learned in high school is not discarded; rather we build on it as we mature and learn.

Remember the situation you brought to mind earlier, one that has recently caused you frustration, confusion, anger, sadness or jealousy? In order to uncover the underlying belief that required some adjustment and is creating your present experience, you can use an old technique called "The Five Whys?" As a child you may recall when you used the world "why" frequently. Perhaps your Mom told you something to which you responded "Why?" When your Mom provided a second answer to the why question, you promptly responded with another "Why?" This cycle may have continued a few more times until your Mom grew weary of answering.

Use this technique to discover the programming behind your actions and experiences manifested by your belief. For example, let's say when you get into a disagreement with your spouse you are inclined to continue the debate or argument, determined to be the "winner." You are well aware of the potential strain the continuous debate and argument could place on your relationship with your spouse, but you press on anyway with your determination to be declared "right" or the "winner."

Ask yourself: *Why am I so desperately determined to be declared the victor?*

You may answer, "It's important to win and I like the feeling of winning."

Why is it important to win and feel good?

"Because when I lose I feel bad."

Why do you feel bad when you lose?

"Because when I lose I feel ignorant and less important."

Why do you associate being stupid or unimportant with losing?"

"Because I believe that anyone who loses is ignorant, incompetent, and will not succeed in life."

Why do you believe failure means you are incompetent?

"Because when I was a kid and didn't meet my Dad's expectations, he told me I was a loser."

In this example, you discover a belief, an old program running in your subconscious, from a childhood experience. The belief that one mistake or disappointment makes you to be a loser has put a tremendous amount of strain on your relationship, all based on a deep-seated belief, **which is not true**.

Everyone makes mistakes and fails and losing does not measure someone's ability to succeed. Yet, every one of us has a multitude of these programs and beliefs buried within us, influencing our thoughts and actions. These beliefs are buried, so deeply within us, that we go to abnormal lengths to ensure these beliefs are upheld most of the time without knowing why. Most of us will fight and die based on a belief that was instilled in us as a child which upon closer examination is not valid or even relevant today.

At times you will not need all five "whys" to get to your answer. Initially, you may even need more than five "whys" or have to try it again focusing on the same issue before finding your primary driving belief. After you have succeeded on many occasions finding this inner belief, you will discover it takes less than five "whys" to get your answer.

This not only takes patience and perseverance, but also honesty to uncover what drives you. This process is not easy and sometimes it can be painful to consciously become aware of long held beliefs that have caused significant pain in your life. At times, you will resist changing or discarding the belief, rationalizing in every way you can to hold onto the belief convinced you require this belief to manage your way in this world! Again, ask: *Why?*

It is your choice to change unhelpful beliefs or continue using them. No one else creates your experiences. No force is causing these experiences to happen to you. You create everything, all of your reality, directly from these thoughts, actions and beliefs. It is your choice.

Each belief generates energy into the Universe. Some of your beliefs may work against other beliefs you have. You may believe you can attract a wonderful person for a great relationship. At the same time you remind yourself daily how your past relationships did not work out as you hoped. These beliefs work against each other. You are simultaneously emitting energies that are juxtaposed to each other. The result is your reality continues to mirror your beliefs being opposite. One day your reality may show you moving forward towards having a great relationship, and the next day you may experience the inability to meet someone special.

Because we all have a significant number of beliefs all working simultaneously, we must examine all potential beliefs that could be helping to create our reality. At times, our beliefs, no matter how well intended they are, can create negative experiences. We react to these negative experiences with increased frustration and confusion.

Well intended beliefs generating negative experiences are one of the most powerful disruptions in our ability to maintain faith,

perseverance, and self-esteem.

How do well intended beliefs cause negative experiences? For example, let's say you believe that it is important to be on time for all meetings and appointments whether it is for business or in your personal life. You consider promptness not only a virtue but an indication of whether another person is considerate of others. You are a considerate person and always demonstrate being on time. This belief and value is so important to you that if the person you are meeting is late you tell them they are being inconsiderate. The result? You create a reality filled with experiences in which the other party often arrives late. Yet the more you experience someone being late, the more you feel compelled to remind others of the value of being prompt. Further, you reinforce this belief to yourself by restating in your mind that being on time is an admirable quality.

So how does this well intended, "good" belief, create a negative experience? It's all about pushing your belief onto someone else or into the Universe. Any time you push any of your beliefs onto others, the energy projected is no longer from a position of caring or love. Looking closer at why you may have a belief that promptness is important, you may discover it is more about the other person having respect of your time, which in turn is really an indication of having respect for you. Pushing this belief onto someone else is not really about value, but about respect to you. As we have discussed, when you respect yourself, others will respect you. If you are not respecting yourself, you will continue to create an experience where others do not arrive promptly; hence, a perfect example of not respecting yourself.

I am not suggesting that your belief of being prompt is not worth having. However, you must stop pushing this belief onto others, as there are other methods to convey the importance of this value and belief. For example, simply being on time for each occasion sends a powerful message to those you meet. Many times nothing more needs to be said. It is often best simply to lead by example. The message will be received by those around you.

Pushing is a negative force, because you are attempting to control the actions of others. The flow of energy must happen naturally. Just as you can not push someone to love you, love will happen on its own, naturally. The same is true for any of your beliefs. They may be valuable, but you demonstrating them with the highest good intended for those around you will radiate the positive energy intended.

Modifying your belief will also help you experience more positive results. Instead of believing promptness is important, consider believing that each moment of your day brings new opportunities to gather information. If you do experience someone not being on time, you can then consider it to be a "perfect" time for quiet meditation or taking in the surroundings especially if your meeting is in a restaurant or somewhere outdoors.

Step 9: Everything you accomplish, big and small, is important. Let's now examine those occasions when you achieved success. It could be something extremely important, or it could be somewhat smaller. Landing a job, graduating from high school, hitting all the green lights on your drive to work to an important appointment, getting into a smooth flow at work, sometimes just everything flowing at work for several weeks or arriving just in time to see your daughter perform at school or score the winning run.

You played a role in all of these experiences. Yet, influenced by years of training, you may believe these experiences are minor miracles. Many believe that miracles only occur when God has appeared to intervene on a grand scale and provided success for us. Too often we remain waiting hoping God will create a miracle for us. God only helps manifest reality based on the energy we generate from our beliefs and actions.

The process works as follows: we put the desired effect and outcome into motion through our energy of actions and beliefs, God helps us get there.

The key concept to understand here is everything about you and what you have in your life is a miracle. Your life is a miracle. The trouble is we believe miracles are something spectacular like the sea parting. God is there whenever we need God to help us help ourselves. If we are expecting God to help us, and we do not help ourselves, we will be waiting a long time. If you insist on believing in miracles, then realize you create them every day. Everything you create is wondrous.

Some of you might be thinking, "How can a four year old child understand she creates her own reality? How does this make sense for a child who is born with a particular handicap, or born into starvation conditions in other countries?"

First, this book is written for adults because we have spent many years using the same beliefs generating the same results to the point of creating considerable frustration, resentment and anger in our lack of success. We are able to think for ourselves and make decisions from quite an early age. We all need to understand these principles as early in life as possible. It often takes people many years to unlearn the unusable concepts and beliefs they grew up thinking were helping them. The stronger the beliefs holding them back, the longer it takes to move a considerable distance down the path of knowledge. In my case it took me well into my forties to put most of the pieces together and that was after starting down the road to enlightenment and success over twenty years earlier!

A child enters this world knowing he can create his world as he desires. Ever watch children play when they put their creativeness to work? For a child, anything is possible and they are absolutely amazing. Children do not doubt their ability to create their world. Their perceptions and creativity, however, are greatly influenced by what their parents and our culture teach them. The actions of their parents and others send a child many, many messages of how their parents and others "perceive" the world. When a child is punished or disrespected for his creativity or his natural curiosity, or attempting and failing at something, he is taught he is inadequate or lacking. On the other hand, if a child is encouraged and supported in her efforts, even when she fails she grows up confident, curious and creative.

Our children must understand their choices create results and they are then responsible for those results. The sooner this is learned, the sooner they can be happier, more accepting, more independent and self-reliant young people. In fact, such knowledge can help them create and have influence in their worlds in positive and productive ways.

Children today learn faster than their parents and have the ability to absorb so much more at an earlier age than their parents. I can see it in my sons and the children of my brother and sisters. All of our children, and they are not exceptional in any way, are smarter and more aware than their parents were at similar ages. Today there are considerably more methods from which to learn, quantity of books dealing with learning, and sources such as the internet to obtain knowledge about any subject.

As a child growing up in the Catholic Church, I never was satisfied with all of the answers provided by the church pertaining to our purposes in life, the ways we must interact with God and what God expected from us. I knew that all over the world many children were being born into undesirable circumstances, possibly a family with an abusive, alcoholic parent; into a community of food shortages and malnutrition; or into war-ravaged areas. To hear the religious authorities claim God is our Father, then say we can not know the reasons these situations occurred and that "God has a reason" for the suffering endured by people, rang very hollow in my young ears. I always found it disconcerting that a loving God would not tell us why God wanted us to experience such difficulty. As a father myself, it makes even less sense to me now. Why would I make my child experience pain (all the while proclaiming my child had free will to make his own choices and endure his own consequences) and never give him a reason? Why would I make him spend years trying to "figure it out" and "learn from it?" From a father perspective that just seems downright cruel.

At times I felt as if the Catholic Church, as with many other religions wants us to fear God as if he will punish us, (hence the numerous prayers we must say assigned by a Priest to earn forgiveness). Again, would a loving parent force us to struggle in confusion, endure hardship and suffering, then punish us because we can't figure out what the rules are for obtaining happiness? What kind of father — what kind of God — would do something like that?

I discovered God does not punish us. We punish ourselves. For now, consider the possibility that the hardship we experience in our lives is **our plan,** in conjunction with God. If an infant is born into starvation and dies shortly their after, could she have created her world before coming to Earth? Since we are all manifestations of God's energy and never spiritually die, then aren't we creating even when not in physical bodies?

Furthermore, when we understand we reincarnate many times during eternity, the concept of experiencing different situations in our physical lives, such as where and when we are born, and to whom we are born, it makes sense that we have control over the conditions into which we are born. In other words, we choose. In other words, we create the reality in which we will be born.

I have a strange and fascinating fear of knives, especially those used for carving meats. I have never cut myself badly with a knife as a child or adult, nor am I a person prone to phobias. I am not afraid to handle knives, but there is a peculiar feeling that sweeps over me when I pull one out of the drawer or dishwasher. Somewhere deep inside it feels as though I had been severely wounded by one at some time in my past, most likely in a prior life.

I was at times a sensitive child and as a young adult, lacked confidence. I know I came here with those traits and placed myself into the situations I have endured in order to address the sensitivity-actually use it to become more in tune with the world around me, as well as address my lack of confidence. Breaking through these issues myself has enabled me to help others who lack confidence. My struggles and the teachings I discovered as a result may help you understand that once you embark on this journey and do the work, you will no longer beat yourself up. Your self-esteem will grow and you will create the world in which you wish to live.

Each of us plays a significant role in the world and reality around us. The good news is we are here to learn from our experiences; in fact, by working through the issue with which we struggle the most, we have an opportunity to create considerable happiness for others and ourselves. There is no question we all face struggles and problems, some of enormous proportions. I have been laid off twice, the first time with the added responsibility of family, including two young children to support. With it came a considerable drain on my savings and self-esteem. I have also experienced the pain of divorce. As difficult as these were, they do not compare to the troubles facing most others around the world. Many may have come here choosing to face tremendous physical and emotional challenges; yet we **all** have the power, together, to create a world in which everyone enjoys peace, abundance and happiness.

I have not only survived but prospered. The prospering came with a great deal of soul searching, examining who I truly am, being honest with myself and having the strength to persevere through the tough times and push myself through the door of uncertainty.

I am no one special, yet I am as unique as each one of you. We are all special in our own way. *You are special.* Always remember that. Every person I have come in contact with has brought something important into my life, at just the right time. Some have shared simple admonitions to live by; some have been friends and walked along with me for a long time on my journey. From each I have tried to become aware of what it is they had to teach me. I, in turn, have done the same for them, yet sometimes I had no idea what I had to offer the other person as far as a lesson is concerned. But there are no accidents in life and every person you encounter is there for a reason, and remember you are drawn into the others' lives to help them on their journey as well. You have a greater impact on the world than you might believe.

When we encounter problems, it is difficult not to take it personally. The first time I was laid off I not only took it personally, but felt stung by the process as well. Faced with such a setback, we emotionally pass through the stages of grief. We move from disbelief to anger, perhaps many times, as grief is not a linear process. Even though acceptance comes, enabling us to move on, it is often common for us to carry some of the anger with us for a long time. We might look back and stay in touch with employees who remain in hopes of hearing our prior boss or company was experiencing difficulty. Several years ago when I was laid off I did not do this. I wished everyone well, and knew it was time for me to move on, although concerned as to where it might lead me.

When I reflected on my prior employment, I wondered what might have been different. What could I have done differently? Could I have said something differently at the right time that may have changed the outcome? And if I had done or said those different things, would I still be employed there? We often look back and wonder how life would have been different, and at times I did struggle with thinking about the past. However, you could have changed the outcome if you chose to, but the key is to learn from the experience, do not focus on the past, make new choices and do not create the old experience again!

One day, after I had left my previous company, while using my computer, my hard drive crashed beyond repair. I was extremely dismayed since the hard drive contained an extensive number of files from the past five years and I did not have copies of them anywhere. I tried everything possible to recover the data, all to no avail. My older son, who is extremely knowledgeable about computers, gave me several suggestions as we tried different options. He finally stated it was a lost cause. For another week I kept talking about the lost data and my disappointment. When my son came to visit and I mentioned it to him he replied exasperated, "Dad, get over it. It's gone." All I could do is laugh at myself for being so stubborn focusing on the past and not using my energy to address obtaining a new hard drive. Yes, my son reminded me of an important lesson.

I realized I had created this situation and received an exclamation point of advice to move forward. I was focusing on "what if" about the past, yet knew I needed to forget about the past and move on. What better way to forget about past experiences in which I could not change the results than for my hard drive to crash? What a superb metaphor for my past experiences. We must learn our lessons and move on.

The same holds true in our relationships. If you were submissive and taken for granted in your last relationship, and you have not changed anything about the way you perceive yourself or others or the world, you will be drawn again into another relationship in which you were submissive. If you attract to you someone who is controlling, it is because you allow it. If you attract someone who is clingy, it is because you allow it. If you find yourself always having to help the other person financially or emotionally, it is because you allow it. If you attract someone to you who is a liar, it is because you allow it. In all of these situations you play the role to which the other person is attracted, and until you change yourself, your deeply held beliefs of others and your world will continue to draw the same kinds of people and experience into your life.

How many times do you want to repeat the fourth grade?

We must graduate the fourth grade before we can move on to the fifth grade. We must learn how to crawl before we walk, and walk before we run. Lessons learned in school provide a fine metaphor for the lessons learned in life. There is no skipping class and skipping grades. You must apply yourself, study how your beliefs affect your outcomes, and then make the necessary changes. I believe we grow "up" mentally, emotionally and spiritually in big steps, as if walking up stairs, not a continuous upward motion. Some experiences will turn the light bulb on in our heads, giving us the wonderful rush of knowledge, understanding and consequential excitement. We will then move along, **somewhat comfortably**, for days, weeks or even months at that level, with anxiety, intensity, and frustration building, until we have another light bulb moment propelling us forward. The effect is like reaching a plateau where we operate mentally, emotionally and spiritually for a while, and then make a big jump up to the next plateau. You can either take years to get to the next level or you can do the work and get there a lot sooner.

As we do the work and begin the steps of creating the world we desire by recognizing our thoughts and beliefs create our outer world, it is required that we maintain balance in the creation process. Up until now we have only discussed one side of the process equation.

Now let's explore the other half of the equation.

CHAPTER 13

The Other Half of the Equation

*"Faith is taking the first step even when you don't see
the whole staircase."*

-- Martin Luther King, Jr.

As much as we create our world, there are two dynamic
forces at work:
Dynamic Force #1 is all about examining our beliefs and
taking the rights steps to create successful results. The people we
encounter along the way, the places we go, the events that occur
combine in perfect synchronicity, providing us rich opportunities
to learn and grow spiritually and emotionally. The power of our
thoughts, actions and beliefs propels our energy into the Universe
gathering with the potential to manifest in our lives.

Dynamic Force #2 – the other half of the equation – is al-
lowing God, in what ever form you perceive God, to help you create the world you desire. It is about faith. We must believe, we
must trust, we must wait, and we must allow the forces in the Universe to work together.

The experiences we create have wonderful meanings for us,
filled with comprehensive learning opportunities that only these
unique experiences can provide. Our learning, like our lives, can
be viewed on a continuum, whole and connected and perfect.
This is an important point. It is perfect. Each experience we create is perfect and just what we need. Every experience on our
journey provides us an opportunity to learn about ourselves, make

changes and grow.

Consider your past experiences and analyze a time when you discovered something wonderful about yourself and felt the warmth of inner happiness envelope you. We have all had such times. We had the opportunities to learn and we did. If, on the other hand, we did not learn the lessons we needed from an experience, we invited the same situation — albeit with different actors — to occur until we understood the message and learned the lesson. Eventually we learn, grow and become more of who we want to be. Eventually we discover and relax in the inner happiness and peace for which we long.

Sometimes, though, we try to force an outcome to occur exactly as we want it to happen. We have the ability to create the world we desire, but there is a difference between creating the world we perceive we want, creating the world we need, and creating the world we truly desire.

If you say you want a new job or a new spouse or a new car, what is it you really want? What does the new job, spouse or car give you? Will it give you power, responsibility, freedom, happiness, love or prestige? What do these things look like when you find them? Do you seek a new job to have more responsibility and challenge yourself or more power to control others to help your ego? You might be able to find one or both of those traits in your current job and with your current company. Perhaps you can find the warmth and caring you seek in your current spouse instead of believing you need a new spouse. Divorce rates show many people who divorce, end up divorcing again. Why does that happen? Because we often do not make any changes in our beliefs and actions and therefore attract the same type of person and same situation to us all over again.

You can have what you want. You must be clear about what you truly want and be honest with yourself about the inner reasons for your desires and first appreciate what you already have. If as he grows up I constantly give my son whatever he wants he may become spoiled and unappreciative of what he has been given. He may never learn to provide for himself. He may take for granted every comfort and opportunity he has been given…until he loses it. Only then might he begin to appreciate what he had. Then he might be inspired to work hard and create what he wants in life. He just might find that creating wealth and sharing it with those less fortunate is more rewarding and much more satisfying than he ever thought possible.

We often need to step back to move forward. In this scenario, fulfillment came in a much different way than what my son might have first imagined. He, like many of us, probably would force and push the process to keep obtaining every toy he possibly could get his hands on. Children may whine and beg for every new toy they see advertised. When they find that what they wanted doesn't ful-fill them inside, they often will look for something new and beg for the next new toy.

Some adults do the very same. We believe the accumulation of goods or the next job or the next relationship will cure all of our ills and fulfill all of our desires. However, pushing too hard leads to frustration. At some point we often throw our hands in the air and yell to the heavens, "I give up!"

I give up. Think about what we are actually saying when we say those words. I laugh at myself when I use these words when struggling with my own issues. When we state, often out loud, that we are giving up, we proclaim to the world that someone else, mainly God, can take over our problems and resolve them as we have decided we cannot do it ourselves. Strangely, we frequently find once we "give up", a resolution to our struggle emerges. Why does that happen? Relinquishing control, no longer forcing what we believe to be the "perfect solution" for our problem, allows Dynamic Force Two to operate. Dynamic Force Two is the time at which we step back and allow God to help us.

Often, although we try hard and with the best intentions, we force and push what we believe is the best solution or answer to the problem we face. At some point, I must trust in God and trust in the process by which we all learn from our choices. I must trust in the creation process through the projection of my energy to the Universe combined with doing all of the right work to generate success. We all have an opportunity to grow from our experiences and my path is not the same path as those around me. When we "give up", we relinquish control of the situation to God and the Universe and allow the thousands of other possibilities to come forth. When we insist the result must occur in the exact format we demand, and insist the result must look exactly as we have envisioned, we are blocking off all other possibilities from occurring. Our minds can not comprehend or imagine all of the possible scenarios that could occur to create the end result we desire. Our insistence on a particular flow tells the Universe we will not accept other solutions and therefore these thousands of other possibilities become blocked from manifesting. The end result is a long delay in obtaining that which we desire and eventually we give up. Only when we let other possibilities manifest do we learn that the result, if we let go of rigid expectations, is almost always, better than we imagined!

Previously I mentioned my relationship with a woman whom I believed was the right one for me. I pushed and pushed, but to no avail. Only when I backed away, and had faith in other possibilities, did I meet someone so much more wonderful than I had ever imagined was out there. I wonder now what took me so long to move on and out of the previous relationship.

Forcing the process is, in reality, a demonstration of fear. To demand a particular path to reach a goal can only come out of fear. Your rationale may be that this particular path is the simplest, or straightest. What you are really saying is this path is the easiest, and in forcing the easiest path you are attempting to avoid the required work and learning process involved in the experience. Forcing the path and particular outcome prevents the best possible outcome and experience. When you block the best possible result for your highest good, you block the process altogether.

Half of the process in our life is creating our reality by our beliefs and choices. The other half is having faith — allowing your projected energy into the Universe — to combine with God to manifest your desired outcome.

Many of us have searched for a new job at some time in our

life, either from the necessity — having lost a job — or choice — needing a new challenge or place to grow. We might set our sights on working at a particular company, and put all of our energy in finding a way to get in the door and land the key first interview. Yet very often we find we do not land a job at that company and walk away very disappointed and frustrated.

However, when we finally reach the point of "giving up" and let all of the energy we have projected into the Universe take its course we end up with a job offer and place to work better than we have dared to dream. How did this happen, when we were so sure we needed to work at Company Y and yet did not get a job there?

While you were busy "creating" the life and experience you desired, your Higher Self — your spiritual self — and God were busy matching up all the possible scenarios to your request. Your initial problem was you kept blocking the other possible scenarios to materialize because your free will stated it had to happen your way. You had it all laid out in your mind how the events would unfold, who would say what, and the company would make you an offer.

When you find yourself in a situation like this, if you will take some time, step back, and ask yourself what it is you are really looking for. It is then that you may understand the answer to your prayers can be found in other options you had not even considered! When we force a solution onto a situation, our energy envelopes the situation and nothing else can manifest. Remember earlier when we discussed how the mind rationalizes that there is no more available other than that it can conceptualize? If your mind can only "think" or "imagine" a few possible outcomes or scenarios to landing that perfect job, you then automatically block out the remainder of the countless other possibilities your mind has not considered even exists. It is impossible to know and be aware of the many possibilities which can materialize to get you to your desired goal.

God and your Higher Self do not interfere in our choices, they only make suggestions. Therefore, if you keep insisting your choice and your solution is the best one, God will let you keep trying to make it work. God knows what you requested and are attempting to create, yet God has the ability to help manifest many other solutions which yield substantially greater results. When we "let go" or "give up" we allow the Dynamic Force Two to go to work and generate the perfect conditions for us to learn and experience everything we want.

Think of it this way: when we go to a restaurant, we don't give the waiter our order, then call the waiter over five minutes later and give the waiter the order a second time. After another ten minutes we don't call the waiter over a third time to remind him of our order, and again remind the waiter of the order ten minutes later, nor do we go into the kitchen and stand watching as the chef cooks our food! We do not carefully review every process to ensure it meets our expectations and it is prepared to our specifications! No! We only order our food once and trust that our beverage, appetizers, entrée and dessert will be just as we ordered and served in a pleasing manner. Furthermore, we are willing to wait for the food. We don't demand the food be brought out twenty seconds after we gave the waiter the order. When we wait patiently, our order is often delivered faster and tastes better than we anticipated.

Further, we were willing to wait to receive that which we ordered. The same patience is necessary when working toward achieving all of our goals.

Often people get frustrated while waiting for their goal to materialize. Consider when you are waiting for your birthday to arrive, or Christmas or some other joyful religious occurrence, or even a long awaited trip you have planned for many years. Each of these events will arrive at a specific date and time. You can not move these events forward. You must wait the days remaining until your birthday again arrives. What you do while you wait is important. But you declare: *"I know my birthday or Christmas is coming, but I am not sure my goal is arriving!"* Yet, belief in your goal's arrival is partly why it can be delayed. If you have believed in yourself and God, done the work required to achieve your goal and prepared for its arrival, the creation process is complete and manifestation is assured.

Spend your time waiting with continued preparation. Around our house at the holidays we never seem to have displayed enough decorations, the right touch of candles, gifts for family, donations to charities and meetings with friends. There always appears more we can do to make the holidays a joyous time for everyone.

Dynamic Force One is similar to putting your order in as it is the creating process. God knows what you ordered. Do the right things to help make your order be fulfilled, and live each day with expectation, anticipation and thankfulness that God is preparing your order.

Dynamic Force Two will occur as you step back and wait patiently as your order is filled, often beyond your highest expectations! Dynamic Force Two is your faith and belief in God or whatever higher power you believe in. We do not have the mental ability to comprehend everything going on in the world as well as to everyone in it.

Earlier we talked about sending out resumes. You can never know whose hands it touches on its journey. At some point we must trust the process, trust in God, and trust in ourselves we have put positive energy in motion. This happened to me a few years ago. While I was still employed I began reaching out to a few key business contacts letting them know I was looking for a new position. About a month later I received an unexpected call from a company looking for someone with my qualifications. I was completely unaware of how this company found me. Later I learned one of my business colleagues through his long line of contacts helped my resume land in front of the hiring manager at this company!

When you think about it, having faith in God to assist manifesting what you desire is actually another belief. Believing in God or a higher power to help you on your journey, providing guidance and advice is the most powerful belief you can have.

In some ways, you might feel this is a contradiction in life. We are busy creating the world we want to experience, and at the same time we are letting God and our Higher Self produce it for us. Actually, it is the best combination of energy and power in the Universe. Can you possibly know of everything going on in the world? Of course not! Therefore, leave it to the one being that can: God.

Our lack of patience and our mindset that everything needs to happen fast causes us to attempt to force the process. When you put a cake in the oven, it needs a specific amount of time to cook properly. If you attempt to raise the heat and cook the cake faster, the result will be a burned cake, causing you to start the process over. The same is true for each goal you set in motion.

From a spiritual perspective at Easter time, the Christian community focuses all of its attention on Good Friday when Jesus was crucified on the cross. Most all conversation, attention, and actions are fixated on Friday, when Jesus died, and on Sunday, when he arose from the dead. Little attention or discussion, if any, is focused on Saturday, the day in between Jesus' death and him rising. Yet consider that on Saturday, no one knew what was about to unfold on Sunday. Saturday is the most important day in the process. The symbolism of Saturday for each of us is to wait patiently in faith that we have generated all of the energy required to reach our goal, and now it is time for the result to materialize. We do not know if it will occur tomorrow or the next day, but we can be assured it will manifest.

If you fully understand the creation process you will not doubt or control the outcome.

Creating is part of our very essence. When you create, putting energy in motion through your thoughts, ideas, actions and beliefs, the outcome is guaranteed. Just like cause and effect, through Universal consistency there will always be a manifestation to the energy you project. The only reason the result may not be as you intended is you either projected contradictory beliefs or attempted to force the outcome preventing other possibilities for manifestation in the form you desired.

In our job search example, you might be networking effectively, sending out your resumes to all the right search firms and companies, attending meetings and organizations helping to find jobs for participants. You keep plugging along every day, possibly with little to show for your efforts, it seems. Then one day you get a phone call, an unexpected phone call from someone unknown to you, who works at a great company, has your resume and requests you come in for an interview. You could not "see" this coming because you can not know everything that is happening in the Universe. You trusted the process, knowing you were taking the proper steps in your job search and knowing the right person, somewhere, would eventually come across your resume and contact you.

The same process is required for all of your choices and desires. Having faith in God and having faith in the Universal laws to assist you in achieving success demonstrates your belief a better life awaits you. Go through your day with a feeling of expectation, trusting God is working behind the scenes for you, and most of all knowing something better is coming. As long as I can remember, the one bit of advice my Mother always gave us — and she says it even today — is, "Believe something better is coming!" She gave us this guidance when we stumbled and fell, giving us the hope and trust in God and ourselves. My Mother may not realize the spiritual magnitude of those words of wisdom, but I have witnessed her live them out. She has endured and adapted throughout her life, believing that something better *is* coming.

When we expect something better to come, we prepare for it. When we are having friends over for dinner, we prepare our house and the meal, cleaning, cooking, and setting the table, as we wait for our friends' arrival. We anticipate a wonderful evening with our friends. We do not go through the day dreading the visit and anticipating something will go wrong! Instead, we look forward to the enjoyment of their company, the good conversation and happiness that comes from being with them. *Expect the same with God!*

Expectation of greater success and belief in God are not ideas to be followed for one day and then dropped, yet so many of us give up after just a short time. Start each morning and live each day expecting more success, more abundance and greater happiness in your life!

God and the Universe's manifestation of your energy into reality, do not work on your timetable. Due to our lack of patience we often want to move from point A to point Z rather quickly, instead of taking the time to hit all points in between. Patience is not exactly my strong suit either, yet I take the time each day and in each event to step back and trust the process. So often the points in between are there for our safety, self-awareness, spiritual growth or prerequisite knowledge to take on the next task. None of us learn how to ride a bicycle until we know how to walk and run.

It is imperative you also let go of your attachment to your goal, and release it to the Universe. If you are deeply and strongly attached to an outcome or desire, by doing so you block your ability to receive that which you desire. By attaching yourself so strongly to the outcome you are in essence telling God you will not be happy until the desired outcome occurs. Further, by constantly focusing on the outcome, you actually are confirming you do not yet possess that which you desire. By continually confirming you do not yet have that which you desire, your world will continue to mirror a reality with you not achieving your goal. When you release your attachment to your outcome, you are releasing the power to God to make it happen in your highest good.

It is important to balance your energy both to focus on visualizing your reality once you have obtained your goal as well as focusing on the daily steps required in order to achieve your goal.

There is an old saying "If a solution exists, do not worry; if there is no solution, do not worry!" Your attachment to "your" solution restricts the energy from flowing into the Universe to manifest itself into the solution you seek. There is no way to control the outcome and therefore there is no need to spend time focused on it and worried about it. Relax and release the power for God to manifest the best solution.

Consider also your fantasies. Earlier we talked about dwelling on something you believe and the opposite also being true. (If you believe you must cheat to earn a living, then you also believe you cannot earn one honestly; hence your experiences will continue to show you nothing will be earned honestly.) The same applies to your fantasies and certain dreams.

Dreams and goals are essential in our lives, but those dreams should be both practical and in your highest good. Be cautious, however, of nurturing fantasies and desires that are not obtainable in your life or not in the best interest of you or those about whom you care. It is possible to dream and achieve what others can consider impossible or unachievable. Yet I am talking about those fantasies and desires you know are not obtainable in your life.

Perhaps you always wanted to live in another country. Europe has always held a great fascination for you. However, because of your life choices, moving to Europe will never come to fruition for you (i.e. you have a great job here, your spouse has a good career here, your parents and extended family live in the same city and you would miss them all very much if you moved to another country.) You could well make it happen and fulfill your dream — you can, after all, create your reality. At the same time we make choices based on important values and qualities of life and closeness to extended family. So if you choose to remain in this country be careful about focusing a significant amount of energy on living somewhere you have *chosen* not to go. Every time you fantasize about the unobtainable you are stating that what you do have is not satisfactory. Soon the world you have here will begin to deteriorate as you have declared it to be unsatisfactory. As you fantasize more, the message plants itself in your subconscious which in turn continues to push for your fantasy even when you are not consciously thinking about it.

Instead, dream about how wonderful your current life is; appreciate it, be thankful for it and by doing so you will allow the Universe to give you even more abundance in all areas of your life.

When we talk in terms of coveting something impossible to obtain, there is no contradiction with the fact that you can create the life you desire. We live in a world bounded by time and space. We can not be in two places at the same time, nor can we go forward or backward in time. Therefore, when I talk in terms of what is not possible, I am focusing on that which is limited by time and space. I want you to dream the impossible, and at the same time stay in this reality as you do your work.

The key here has to do with your energy. It is important you focus all of your energy on your goals, dreams and desires which are in your highest good, and not put energy into dreams which you know are not. If you desire to live in another country because you want to escape your life here, then you are simply running away from issues that must be dealt with no matter where you go. Consequently, your issues will be resolved much sooner if you put energy and focus into those issues, than dreaming about an escape. Each day you have a certain amount of energy to project outward. Using some of the energy on unrelated goals, unobtainable goals, or negative thoughts leaves you less energy to generate for manifestation of your goals. Consider your energy to be similar to your car's gas tank. Using up two gallons each day on negative thoughts or fantasizing leaves you fewer gallons, (energy) to use to move you forward.

To ensure you achieve your dreams and goals as soon as possible, place all of your attention on your goals and current reality. I am not saying you shouldn't spend time with your children as you are working on your dream of building a business. Both of those are priorities in this realm. However, if you spend part of your day dreaming of being an NBA basketball player, are short and have never played basketball, then your valuable energy is being used up on the wrong dream. The greater amount of energy you project into the Universe related to your main goal, the quicker it can materialize in your reality.

Balance is a critical ingredient in a healthy and abundant life. Open minded thinking helps create balance, and balance creates harmony. We must balance our activities. All work and no play is not a healthy balance, nor is all play and no work. There is an old adage that states "Everything in moderation." I heard this saying frequently from my parents as a child. It holds so true for today.

Look at the great debate today about whether to eat a high protein, low carbohydrate diet, compared to a low fat diet. In the end aren't we simply talking about balance? Scientists have told us for years the body needs all three: protein, fat and carbohydrates. The answer is eating all three in moderation and balance.

The same approach holds true in working toward your goals. If you are constantly visualizing the end result you will miss the lessons to learn along the way. If you concentrate too heavily on the day-day-day experiences, you will be too easily swayed by emotion and can easily get derailed from maintaining your course to your goal.

Work hard, do the right things and then sit back, relax and enjoy what you have already created by living in the moment. Living in the moment - the only moment you have - helps open your heart to new possibilities.

Maintaining balance is the most interesting and exciting part of the whole human experience because you get to taste everything from both sides. You can create greater balance by embracing all events in your life, either deemed fortunate or unfortunate, as opportunities to grow and learn about yourself.

No one enjoys unfortunate experiences, like being hurt in a relationship. However, the result is our appreciation for the opportunity to learn from it, to grow, and make our next relationship more powerful.

I experienced the depth of great disappointment, fear and rejection of being laid off, but also by making the necessary changes I became much more than I thought I could be. The first time I was laid off over fifteen years ago, I was depressed and beaten. Although I went through the outplacement process, I had a "Why did this happen to me?" attitude and did not believe this should happen to me. As you know, this mental attitude kept me from achieving as much as I could.

The second time around I had a different attitude. I knew I had a lot to offer another company and was determined to find an employer and boss who valued my experience and respected my ideas. My former company allowed me to use the services of an outplacement firm they hired to assist me in finding a new job. I dove into the process with full intensity and determination to make every aspect work for me. In the end I was so effective at networking, effectively presenting my extensive experience and skills, writing a powerful resume and landing an interview, the outplacement firm was referring newly unemployed workers to me to give them guidance! In addition, I wrote three articles for a national magazine on how to obtain a new position.

Go through your closet and find as many items as you can to give away. Bundle them together and give them to your favorite charity. In doing so you are giving to others and can help create some greater abundance in their lives, while you now have space in your closet. The space in your closet is a metaphor for the space in your mind and heart for greater abundance to materialize for you. If your closet is full of old, out-dated clothes, just as some of your beliefs and thoughts may be out-dated and no longer serve you, then by giving away or discarding some of them, you make room for new thoughts, ideas and abundance in your life.

There is an old saying that nature abhors a vacuum. Basically, the Universe will help you fill the void with something new. But note, the "new" may end up being the "old" if your beliefs do not change. For now, discarding what you no longer find valuable is a positive signal to God you are preparing for a change in your life.

As I write this chapter, I am on an airplane heading back to Dallas from Seattle. A strange set of circumstances just unfolded before and during this trip that exemplify expecting good things can happen in your life. Sometimes even the smallest ones show the power of belief in expectation. Early this morning I discovered I was booked for a later flight than I anticipated and my seat was at the back of the plane. Upon quickly accessing the internet I discovered that access was no longer permitted the day of the flight due to national security regulations. I was instructed that my only option was to change my seat, and possibly my flight, at the ticket counter.

At first, I was frustrated, but then I relaxed knowing everything would work out just right. Arriving early at the airport, to make matters worse, I discovered my flight was now delayed almost two hours. Once I reached the reservation counter I asked the agent to change my seat assignment, and then proceeded to wait in the security line for over forty-five minutes. Upon clearing security and reaching my gate I was surprised to learn an earlier flight scheduled and heading to Dallas had not yet departed. I quickly approached the ticket agent at the gate inquiring if there were any seats left on the plane, although I was doubtful, as a rather large crowd of passengers waited to board.

Within a minute after checking, the ticket agent called my name handing me a boarding pass while informing me I obtained the last seat available! My original flight with its delayed schedule would have brought me into Dallas very late in the evening, and I was quite appreciative to now be arriving much earlier than planned.

I was one of the last to board and of course, was unable to locate a place to put my carry-on suitcase, and was hoping to not check it, which would delay my return once I arrived in Dallas. As I stood waiting for the flight attendant to take my suitcase to who knows where, I relaxed again knowing everything would work out right and expected good things to be made from this. Right then, a man in the row behind me jumped up and said he could move his smaller bag from the overhead compartment and store it under his seat, giving me room to place my carry-on suitcase right above my seat in the overhead compartment. I was overjoyed and thanked the man several times.

Oh, one more thing. Once we were in the air the captain came on the intercom to announce we would be arriving at Terminal A in Dallas. Unfortunately, my car was parked at Terminal C. At DFW airport, to get from one terminal to another requires taking a shuttle or taxi. (They now have a great air-tram system for moving between terminals) Despite an earlier-than-expected arrival I would still reach Dallas late and was not excited about taking additional time to wait for a shuttle to Terminal C. However, I knew it would all work out just fine and expected no problems in getting to my car. Two hours into the flight the captain came back on to announce our status and said, "Oh, and we have a new gate assigned to us, we are now in Terminal C". I just smiled and thanked God for rewarding my optimism and acknowledged once again another example of how I helped create my world!

You can achieve magnificent results. Jump in and do not be afraid of what lies ahead, or what you can create by believing in yourself. Too often we do not make changes in our life because we are afraid of the unknown. We may struggle with some difficult circumstances and still be reluctant to make changes knowing full well an opportunity for greater abundance lies ahead. Our fear prevents us from acting, and we leave ourselves stuck in the same routine dealing with the same issues, pain, hurt and frustration.

Now is the time to take the challenge, because something better awaits you. Remember, if you do not make a move forward, you will create experiences continuing to keep you where you are. You will continue to experience the same frustration, disappointment, rejection, or disrespect over and over again. Once you take a long look at this process, you will understand you are constantly creating new experiences in order to get you to move forward, because deep in your heart you seek to have more than you have now. That deep desire is the driving force.

You can either awaken each day knowing each experience is waiting for you to learn from it and you can leave behind the fear and rejection of the past or you will be trapped in the same experience again and again. It is your choice.

This is a time to be excited, assertive and persistent, because:

The meek inherit very little.

CHAPTER 14

The Meek Inherit Very Little

*"God gives every bird its food, but He does not
throw it into its nest."*

-- J.G. Holland, novelist and poet

Perhaps the title of this chapter struck a nerve. Many of us were taught by our respective religions that the meek would inherit the earth. The definition of meek came to include being good, timid, pious, humble and patient. We were instructed that by demonstrating these meek traits we would "win" by inheriting the earth when the time came for eternal justice and evaluation. This concept always appeared strange to me. I realize inheriting the earth is somewhat of an analogy, but you can see being weak or timid is what got us into this mess in the first place. We wanted it easy, fast, with no responsibility and no pain. Church leaders instructed us to follow them and follow the rules. Remaining poor somehow made us pious and would help us gain spiritual salvation.

Being pious, humble, patient and good to our fellow man are admirable traits. Yet, over time we have found exhibiting these traits did not provide for our success or abundance. With each unsuccessful journey our patience grew to despair, being good to others grew into giving less, and being humble heightened our lack of self-esteem. After all, being told we started out life with original sin made us doubt our ability in the first place.

Further, we never felt we could question this information. Being meek and treating others good seemed logically to be the right formula for success and abundance. At best, it is only part of the formula. More is required. Until now we were never told we create our reality. Meekness only begets more meekness. Self doubt only manifests greater self doubt. Being humble, being patient, being good to others *and* believing in ourselves, trusting our ability, and believing everyone on earth can have abundance creates a positive reality.

There are some wonderful churches out there that do wonderful things in the world. At the same time there are some religions, churches and church leaders who have become more focused on gaining more members than helping their members grow spiritually and emotionally. They reasoned and **feared** that if we learned we had the ability to create our world within us, we might not come back to hear the same message each week that we were sinners. If we learned we create our reality, we would not be interested in continuing to hear we had sinned nor continue to be taught that only a chosen few who stood preaching to us were the only ones who knew the way.

I am not recommending you abandon your faith or your church. In fact, I encourage active participation in the faith of your choice. Obtaining information from any well-intended source is always beneficial to our growth. Not all instruction is as valuable as intended. If my doctrine demands that specific rules be followed and makes you believe you are inferior in some way, I am not helping you; in fact I am attempting to control you.

There are religions, churches and individuals who preach week after week that we are sinners, imperfect and subject to God's punishment when we "sin" or fail to keep God's word. What are God's words and rules? Some would say the Ten Commandments are the most important rules to follow, while others would say what is written in the *Bible* are the correct words and rules. Then there is the New Testament and Old Testament. However, there are various translations and interpretations of what is written in the *Bible,* and yet there are other books considered holy by millions such as the *Talmud,* the *Bhgavad-Gita* and the *Tao-Te-Ching*, to name a few and all deemed by their respective followers to contain "God's" words. There are also individuals who claim to have inside information on what God wants. Countries have gone to war over the correct interpretation of God's words.

Can it be that the only message God - or whoever you believe to be the highest power - was only trying to give examples of how to create your own experiences so you could understand the depths of your own being? Can it be for Christians that Jesus was one of the greatest teachers providing examples of how to create your own experiences? Could it be that Jesus did not die to save us from our sins but simply and magnificently to show us our spirit never dies demonstrating the perfect analogy for reincarnation? Believing God chose your life for you denies the truth you create your world and have the power to change it. When we see that the true message of compassionate, loving spiritual leaders such as Jesus or Buddha is our ability to create our world, then the only reason the term "born again" is relevant is that the soul has eternal life and we continually create new lives in which to reincarnate!

Why would God desire us to control others, evidenced today by some men who believe that they are better than women or some people from certain races or origins believing they are superior to other races? Why would God desire those who do not follow the ways of God be punished or killed when God knows we create our own heaven and hell through our own choices? Why would God favor one religion over all others and why would followers of that religion be favored by God? There are no valid reasons God would desire any of this behavior because God knows our realities will mirror our beliefs. Through our free will and our own choices we create our own heaven or hell on earth. Once we align our beliefs and goals for the highest good of all people the wonder of God will appear in our lives.

Preventing any people on this earth from creating, learning and growing from their own experiences goes against the idea of a loving, caring God. To interpret from any book, word or transcript that God wants us to control anything or anyone goes against the concept of free will and the inherent nature of a loving God. Further, if God wants you to control others, the idea of him simply deciding who was born to control and who was born to be controlled is contradictory to giving us free will.

Some religious teaching urges us to fear God when in fact this is a tactic born of control. We are much easier to control if we are afraid. Upon further examination one easily discovers the "interpretation" that God wants one group to control another group was actually proclaimed by those who want to control others!

Although anyone can make any choices they desire, choices which are made from the heart and from love experience a manifestation of happiness. Considering God is pure love, we go against the natural forces of God and the Universe if we desire to harm others physically, mentally or emotionally, or if we cheat or steal. If we choose to use our power to create in negative ways, we will create our own unfortunate experiences. Remember, if you believe you must harm and control others, then you draw to you experiences and people who will attempt to do the same to you. If we attempt to create our experiences with the idea of growing closer to God and being more connected to every other living person and creature in the Universe, then our experiences reflect those wonderful qualities.

It is disconcerting that some churches and religions preach to us about how we were born with sin and God decided after thousands of years to put his son here to be sacrificed so God would forgive all of our sins in one giant process. Does anything sound strange about that? Maybe its more likely Jesus helped us understand we have the power within us to do anything. He was a superb example, and a masterful teacher. Maybe if God is the loving God we say and believe God is, God forgives us every second for what *we* believe are our imperfections and transgressions against each other. Knowing our destiny is to move down the path of enlightenment, it is possible that forgiveness is not God's main concern. Through the process of creating experience and learning from each one, we grow. God does not need to forgive us, because when we decide to grow, we will learn to shower compassion and love upon everyone. In the end, the message is this: we only need to forgive ourselves for any of our past mistakes.

The only "sin" we ever commit is not attempting to be all we can be by creating the most wonderful reality for us to experience, grow and learn. Creating from love is what we do best. To refuse to grow and learn from the experience creates our own "hell" right here as we live without reward and live without abundance. But it is our choice, and we punish ourselves.

God does not punish. For centuries people have believed God rules with an iron fist casting down justice, continually forgiving our sins and punishing those who do not follow God's laws or will. We have projected our human nature and emotional bias onto God, assuming God behaves as we do. The truth is God has no "need" to punish us. When my son does not study and fails a test at school, I do not punish him. He ends up punishing himself by creating a world around him which shows missed opportunities and lack of effort.

We are created in God's image, and we are designed to live our lives in God's emotional and intelligent image as well. God's power and design is to create. Therefore, for us to live our lives in God's likeness creativity is the most natural and God given ability we have.

We mistakenly believe God is limited and influenced by our fears. When you fully understand you create everything in your life, fear is no longer a factor. When your fear subsides, your anger, resentment, jealousy and the need to control everything in your world subsides along with it. You can see how all of these negative emotions influence our daily actions and choices. Where did we get this concept that God's main objective is to punish us? How did we come to believe we must be punished while often we aren't sure what the right course of action is to prevent being punished? Is that a way to have a relationship with God?

Some churches and religions have taught us to fear God, when instead they should teach us how to connect to God, to view God as someone who can help us grow, and as a loving God, who loves us no matter what we do. True, we have consequences to own up to if our actions are not in our highest good and others. The message of this book is to give you hope and encouragement. You already have a deep connection with God if you open your eyes and minds to it. Most of us at some time in our lives struggle with the belief that we are undeserving of God's love. We believe we were not worthy to receive love from another human being, a belief that is often based on prior disappointing relationships. We may have failed at prior attempts to reach various goals creating the belief we were not worthy of success. Struggling with our daily lives, we turn to our religions and churches for assistance, and we find little relief. After a week of battling job pressures, school tests, sick parents and a myriad of other issues, the last thing we need is to walk into a church on Sunday, be told we are sinners and to take heed because we will be punished. Is there any wonder the biggest problem people face today is that they believe they aren't good enough? People who realize they create their world believe in themselves. Successful people believe in themselves.

Many of us were taught if we were a good person, then good things would happen to us. (There is that "happen to us" concept again!) There is some value and truth in this belief. However, we were led to believe being "good" was the only requirement for happiness, success and abundance in our lives. And we all know from experience, it is far from the truth.

Myth: The act of being "good" is the key ingredient required to achieve success, happiness and abundance.

Each day we work hard but watch as others with lesser values achieve some apparent success. We try to enrich our lives and the lives of those around us. We let someone move ahead of us in line at the bank or store. We open the door for someone. We lend a helping hand to a neighbor. We believe in God and pray or meditate. We are ethical at work and put in the time necessary to get a promotion or advancement in whatever endeavor we undertake. Yet, as I have explained, this effort is not enough, although it all gets easier once you understand all that I have written in this book. We call out for justice and try to make some sense of this confusion. We struggle mightily day after day to achieve success because we believe this one concept — that being good will ensure our success and happiness — is supreme. Treating others with respect, honesty and integrity is important. Whatever energy you project out into the world comes back to you. Plus, since God is a being of love, love should be the basis for all of your actions. Yet being good by itself or even added to a work hard mentality are not enough.

We were led to believe good always wins out over evil. Day after day we worked hard to be honest, ethical and fair towards those around us. We watched in frustration as our success was sometimes surpassed by those paying much less heed to being "good".

Confusion results if we believe that being "good" is the only trait required for success. To reconcile the confusion, remember we create our reality based on our beliefs. The strongest beliefs always manifest the quickest and the strongest. You may very well have a strong belief being honest and forthright in all your dealings is of utmost importance. However, if you have a stronger belief that you are not worthy, this belief generates and moves stronger energy into the Universe, returning experiences to reinforce the belief you are unworthy. You will also have experiences that manifest the values of honesty and compassion, but because your belief of being unworthy is stronger, its impact in your life is, unfortunately, stronger.

When I was growing up, the Catholic Church taught me that God had mercy on the poor and the meek would inherit the earth. Being poor does not serve anyone. I am a caring, sensitive, compassionate, honest person, and believed those traits would never change in me if I had financial abundance in my life. Further, if I had this kind of abundance, along with a higher understanding of life in the earthly and spiritual realms, I could use my abundance to help others. Having and sharing abundance is the ultimate display of being all you can be.

Abundance does not always mean money. Abundance could be intelligence. Sharing your abundance is the beauty of God. Therefore, being poor does not help anyone, is not pious, nor gives you a better chance to achieve abundance.

Do you really believe God wants us all to be poor or meek? Do I want my sons to be poor? We are all children of God, and God wants you to love everyone and have abundance in all areas of your life. Therefore, just as I want my sons to have all the abundance they can have in life, God wants us all to have abundance of whatever it is we desire. Believing that God wants some of us to be rich and others to be poor is simply a projection of our fear beliefs and own lack of success onto God. The truth is God does not decide who will have abundance or success and who does not. You choose it. I choose it. We all choose it for ourselves.

When you strive to be the best you can be, you can share your talents, knowledge, money and time with everyone you meet. Each time you learn and grow you have the opportunity to positively impact those around you. There is so much value in growing and sharing your knowledge and abundance that to consider being poor as constructive, is actually destructive.

Remember the myth of the zero sum game? There is enough here on Earth for all of us to have an abundance of everything we want.

Successful people have learned this concept of abundance. There are many successful people who share their wealth and knowledge, giving millions to charity and their time to help the world. You, too, can be successful.

Successful people do the work. What "work" do they do? They examine their actions and their beliefs. They push themselves to determine why they react to situations with the behaviors they exhibit. Do they refuse to open up in a new relationship because they got hurt in a prior relationship, and do not want to be hurt again? Do they approach every business opportunity with fear and timidness because they remember all the times in the past they "failed?" As a result, do they tell themselves they are losers who won't amount to anything? Do they lack self-esteem because they experienced mental, emotional or physical abuse as a child and now believe they are unworthy or undeserving? No, no, no and no.

I do not judge any of these behaviors or actions. Many of us have felt these emotions and exhibited these behaviors at some time in our lives. Our reactions are very normal.

The "work" involved is changing our beliefs, behavior and re-actions. Is it fair to take out the emotional hurt you suffered long ago on someone new who comes into your life? You may have long been asking God to bring you someone special who cares truly about you. When a new person arrives in your life are you so focused on your past pain that you somehow expect this person to make up for all of your previous emotional pain and losses? Are you then disappointed because this new person is incapable of fill-ing all of your needs? Are you expecting this person to tell you they are sorry for what others did to you? Isn't this behavior not only attempting to seek compensation from someone else for your past hurtful experiences, but also controlling and psychological blackmail? Yes, you were hurt, treated badly, possibly immorally sometime long ago. And feeling pain and hurt is a natural part of the healing process. But you can not change the past. You can only change how you react to it each day.

This path is difficult, and takes time and patience, but it is es-sential to create your new world. I have been through this process, felt many of the painful emotions you have. I have persevered and courageously walked through the door into a new world. You can do it too. How badly do you want it? Isn't it time you received and created the world you so desired? Anything you put your time and energy into is worth it, and as you know from prior experiences, when you did do the work, the results were wonderful. No one can take that from you.

A former co-worker used to say "That is why they call it work!"

Almost twenty years ago I decided to enroll in a Tae Kwon Do school. I was in my mid-thirties at the time and my body just didn't stretch and bend the way it did when I was twenty. I had been playing tennis two to three times a week for fifteen years prior to enrolling in this class. I knew it would be strenuous but assumed I was in fairly good shape from the years of playing tennis. I quickly discovered I was quite mistaken as just the stretching and twisting moves for the first half of class proved to be rather discomforting. The remainder of the time was spent on kicking and punching workouts. The class lasted only fifty minutes but was the most strenuous physical work I had ever done and required extreme mental focus as well as physical effort.

Since childhood I have had a fascination and respect for the martial arts. Furthermore, I knew the mind and body must work together to perform each movement, and I believed this was an additional benefit besides self-defense and exercise. The difficulty of each new physical movement was increasingly stretching my patience and my body. It was work but I was determined and cherished the opportunity. Many bruised bones, a broken rib and three years later, I earned a black belt, which I proudly wear. The feeling of accomplishment and the lessons I learned from the process are things I will carry with me always.

It is time for you to do the work. This is not the time to be timid or meek. Your wonderful reality you will create awaits you!

Trust me when I say you will receive ten times back what you put into it as long as you do the work with an open mind, a willingness to learn and grow.

Perhaps, at this point, the word "work" needs definition and clarification here. "*Work*" has connotations of being painful, boring, intense and possibly exhausting. Yet, it's only "work" if we perceive our growth to be difficult. Rather, doing the "work" can be fun. "Work" for this book means the dedication and perseverance you must have to look inside yourself at your beliefs and actions and examine the rationale behind them. I do not like painting, as in painting walls inside or the outside of my house. Yet, many people enjoy this type of work as a feeling of expression or creation. Conversely, I enjoy planting flowers and growing a vegetable garden. No doubt there are those of you who would find it rather uncomfortable digging in organic soil in the mid-day sun. It's only going to be "work" if you perceive the process as painful. It's work if you are resistant to change. It's fun when you approach the journey with curiosity and a feeling of expectation.

Approach growing and learning from the viewpoint of a child and it all becomes play. Examining yourself — and best of all — changing yourself, creates rewards far beyond anything you can imagine. Begin to approach your life with expectations of new and greater abundance and happiness in your life.

This may be difficult for some of you. In your way stands a figurative wall we created by the emotional pain and suffering we have incurred. This wall is the feeling of guilt. We all have feelings of pain and regret over past experiences in our lives, either by those from our specific actions or due to improper action by others towards us. In both cases our deep feelings of pain often turn to guilt as we blame ourselves, no matter who caused it or how it was inflicted upon us.

When I separated from my ex-wife, I felt a tremendous amount of guilt moving out of the house away from my sons. I moved to an apartment just a few short miles away so I could see my sons often. Every day we talked via computer and sometimes via phone, and I continued to support them financially. Even so, I continued to feel guilty, and, as many people do, at first I attempted to compensate by giving my sons money and gifts.

I quickly realized providing gifts and money was not helping them. They still needed a father providing guidance. I will not place blame here, but my marriage to my ex-wife was not working. We tried to make it work for many years, but we were headed in different directions. My ex-wife and I were not presenting our children with an example of a happy, loving marriage. Over time I have been able to discuss openly with them the mistakes I made and to help them learn and understand what was missing in our marriage and the keys they needed to seek for a healthy, lasting relationship. I am often amazed and pleasantly surprised at how perceptive my sons are regarding relationships.

Moving out of the house was one of the most painful things I've ever had to do. To call it work was an understatement. Today I have a wonderful relationship with my sons as they finish college, and I have a wonderful, deeply connected, supportive relationship with my wife Michelle. My sons now see how happy a marriage can be, and my sons see the work Michelle and I put into the relationship. Michelle and I do not believe it is work, since we love each other, yet we spend the time and energy required for a healthy partnership. We have learned that caring for each other is very easy, and taking the time provides great reward.

There are times when we all feel guilty about prior choices and decisions.

We all make decisions in our life we wish we could reverse or attempt to do again. We all have endured hurtful actions from others. Today, and every day, we can make a conscious choice and decision to either let the pain from prior experiences continue to beat us down or we can rise up beyond the pain and move on to a happier life.

Sometimes we choose to be stuck and believe that we cannot be happy if justice has not been served. Or we may try to find ways to get back what was taken from us — even if that's impossible. In either case, we do not have control.

What does justice look like especially if that person is no longer living or it is impossible to meet up with that person again? However difficult the situations were that you endured, they were there for you to learn about yourself. Some people have overcome amazing odds, significant injuries, disease, loss of limb, or financial loss and have used their experiences to propel them forward to greatness. Our world is full of people who have overcome incredible odds. Many of these successful people faced disadvantages at an early age; some have had doors closed to them and had to fight to finally be noticed.

Recently there was a story in the newspaper about a man who had lost both his legs below the knee after being hit by a drunk driver. This man had to endure his own rehabilitation while caring for his young daughter. Now fitted with artificial legs he is continuing to be positively focused on his future and has forgiven the man who hit him! I greatly admire him and so many others as they are the epitome of not letting the past affect their actions today. They demonstrate the positive attitude and will power to obtain happiness and abundance in their lives.

Consider this: if you continue to hold onto the pain, anger and resentment of the past, are you not giving power every day to the person who caused you the pain? When you carry around the pain, sorrow, anger and frustration from your circumstances, it is as if the person was inflicting the pain all over again, each day. Why give that person so much control? It is time to take back your power and no longer give it to someone who hurt you in the past.

There is only one way to release your hurt, anger and resentment. You must forgive both those who hurt you and especially yourself. Most of us have an extremely difficult time with the concept of forgiveness, especially when it comes to forgiving someone who hurt us. Sometimes we are angry at God. There is, of course, a normal time for crying, hurting, mourning and even being angry over hurts and losses of the past. At some point we must pick up the pieces and move on with our lives.

In all cases, step back and view the situation from a broader perspective. Can you see you helped bring the situation into your life to help you look deep inside yourself? These experiences push us to examine our behavior closely, examine our beliefs and push us to a point where we must change.

Please understand, when I state you helped create the experience, you must not view the process as punishment. We discussed in earlier chapters how we attract experiences to us in order to help us learn, grow and be closer to God. Some of us have enormous challenges as we progress down our paths of life. In no way am I attempting to state you should blame yourself for the events that occurred. There is never a time when you should "blame" yourself.

All of us have trouble forgiving someone that harmed us in some way. Maybe it was a bad relationship, maybe an unfortunate family life, maybe a difficult boss at work. In all situations, when you resist forgiving, you are going against the nature of the learning process. Remember, you created the experience from the energy and actions generated by your beliefs. Your belief created the experience, and the experience is the opportunity to learn and grow and modify the belief.

For example if you believed all men are liars, and each man you dated truly lied to you to and hurt you, forgiving them is forgiving yourself. You created the experience and attracted this man into your life that lied to you. Your choice is what to do with the experience: learn from it or let it continue to validate your incorrect belief. Only when you move past your illogical belief that all men are liars, you find a man who does not lie, who believes strongly in truth. You then will have attracted a man who is honest because you now believe having a relationship with an honest man is possible.

Examine for a moment your old belief. In believing all men are liars you were asking for someone to come into your life that was dishonest. Further, when you changed your belief system you then attracted honest men into your life. However, realize that forgiveness is seen as automatic but it is actually unnecessary and illogical! When that person appears you must be joyful and thank yourself and God for helping manifest the process. *Who is there to forgive when the Universe provided exactly what you desired?*

Congratulations! It took work and perseverance on your part to change your deep belief. Your success did not arrive until you moved past the traditional meek or victim approach. Therefore, forgiveness is automatic, as unnecessary as it is illogical.

With all this said, the first act of release is forgiveness. Forgiveness now becomes much easier when we understand we have been holding on to anger and pain when neither was necessary. Rather, our feelings turn to joy knowing the gift we gave ourselves. Best of all, we know we love ourselves to have created the perfect situation for us to grow. We now are able to easily forgive others for the pain they caused to us.

Some of us can make the first step to forgive others, yet remain unable or unwilling to forgive ourselves. We beat ourselves up daily telling ourselves "My whole life would be different if only...."

Let me explain something: Your life would not have been any

different, or it would have been different to some degree, but the impact would have been the same. Consider everything we have discussed up until now. We create the exact experience we require to move us in the direction we desire. If you turned left and ended up in a car accident, you very well could have turned right and ended up in a different car accident. If it wasn't a car accident, the injury may have occurred another day in another scenario. If you didn't get passed over today for a promotion, you will get passed over for something else in another opportunity. Why? Because if you held onto the belief you were not deserving or unworthy, (or some similar negative belief) you were going to continue experiencing being passed over for a promotion at any company. Or you might experience feeling undeserving in some other experience. But if you need to learn how to gain confidence you will produce experiences testing your confidence.

There is something very special to understand about our experiences. The experience itself does not give you confidence. The experience is a gift you give yourself in order for you to *decide* to have confidence in yourself instead of feeling unworthy as you did in prior experiences. The experience creates an opportunity for you to choose the next course of action, for you to change your beliefs, for you to change how you perceive the world, and for you to change how you perceive yourself. If there is a lesson to learn, if there is something you need to experience in order to push you to change your beliefs or habits, the experience will present itself. Sometimes we are smart enough and heed the early warning. Consequently, we get the point and learn our lesson without enduring a major hardship.

Now is the time for you to forgive yourself. The only "mistake" you make is by not learning from the experience and having to re-do it again and again until you get it right. How many people do you know who continue to meet the same type of person in every relationship, never finding the right one? How many people do you know who move from company to company never realizing they get looked over for promotion because they don't come to work on time?

179

Begin to forgive yourself today. Start now. You deserve it. If you have strong faith in God or a higher power, be comforted knowing God never faulted you. God loves you like a parent loves his child. Love yourself. God loves you. What a relief to have such a heavy burden removed from your shoulders. You only have so much energy to expend each day, and previously so much of your energy was consumed holding the anger towards yourself inside of you. Release the anger, forgive yourself and immediately you will have a surge in energy. You can only move forward toward happiness once you have forgiven yourself, especially when you discover you created the experience out of love for yourself.

Another example of meekness is procrastination. Procrastination is an attempt to not do the work, not face your fears, not demonstrate your desire to achieve, and an attempt to continue being a victim.

We all know we should exercise, eat right, not smoke or do drugs and many other forms of destructive behavior. Why is it so difficult to get up off the sofa and start our exercise program? Why is it so difficult for many of us to go to the library and check out a book on self-improvement and take the steps to change our lives? Why is it so difficult for us to find the time to give our minds and body the refreshment it needs in the form of meditation, yoga, sight seeing, and hundreds of other hobbies? The answer can be found in the first few chapters in this book. We have grown up in a culture that pushes and perpetuates the belief of instant gratification and little, if any, patience.

Short-term thinking is timid and meek. Long-term thinking is bold and daring. Our short-term focus is so strong that we have lost sight of what the long-term can look like, and therefore lose any potential attachment to the long-term benefits and rewards of any efforts we put in place today. We eat, smoke, drink, watch TV and many other activities for many reasons, but the most important is the instant gratification each activity provides. When we take these actions for the purpose of medicating ourselves, we want instant relief. The strongest message of every medicine advertised is it provides quick or instant relief. We have not time to wait, or patience for a medicine to take more than a few minutes or moments to provide relief.

Understand this short-sighted view is a mind set and a belief system which we must change in order to be successful in our lives. We are not eager to examine our actions and beliefs to determine how we can change them for the better because this process takes work, time and effort. Most of all, the results are not seen overnight. Often ten, twenty, even thirty years may have elapsed as we ingrained beliefs into the very essence of whom we are. Yet we expect to resolve our inner conflicts and change our beliefs and habits in just a few hours, days, or weeks. All of our reluctance is due to being programmed into a short-term focus and mentality.

Unfortunately, since there are no accidents in life, all actions are connected. The key here is changing our mindsets to view each short-term action as part of the long-term. But in our world and society of having to touch, see and feel our success we lose patience because we can't see the light at the end of the tunnel. Actually, we just think we can't, and our thoughts create our reality. Successful people have no concept of time. To them, their actions and processes are all part of one giant project which is in the here and now.

When we set off to go to college and have a goal to not only complete a four year degree but take additional years towards a law or doctor degree or MBA, we all are able to manage the lengthy process. The difference is we can see the end of the process. Successful people see the end of the process for every one of their goals.

Stop for just a few minutes and imagine how you would view your world, yourself and others if your mental focus was all long-term. Imagine how different our entire world would look as every law politicians enacted was done so only with the long-term good of the society in mind. Just imagine the difference in our world if every company made its decisions based on the long-term benefits for its staff and customers and not short-term profits. Imagine how differently you would treat your friends and family members, how you would approach your job and the world around you if your focus was long-term first.

Every thought, belief and action you take would all be oriented in a long-term focus. For some, long-term might be fifty years, for others maybe ten years, and for other it may be a month. "Long-term" does not necessarily mean the next century! Anything beyond tomorrow or the next couple of weeks for most of us is considered long-term. We can all have different views on how long is long-term. The lack of success is due to lack of focus on the short-term.

Successful people who are always creating a most interesting reality do so by *always* looking at the long-term. Yes, they are *always* viewing their thoughts, beliefs and actions with long-term implications. If there is any secret to their success, their long-term focus is the secret. Successful people are not only making deals happen in the short-term, every action they take today they do as part of a long-term strategy to obtain the desired result they seek. And where are the rest of the unsuccessful people focusing? On the short-term! Is it any wonder why so many of us struggle day after day, living paycheck to paycheck, considering our inability to focus on goals that seem too far away?

If you were building a house, after drawing blueprints and having contractors in place, you might first start with the foundation. Your focus would be on getting the lines laid out, the foundation dug and ordering the cement needed to build the foundation. *At the same time* you would focus on obtaining the wood, nails, tools and fixtures to build the framework for the walls of the house. Your focus would be on obtaining all of the necessary materials in the order needed to complete the long-term project. If this was your house, you would automatically view your task of obtaining wood and materials for the house as an important function today knowing its long-term implications. If you were busy laying the cement foundation and didn't bother to order the wood for the framing, you know your project would not continue without having the wood in hand. Notice how each short-term action has a long-term focus to it. When we are involved in a project such as building a house, we do not perform each action on the basis of its potential to provide us instant gratification. There is little instant gratification in buying wood which won't be used for a couple of weeks. Yet we would never question our action of purchasing the wood today. Consider how differently we view our short-term actions in this case. When you evaluate each and every thought, belief and action for its long-term effect, you have the drive to make progress today.

> *Successful people never work on today's tasks for today's results. Instead today's tasks are addressed to achieve tomorrow's results.*

> *Successful people view the long-term as if it is a reality today.*

Successful people do not view the completion of a project as years and thousands of hours away from obtaining any enjoyment. They view their project as already completed because they can not only envision the completed project in their minds, they can also see the results and benefits from the project itself. If you believe you have already achieved a goal then the Universe and God works to manifest this occurrence! This exact approach is why successful people are successful. Their focus, although preoccupied with the future, manifests the result into reality automatically by visualizing and believing the end result already exists.

To enhance your vision of believing the result already exists, begin to claim and proclaim what is yours. Set aside meek and timid behavior and lay claim in the Universe what is rightfully yours. Say it out loud. Hear yourself say it strongly. If you have done the work, if you have prepared for manifestation of your goal and have let God complete the process, then proclaim your joy for obtaining your goal. When you understand that the process of creating is natural and always consistent, the result is always manifestation of what you seek, once you put the energy in motion. There can be no exception.

When creating occurs-manifestation is assured!

At times we may be disappointed that the manifestation is not what we sought. We have discussed that if this is the case, that it is necessary to re-examine your beliefs and actions to determine which ones provided the strongest overriding energy. Then re-energize your process and the correct manifestation will appear.

There is a magical aspect to claiming and proclaiming your goal is already achieved and the result is in your grasp. You can only claim and proclaim that statement if you really believe and have faith the result is certain. Any doubt you have will cause you to feel uneasy when you claim and proclaim your achievement. This is a key step in the creation of your reality.

Another way to claim and proclaim your success is to write out a detailed description of your goal by hand. This must be done by hand and not by other methods such as typing it into a computer file. Writing by hand puts your energy to work using the power of your beliefs and thoughts to project the energy into the Universe. Further, when writing by hand, your whole body and mind are committed to the words you write on paper. The power of the mind and body united together acknowledging your success is a powerful force.

I have used this technique several times and each time the result has been as good as or even better than what I wrote on paper. This is not a casual technique. On the contrary, it is an extremely powerful technique. Do not underestimate the power of your beliefs and the energy generated by your thoughts. This process is to be used in addition to doing the work, preparing for its arrival and having faith in yourself and God to help manifest what you desire. Writing down what you believe is yours, knowing your hard working energy is in motion is validation to yourself that the creation process is complete.

When you are finished proclaiming your success take time to thank God and everyone you know who has helped you on your journey. Begin and end each day by thanking God and appreciating all you have accomplished and obtained. Make a point to share your wealth of abundance, knowledge and health with those around you. Although the task is to be assertive, each day be humble in acknowledging all you have received.

To move forward with assertiveness and limit meek behavior

requires that we must demonstrate the belief in ourselves and in all of our actions. To do so we must stop enabling ourselves and more importantly, stop enabling others. Just look around us and see how blaming others is an acceptable mindset, and further more, this behavior and belief is constantly reinforced on a daily basis by those around us. Enabling others just takes away their power to create; they become dependent on you for their happiness until it becomes a way of life.

If, for example, one of my sons dropped out of college with little money, no job and nowhere to sleep. As a parent my first inclination is to give him some money, help him get into an apartment and maybe even help him get a job. If he loses the job because he didn't make it to work on time and he spent the money I gave him for his first month's rent on a killer stereo system for his apartment, is he helping himself? We often believe that if we just help people out, they will weather whatever crisis they are experiencing and get back on their feet. Sometimes a little help is all that is needed. But what if I keep giving him money, month after month? As a loving father I do not want my son to be out on the street, yet what happens if he continues to be irresponsible? What then? If I continue to help my son yet he does not demonstrate any inclination to help himself, am I really helping him? I am trying to enable him to do better. Yet consider this: I am actually "dis-abling" him. Yes, my helping hand is working against my son. Giving him assistance is preventing him from helping himself. Too many people today are "disabled" because they have been helped by others for too long. When someone has been helped for too long while making few, if any, changes, dependency is created.

It is time to stop disabling others and stop disabling yourself by expecting someone else to create the world you desire for you. Start today to build the world you desire. Demonstrating meekness creates greater meekness; enabling yourself or others is a form of being meek.

One saying we may have heard for years and hear it louder today is "the rich get richer." And you know what? This statement is

EXACTLY true, but not for the reasons you believe. We often think the "rich get richer" at the expense of the poor or middle class. The rich get richer because they demonstrate all of these assertive thinking traits. You have learned the myths of the zero sum game and the fixed size of the pie.

Successful people take all of these steps with self-confidence, believing in themselves, and taking responsibilities for their actions and their results. We have heard this before, so there is no magic formula for success. Successful people don't blame others for their mistakes and they don't beat themselves up for what did not work. Instead they learn from the experience. They figure out the successful parts of the process, as well as the ineffective parts of the process. They adjust what didn't work and try again. We view scientists as people who try something, examine the result, take notes, determine the effective and ineffective tests and try again. Testing involves patience to try and try again different approaches or combinations until they find the right one. Scientists probably have at least ninety-nine failures for every success. Yet, we do not consider them failures for those first ninety-nine attempts. Strangely, in our own personal affairs, when we start out on a new endeavor and we do not achieve our goal, we consider ourselves a failure. Successful people do not *ever* consider themselves failures. They simply remix the formula or strategy and try again. They try until the process works. Successful people are not meek. They persevere and are determined to try again.

People who are busy creating the world they desire display the extremely important trait of adapting. The ability, desire and willingness to adapt are of utmost importance for our happiness. Look around you. Is the world different today compared to when you were a child? How about compared to several years ago before 911? Is your own personal world different from five or ten years ago? Change is inevitable. My sons are no longer children with countless baseball practices and games to go to, but now are off in their own world as they graduate college and find a job. My conversations with my sons grow more fascinating every day as they make major life decisions and view the world from a maturing perspective.

My mother is the epitome of adaptability. At eighty-eight, she is active and involved with organizations and my siblings and I find it difficult at times to keep up with her! My mother never stops growing, and she is always willing to try something new. She didn't learn about computers until she was eighty and you should see her today surfing the internet!

My Dad passed away four years ago, a man with whom she spent over sixty years of her life. My mom could well have packed it in, felt she had a good life and buried herself in her home, watching TV all day. But that's not my mother. She has never been one to back down from any challenge life threw at her. Having endured through the Great Depression, she has internal fortitude to take on the issues of today. My Dad spent the last year of his life in a nursing home designed specifically for treating patients with Alzheimer's disease. During his stay, my Mom was there every day helping to care for him. Since his passing, Mom has visited the nursing home regularly to help others she got to know there. She gathers with fellow church members for lunch once a week, and once a month serves food at a soup kitchen. Periodically she drives (yes, she still drives a car!) to the nearby recreation center to walk one mile in the indoor track, and let's not forget her daily time spent in the yard planting flowers and pulling weeds. Adapting is all she has ever known, and has kept her mentally strong. Has she created the world around her she desires? Absolutely.

Adapting can be fun. We often resist because the process involves changing some of our routines and habits. Do you wear the same style clothes you did ten years ago? You have adapted to the cell phone, the Internet and 500 channels on cable.

One of the most important places we must adapt to is in business. The number one cause of failure of any business is from complacency by upper management. Upper management works hard to get the company running on all cylinders, profitable, customer and employee friendly, and then tries to coast for a while. They spend so much energy and passion getting there, they make a major mistake in wanting to sit back and enjoy it. Definitely enjoy the ride, because most of us get tired pretty fast of the merry-go-round. Adapting is trying each new ride at the amusement park. In the business world, the economic climate is ever-changing, fast paced and extremely competitive. Successful people ride the wave and adapt to the changes. Actually, they often do better than that; they anticipate the changes to come.

I have worked in the business world for twenty five years, and the environment changed every year. Each year we were required to dig in and work smarter and sometimes harder. Each year there was the annual challenge to examine the methods and systems we used and determine new approaches with the goal of saving both time and money. I worked at companies that acquired other companies, and worked for companies who were acquired by larger companies. My challenge was and is to adapt, to continue to evolve to meet the demands of the business world, and the demands of our own personal world. No matter what our path is, no matter what course we choose, we will always encounter challenges. Our ability to adapt gives us the ability to surpass any challenges.

There are extensive changes occurring in your personal world every year, whether you acknowledge them or not. Have fun with the changes, embrace them, because they are opportunities to grow, learn and develop a skill you always wanted to explore but never had the chance. Now you have the chance. On the other hand, you can sit back, relax, take your shoes off, and take it slow and easy for as long as you want. If you desire the slow, easy pace, then you have the right to create exactly that world and reality for yourself. However, if you find yourself falling behind financially, or socially, or emotionally, don't blame those around you. Time marches on and no one can control the clock. How you manage the clock is up to you.

Sitting and complaining or feeling sorry for past events and perceived mistakes will not help you move forward. The meek do not inherit anything except further meekness. The bold, the confident, and those believing they will learn from their experiences, adapt and change their strategies knowing they will succeed, and do succeed in obtaining what they desire. Stand up and claim what is yours. It is yours not because somebody owes it to you, or you believe God owes it to you, but because you are a deserving person, who is compassionate, caring, honest and works hard and tries to change and grow.

Conversely, if you desire revenge, or seek to inflict harm on someone or cause hurt to anyone, you will attract to you and upon you that which you seek to do to others. Your own energy is transmitted into the Universe and it comes back to you. It always does because it is your energy. But if you truly look inside yourself to examine how you can change your beliefs which are causing your lack of success, it is time to claim what you desire.

When I was searching for a woman to be my wife, I believed I had a great deal to offer a special person in a relationship. I spent years of introspection transforming myself, being honest with myself about my beliefs of how I viewed the world and how I viewed myself. This was not an easy process. Building something magnificent generally is not without struggles. However, the end result is priceless. No one can put a price on inner happiness, contentment and joy. For me, every struggle, every challenge and every time I pushed myself to break through old patterns resulted in a greater amount of happiness than I had anticipated. The results were always better than I had anticipated. I had done the work and was ready for a woman who had done the same. We did find each other, and every day I am amazed how we are uniquely connected on so many levels. To find someone who is working hard to grow and learn while at the same time encouraging me as I push myself through each new door of opportunity is everything I desired and more.

Another form of strength not associated with meekness is our free will. We all have the free will to make choices and any decision we deem appropriate. It is our God-given right to make our own choices. Having the ability to make our own choices, then proceeding to choose, is one of the strongest connections we have to God. When we *choose* we are creating. God lets us choose whatever we want, and better yet, God helps us obtain what we desire. Unfortunately, we sometimes make choices with less than pleasing results. God's role is to help us achieve what we desire, not to push us to what God wants. After all, if God wanted us to do something, don't you think God could manage to do that? What fun or purpose is there in God forcing God's will on us? As a father, there were times I wanted to push my own will onto my sons, thinking I knew best what they needed. I realized I needed to let them make their own decisions, and bear the fruit or discomfort of their choices. If I made their choices for them I knew I was taking away their creativity and a part of me was lost as well. Instead, I offered emotional support and guidance as they made their choices, which is similar to what God provides for us. God wants us to create our world and experience all there is to have. Being connected to us, God gets to share in our experiences and help us create more of them.

Free will, and just as important, willpower, are important traits you will find in successful people. People who create the world they desire feel free to make their own choices, experience them, learn from them, enjoy the learning, and never look back. Further, they exhibit willpower. Many times I have heard the phrase "He willed it to happen." For years I was fascinated by that phrase and wondered if it was possible. Could someone really "will" something to happen? A most definite, yes! Willing something to happen is an expression of our deep, most inner belief in what we are doing.

As a sports fan, I have seen a variety of athletes demonstrate this behavior. These successful leaders, appeared to almost literally take their team on their back and carry it to victory, because nothing less than victory was an option. We have the will, because it comes with having the free will to choose freely. When I think back and examine the many times I created abundance and success in my life, it was partly due to my will and determination to succeed. When I had no doubt I would achieve my goal, no matter what stood in the way, my will was strong and there was no stopping me.

To be assertive in all of the ways I have described here requires strength. This strength can not come from around you, but can only come from within. It is widely known that in order to harness your energy it is recommended you spend some time in quiet contemplation. During this time you have your choice of activities to free the mind of *thinking.* Relax with soft music, meditate or immerse yourself in a hobby.

Attempt to get in tune with your inner self, gather your inner strength and listen to your inner voice. This inner voice, your Higher Self, which comes through as intuition or in dreams can provide you with the reassurance you are working in your highest good. Through your intuition, meditation or dreams you can also receive insight about yourself and your current struggles.

God never said we had to do this alone.
God is always there ready to provide guidance if needed.
Take the time necessary to look inside.
The answers you seek are within you.

CHAPTER 15

Look Inside for Guidance

*"You have to leave the city of your comfort
and go into the wilderness of your intuition.
What you'll discover will be wonderful.
What you'll discover will be yourself."*

-- Alan Alda, actor, director

Ever since I was young each morning I could recall my dreams experienced from the prior night's sleep. Many dreams were easy to remember due to their vividness and intensity. There were countless other dreams of a milder nature that never made it through to my consciousness when I awoke each morning. No one ever encouraged or discouraged my awareness of the dreams or their importance or relevance. I considered my dreams to just be a part of me like breathing, as I did not give them a lot of thought, yet at times found them interesting. It wasn't long before I began to understand the strategic messages and valuable guidance contained in my dreams.

In my late twenties, I began to have an unusual dream. This dream occurred two to three times a week, and continued for well over a year. I was not frightened by the dream; rather, the dream seemed rather comical. In the dream I was playing a game of hide-and-seek, and I was always the one to go hide. The dream's location often varied, but the basic game of hiding and waiting to be found was consistent in each dream. There were two strange aspects of the dream: first, when I was "found" in the dream, the game would start again with me running off to hide, and second, every time I had secured a hiding place, I was always "found" in the dream. The most significant aspect of the dream was that the "other" person always searching to find me and who always found me — was me! I know that may sound peculiar. In the dream there were clearly two people, but both of them were me. The frequency and consistency of this dream left me confused yet fascinated. One day at work I was describing the dream to my boss and his secretary. Once I completed telling my story, his secretary, Gayle, jumped up and said "I know what it means. Gary, you are trying to find yourself."

Her profound statement left me standing there totally amazed and speechless. Simultaneously, I marveled at how the interpretation was so clear to her. I had never considered examining the dream's specific actions and characters to decipher the magic message. Up until then I had never considered there was a message being conveyed to me! Yet, Gayle's ease of interpretation changed my whole perspective of dreams.

For years I had been trying to discover the road to happiness and connect to my inner, spiritual self. I had no clue where to go, and was not sure how to even start the process. As for most people, my inner desire was over-shadowed by my daytime focus on succeeding at work and caring for my family. The increasing frequency of the dream was a direct message suggesting it was time to move this inner desire to the front and center of my attention.

This dream was important to me in many ways, yet none was more powerful than understanding someone, somewhere, somehow was communicating to me. Over time as I continued to have more dreams it became evident that my mind was not the initiator of the message. These images and messages were not bi-products of my mind left to review the prior day's events. Rather, the messenger was another entity, which was God, my Higher Self, or the Spirit Guides who watch over me. No matter who was delivering the message, I knew there was valuable information and guidance to discover by going within. Receiving information via dreams just happened to be what worked for me the best.

194

One more thing: I never, and I repeat, never, had that dream again. I quickly learned once I understood the meaning of a dream, the need to communicate the message was eliminated. This rule has been consistent for all the dreams I have interpreted subsequently.

From that day forward, I have always turned to my dreams for guidance. On many occasions I have received valuable information guiding me on my next course of action, especially when I was about to make a major decision. On many other occasions I was provided with objective perspective on how my current actions, beliefs and behaviors were not serving me properly.

One major theme runs subtly through this entire book and I hope you've caught on to it. We have discussed how we each have the ability to create our outer worlds and obtain the success and happiness we have sought all of our lives.

The most fascinating path to creating the outer world we desire is to first create the world we desire within us.

If we seek peace, happiness, love, self-esteem, even abundance, we must look first inside each of us and create a new us. Looking within for guidance provides the perfect vehicle at any time to stop, contemplate, evaluate and even validate if you are heading in the right direction to achieve success. Listen to the inner voice within you and hear it give you direction.

To use your inner guidance to the fullest requires that you let your Higher Self and God come through and speak with you in quiet times. The first step is to step back and examine what you have learned from each experience. Quiet introspection allows you the opportunity to fully focus your mind on what occurred, and open your mind to receive key information from God. Ask yourself what emotions and feelings grew quickly in intensity in you as you endured this situation. Could you have made different choices? Can you now change your perspective and beliefs, just slightly, in order to not repeat the same experience? Is there key learning which will help you transcend the experience and move you to a whole new perspective and understanding of your world?

Information from within can come from many avenues besides dreams, such as meditation, prayer and our inner voices. My wife Michelle and I are animal lovers and our dogs and cats are considered members of our family, showered with love and care. Big Gus, at a fluffy fifteen pounds, was the largest of five cats. He was also diabetic, requiring a shot of insulin twice a day. His personality matched his size as his presence was felt when he entered a room. Even our two dogs, both over sixty pounds, knew Gus was the boss and respected his reign at the top of the family animal pack.

One day while Michelle was at work she developed a strong stomach-ache. At the same time she felt compelled to go home. On other days Michelle would have managed through the discomfort, but the urgency of her intuition telling her to go home coupled with her physical symptoms caused her to listen and respond. Gus always met her at the door when she came home but he wasn't there to greet her this time and did not come when she called his name. Frantically she searched for him, found him lying prone and unresponsive, quickly scooped him up and rushed him to the veterinary clinic. The veterinarian diagnosed him with extremely low blood sugar, treated him successfully and he came home a happy cat. Had Michelle dismissed her intuition, Gus would have died that day, alone.

Intuition is nothing more than listening to your inner self, your Higher God-Self or spirit, which connects you to God and the Universe. How many times have you "known" something was going to happen before it occurred? Or, when attempting to find a new location, you may have "sensed" you should turn left vs. right even though the directions provided said to turn right. We often call it a feeling. A woman might call this her feminine intuition, whereas a man might call it his gut instinct. In either case, it is much more than a feeling, rather a "knowing" of what is to occur. When we look closer and trust our intuition more, we will find it often gives us the important information critical to us at that time.

Intuition is just one of many ways to receive information from your Higher Self to help you learn and grow. God leaves clues every day; actually you and God together leave clues for you every day. Too often we miss these clues or opportunities to learn or experience something helping us to grow. Remember, all experiences are presented to help you get where you want to go and achieve what you desire.

Directions and advice will manifest in clues in the outer world. Consider how many messages and images bombard our senses each day. We have learned to filter out almost all but a small percentage of this information. And yet, if we take the time and become aware of the information coming through to our senses, we will find some of it is was designed to help us on the next step in our journey. Maybe we will hear a song on the radio that brings back memories of someone or some happy (or even sad) event. There is no accident we hear that song at that time. It was there to help us focus on something valuable.

You might pick up a book randomly at a store, or a magazine lying on the table at a friend's house, and a particular passage or article catches your eye. Upon reading it, you discover the words strike an inner cord, as if they were printed only for you. A co-worker might be telling a story of her discovery of some interesting web site during her search for some data unrelated to your goal. However, the web site she found just might hold some information you have been in search of for several weeks. Normally you might filter out her story and miss the message actually intended for you! Just think how difficult it is for God or your Higher Self to break through to your awareness when competing with the thousands of other messages you potentially filter each minute of every day! It is extremely valuable to take some time each day to quiet your mind and allow the key messages to come through to your awareness.

There are hundreds of these types of events happening for us every day. We must be aware of them in order to receive them. We are often too busy focusing on our work or children, or worrying about financial matters, or our health to take notice of these clues. Also, because our senses are bombarded with information every minute, we filter out what we believe is extraneous and only let through what we feel is most important. Too often what we permit through the filter is what we *want* to hear or see. We are able to hear and feel God or our Higher Self when our mind is still and not multi-tasking and filtering. Meditation is a very effective method for connecting in this way. However, our mind simply needs to be at ease, not necessarily in a deep meditation. Our best ideas come when performing simple tasks where our mind can relax, such as gardening, playing music or indulging in a favorite hobby. At those times your filtering is at a minimum and your mind is focused and not running at full tilt, thereby allowing information to come through from your Higher Self and God. For me, my dreams have always been the most powerful source of information, yet I have had great revelations while taking my morning shower! Prayer is valuable, but prayer often involves talking to God, whereas meditation is listening to God. Whatever method you can use to quiet your mind and listen to the voice inside is the best method for you.

When major events put the information front and center, we tend to view these as miracles. In fact, if we regularly filter out the subtle messages that come our way, it is indeed a miracle the message actually gets through! The "miracle" was nothing more than our Higher Self having to make the message so strong that we could not help but take notice. Unfortunately, the experience we encounter to finally learn or obtain the valuable information was more than we bargained for!

We could be driving our car one day and notice a slight squeak or noise from the engine, but we ignore the sound believing it will go away. Days go by and even weeks go by, yet the sound does not stop and furthermore, the sound slowly gets louder. We convince ourselves the sound is nothing, maybe just the car getting old, because otherwise the car runs fine. Somewhere in the back of our minds we know we should take the car to a repair shop or the dealer, but we don't have the time so we continue onward. A few more weeks go by and by now the noise level requires us to keep the radio on to drum out the sound of the noise. Finally, on a day when we need our car to transport us to a very important engagement, the car engine finally has had enough and stops working. Our day is now totally interrupted, our important appointment missed, our car has to be towed and the icing on the cake is we are informed the repair cost will be over $1,500! The mechanic tells us if we had brought the car in weeks earlier, the cost would have only been $100 to replace a small part. At this point we are so mad and we scream "God, why did you do this to me?" God is smiling back and explains, "Why do you think I helped you manifest the noise; it was there to warn you earlier?" Later, you learn from the mechanic that some other vital component in the car was just about to break, and if it had you could have been in a major accident. Only then do we realize we aren't alone in this process, and just maybe if we open up our minds, we can understand we have the power to create everything in our life. Just maybe if we open our minds and listen we will receive information to help us navigate the sea of life.

Sometimes a radical change of significant, immediate impact will occur in our lives to ensure we get the message. Inside you knew that a change was necessary. In your outer world, there had been many clues, many opportunities for you to make step, a choice to move in a new direction, but you chose to remain with the status quo. Then one day, a dramatic event occurs. The energy you have projected for so long has built up so large that the manifestation cannot be stopped. Although the change is significant and scary, you strangely feel an inner peace. The inner peace is knowing that the world mirrors what you were creating all along.

Perhaps you wanted to break away from your current job and company knowing something better lay ahead for you, but you were afraid to move out on your own. Then one day you reached work only to hear your company is moving its offices to another city and you are out of a job.

Maybe you were afraid to let go of a long dead relationship because of the fear of the unknown of new relationships. One day you arrived home to find your partner has moved out leaving you nothing more than a note saying good-bye. The changes that come in these circumstances are extremely dramatic and represent the energy built-up and final manifestation of what you were projecting from within.

These dramatic events do not have to come by surprise. About fifteen years ago I was laid off and it took me over two years to gain employment in my career field and industry. Several days before I was laid off I dreamed of driving in my car and I was going down a steep slope that never seemed to end. I just kept driving down, down and farther down. The morning I awoke from that dream, I knew there was a strong potential for some unfortunate incident to arrive soon in my life, but did not know exactly what it was. This dream clearly forecasted not only my long unemployment but the severity of it. Although the dream was an unfortunate prophecy of what was to come, it reinforced my ability to rely on my dreams for direction.

Many positive dreams have come to me indicating I was on the right road to success. I learned to not fear "bad" dreams as these messages were intended to help me see the possible impact of negative energy generated by my out of step beliefs and actions.

After having that significant dream in my twenties I began to take notice of the power of my dreams. From that point on I read every book I could find on dreams and began to learn about symbolism. There are both universal symbolism and symbols which are specific to each of us. Our personal symbolism is based on our own experiences and the ways we view ourselves and the world. The key is to examine what each person, place and thing in your dream means to you in your conscious state. What feeling or impression does each person, place or thing invoke in your conscious mind? My father was a disciplinarian, yet was loving and intelligent. When he appears in my dreams I know it is important for me to take notice of my impending decisions. Someone with an abusive father would have dreams in which his father's presence would represent something completely different.

Many years ago when I was working at a major company, I was approached by an employment firm looking to fill a position one level above me. The idea of a potential promotion was intriguing and I agreed to an interview. The interview process progressed successfully to a second and third interview until it was time to receive an offer. I had mixed feelings about this new job as I was doing well at my current company and intuitively it seemed there would be an opportunity for advancement although none was immediately apparent. The search firm pressed me for my decision anticipating an offer coming from their client company. I "slept" on it, and had a dream of my dad. As I indicated previously, my dad represented wisdom in my dreams and in this one he indicated I needed to be careful in my decision. The next day I turned down the job offer. Within 3 years that company offering the job had gone out of business, *and* I was promoted at my current company! This was just another example of very many dreams and intuitive feelings I have experienced in which I received and listened to the inner guidance. Notice, I wasn't told what to do, the dream simply provided insight. The free will to choose was still mine.

Considering we spend almost one third of our life sleeping, it is understandable why most people hope to receive some insight if they "sleep on it" when facing a major decision.

I do not remember every dream each night, nor can I interpret every one of them. Over the last twenty-five years I have studied my dreams in light of my reading. In addition to writing down my dream, I make mental notes each morning after a vivid dream and at the end of the day examine if anything I experienced that day matches anything in my dream. Sometimes days or weeks would pass before an event occurred which seemed to match up with my interpretation of the dream. After several years I was able to notice trends in themes and the repetition of certain dream symbols.

In high school I played basketball for our high school team, and although I enjoyed it greatly, my skill was average at best. Over fifteen years ago I had a dream one night in which I was playing basketball and I was successful in always ending up with the ball and shooting. If the other team had the ball I would steal it and shoot it. Upon awakening I remember in my dream that I must have taken twenty shots and none of them went in! Boy was I upset. All during that day I thought about what missing all those shots meant, besides validating I wasn't a very good basketball player! I already knew that.

I closely examined the symbolism of the dream. What was actually occurring? When you put the ball in the basket you get points. That was it! My dream was telling me I wasn't getting the point! The point was the concept or lesson I was working on for my emotional and spiritual growth. The message was my Higher Self telling me I needed to look beyond my current frame of reference. Fortunately, I have had other dreams in which I "make" all the points. What a relief to wake up knowing I have indeed gotten the point!

We often wonder what our purpose is here on Earth. We wonder if we are destined to follow a specific path. We create our reality here on Earth and continue it as a spiritual being when not in the human body long after we have left the Earth. When we decide to return, we again create the potential path or destiny we will encounter back on Earth. Listening each day to our intuition, to the voice inside us, we can gain insight about how to maintain our course or correct our actions to get back onto our chosen path. You may have noticed times in your life when you felt totally in sync with life. Maybe a new job opportunity, new classes at school or using your abilities in a hobby provided an opportunity for you to feel at one with God and the Universe. The more we stay on the path we have chosen as our destiny and the quicker we make corrections to move back onto the path, the faster we create the true reality we always sought.

You may have always wanted to be a teacher. Someone can display teaching qualities in numerous places, many beyond the standard classroom. Someone can teach or coach sports, teach musical instruction, teach managers how to be more effective or mentor kids in your neighborhood. Finding your place in teaching or coaching helps you feel connected to God and Universe knowing you are creating the reality you have chosen. Staying on the path you have chosen helps you more quickly create the world you desire.

With all this said about how to manage our time asleep or going within, is there something we can do to better manage our "awake" time?

We, too, need to slow down before we can receive the messages and be aware of our surroundings. We believe we have too much to get accomplished each day to stop or slow down and mentally rest for awhile. Often, when I am at work and faced with an unexpected issue, I take a deep breath before I react. Sometimes I close my office door and for just two minutes I turn inward and relax, stopping my world and head from spinning. This process allows my thoughts to focus on the issue and possible solutions come forward. In the end, taking a few minutes saves me a significant amount of time compared to if I had jumped into the process immediately.

Often when a problem presents itself, our first reaction is one based in emotion, and can lead us in the wrong direction. Backing away, in essence, slowing down, for a few minutes — or even a few seconds — can lead to a more centered and effective answer.

Find time in the morning when you first awaken and in the evening to take a few minutes for yourself. Turn off the radio, the TV, the cell phone. If you go for a run or swim in the morning, listen to the sounds around you. Begin to quiet your mind and listen to your inner thoughts. Most of us believe in intuition or a gut feeling. Even if your mind wanders to a singing bird or the sounds outside your window, quieting your mind will relax you and open yourself to new thoughts and ideas. Every day after work I make a point to spend some time outside, connecting to nature. I feel the breeze against my face, watch the birds flying by, and even insects scurrying on the ground. I smell the rain, see the leaves on the trees gently sway in the breeze, glance at the interesting cloud formations, or marvel at the sunset or stars. We are all part of the Universe and when we re-connect to the Universe, our minds open to new possibilities, we relax, and time slows.

When making an important purchase I often stop and tune into my body. I ask myself "Does this feel right?" I quiet my mind for a few moments and let my body and intuition speak. My inner voice and body always give me the right decision, if I listen.

Instead of hurrying from one issue and event to another, take time to reflect on each one as you proceed through your day. As each event unfurls, notice if you get emotionally involved in an is-sue. Did something someone said cause old memories to come to mind? Did an event occur which caused you some strong emotion such as anger, anxiety, jealously? When a person in your office made a comment did it set you off emotionally? Why is it when you see a particular type of news on TV it creates great frustration or bias in your mind? Instead of looking around for the lottery numbers, the wealth and abundance can be found in noticing how we react to our surroundings. Take note of those experiences, as they are the clues you and God have created to help you examine who you are.

If you sleep as late as possible each morning, hurrying as you get dressed and drive to work, you create a reality of being hurried all through the day. Remember, your actions state to God how you desire to live your life. And, your actions, born from your belief that you accomplish more by rushing throughout the day, ensure your world mirrors your belief.

Unfortunately, hurrying does not imply greater success. Do you know someone who always appears to be in control, talks softly, is always in a good mood, never appears rushed but gets all her work done on a timely basis? How can she accomplish this if your belief states moving and acting quickly is the best approach to accom-plish your tasks? Speed is not an indicator of success. Rather, the key is to be in tune with your surroundings and the flow of energy of life. Most successful people do not move in a rushed manner. They understand their world mirrors their beliefs, and therefore, they move through the world in sync with its flow, instead of striv-ing to control the energy flow.

When we slow down, we move faster. Although that may sound strange, it is very true. My son, Chris, played soccer when he was young. At eight years of age, he was one of the fastest players on the field. He could kick the ball forward and outrace everyone around him to the ball and continue down the field. Un-fortunately, he also out ran his teammates, and soccer is a team sport. Sometimes as he maneuvered with the ball from one foot to the other, he out ran the ball. I recommended he slow down just slightly, and once he did, he was more in sync with the flow of the ball and the game. He then began working in tandem with a team-mate and scored more goals than ever before.

Learn to be still whenever possible and listen in silence. You probably have experienced a time when you have worked on something steadily for many hours each day for many days or weeks. At some point you took a small break, maybe went for a walk, sat and watched TV or indulged in your favorite hobby. Too often a key piece of information flows to our consciousness either during this break time or as we return to our major task with a fresh mental approach.

We all are busy each day, with so much that requires our full focus and we also have plenty of distractions. Taking fifteen minutes each day to rest your mind and listen to your inner guide will allow for valuable information to come through to you, open your mind to possibilities, and give yourself a feeling of well being. What you learn during this quiet time can help you reach your goals much faster.

It's time to create. It's time to be a painter with a new canvass on which to paint the reality you desire. The painting does not appear in just a few minutes, as completing a beautiful picture may take days, weeks or month. Once completed the painting is unique. The most wonderful design and amazing aspect to our life is we can then take another blank canvass and create another beautiful painting.

You have all of the tools to create the life and reality you desire.

Now, it's all up to you.

You have all the pieces to the puzzle.

CHAPTER 16

All the Pieces to the Puzzle

*"If people knew how hard I worked to achieve my mastery,
it wouldn't seem so wonderful after all."*

-- Michelangelo, artist

We have explored a wide variety of pieces to the puzzle of life. We have examined how each piece of the puzzle fits together to create one's reality. One does not get the full view and appreciation of the picture until all pieces of the puzzle are connected. An engine with one hundred parts does not run and produce until the last piece is in place.

As you put each piece of the puzzle in place, you do gain greater insight into what the total picture displays. And yet, there is a synergistic effect when all the steps are completed. Along the way you will achieve successes, much like climbing a ladder or a stairway. With each step you can see farther and with greater clarity and perspective.

Most people believe we grow gradually in the same proportion. In reality, our growth is more like climbing stairs or reaching a new plateau. On our journeys we walk on the same level until we have a breakthrough in changing our beliefs or perception of our world. With this breakthrough, growth is a quick step upward to the next level, as all of the pieces fit in place.

Achieving the reality you desire takes effort, persistence and faith. However, the results will be greater than you imagined. This process can be as simple as you make it or as hard as you make it.

Examining our actions, thoughts and beliefs takes us on an extremely fascinating and compelling journey. You must be willing to be honest with yourself and face your fears, face your out-dated beliefs, and be willing to grow.

Let's review the 10 key steps you must take to create the exact reality you desire:

1. *Be willing to go on an amazing journey to learn and grow, requiring patience, persistence and curiosity.*

2. *Understand that the zero sum game concept is a myth, while abundance and success are achievable for everyone.*

3. *Learn to perceive and view yourself, others and the world differently.*

4. *The greatest force impacting your ability to manifest your reality of achievement is the Universal Law of Attraction.*

5. *Your thoughts, actions and beliefs created every experience you have ever had and ever will.*

6. *Discover which beliefs are giving you undesirable results knowing your world mirrors your beliefs.*

7. *Learn to expect, prepare and receive abundance as you live with faith and trust in a higher power. All goals should be in your highest good.*

8. *Claim and proclaim the experiences you desire to create; this is no time to be meek; persistence and perseverance drive results. Always show gratitude and appreciation for all you achieve.*

9. *Go within to help connect to God to provide powerful guidance on your journey.*

10. Know it was you all along.

1. ***Be willing to learn and grow.*** Take time each day to give yourself a chance to think about and prepare for the reality of which you have always dreamed. Consider each step as a new wall to break through to achieve even greater abundance and awareness. If a goal is easy to achieve, there would be little opportunity for you to face your fears, test your resolve and perseverance. The resulting benefit and satisfaction would be minimal. Rejoice in the challenge, for its reward is plentiful.

I remember the first time I took my older son to a professional baseball game. At age seven he already greatly enjoyed playing baseball. A close friend helped me secure seats very close to the field. My son never sat down for the first four innings as he stood with amazement as his senses filled him with the sounds of the crowd, the night air, the hot dogs, the towering walls of the stadium, the green grass, the colorful jerseys, and bright lights. Proceed with the fascination and the wonder of a child as you look inward and outward and adjust your focus knowing your reward is waiting.

Be willing to do the work. No matter what your goal is, no matter what you seek to achieve, effort is required on your part. If you desire to be a great golfer, be willing and eager to spend the time necessary to learn everything you can about the game and practice, practice, practice! If your goal is a promotion at work, then seek out the requirements of someone in that position and find out how you can learn more about those functions. Years ago, I did just that when I was a manager. I wanted my boss's job someday, so I made a list of all of his responsibilities. Upon discovering I was well versed in six out of the ten areas he managed, I selected one I was less familiar with, walked into his office and asked how I could become more involved in that function. He immediately gave me some work on a related project and I was on my way. Over the next few years my expertise in this function grew significantly until I was in position to make major decisions on behalf of our company in this regard.

You must do the work, but it can be play when you approach everything with passion. My father used to say if instructors would learn how to have rock music contain math or science teachings, every teenager would get A's in class. He knew the secret of having fun while you learn. Your success and achievements are waiting.

2. ***Embrace and understand the Universe does not work on the basis of a zero sum game.*** That idea is a myth. When someone else wins, you do not lose. You only lose if you believe you lose. The Universe is ever expanding, and just like your imagination, the possibilities for you to achieve abundance and success are endless. If you experience a setback on your path it is imperative to understand you created the impasse. Examine how you created the impasse and you then have the opportunity to take the necessary steps to change your direction, modify your approach, or realize it's time to discard a belief that is no longer working for you.

Each of us has the opportunity to create a world of abundance. We prevent ourselves from achieving abundance out of fear, believing there is not enough for everyone. Believing there is not enough we attempt to protect what we have. Doing so creates our reality of limited abundance. The simple act of attempting to hold on to what we have has buried in it our belief there is not enough for everyone. Our belief then manifests reality by creating a world for us of limited abundance.

Expand your mind to allow the possibilities of experiences you cannot now comprehend. When you set aside your fear, and walk through the door of opportunity, you will experience more than you have believed was possible. Your mind may limit your thinking and perception of what lies ahead. Yet your reward is limitless, and the possibilities infinite.

The problem occurs when we believe the amount we can relate to is all there is!

Whatever you can visualize you can create.

3. ***Learn to perceive the world differently.*** When we recognize the Universe works on the law of attraction, our approach to the world will change dramatically. Wishing harm, destruction, violence or abuse onto anyone else causes the same type of negative energy to materialize in our world directed right at us. Harm may come into our lives if we wish harm to others. This process does not mean you are not to defend yourself from harm. When we desire wealth, happiness, abundance and success, then we must believe everyone can achieve it and happily wish good fortune to everyone around us.

Realize that there are never any accidents in life. You created all of your experiences; hence, nothing you experience is by accident. The Universe functions consistently, always. What you perceive as "accidental" or "coincidence" does not occur part of the time. The energy you project by your beliefs and actions will always manifest the same way. The Universe is full of "no accidents."

Examine each of your beliefs and recognize how each belief paints your reality. Each belief causes you to see the world from a different point of view, as if wearing glasses filtering out what you do not wish to see and only allowing in the visuals you believe are correct. Step back and examine your beliefs one by one. Challenge the basis for each belief. Many will address your conclusions related to other people. Many will be solely about you.

Too often these beliefs will negatively affect your self-esteem, as you have deep-seated beliefs you hang onto and remind yourself of each day. You may believe you are not enough: not good enough, not smart enough, not good looking enough. Someone may have told you that you would never amount to anything. The list could go on and on.

Resolve to see the bias in your beliefs and change them. Your beliefs are creating your reality and once you destroy old, unnecessary beliefs you will no longer find that events in life happen to you. Nothing happens to you. You happen it to yourself. If you perceive that unfortunate events, bad relationships, and negative experiences happen to you, you will be forever locked into a reality of limited abundance and success. Fully understanding you create your world and all experiences within it changes your perspective on the world. Each day becomes a fascinating journey of how to grow through your experiences on the path toward your goal.

Nothing happens to you. You create it all. I create it all.

For every experience in my life, it did not happen to me.

Rather, *I happened it to myself.*

4.   *Your beliefs, thoughts and actions create every event, every interaction with people in your life, and always will.* We are beings created by design to create. Through creation comes experience, and through experience comes the opportunity to know and understand the total all-knowing of God. If you take a drop of water from the ocean, that drop of water contains the very essence of the ocean. You are the drop of water, a duplication of

God. You have the power to create wonder and magic in your life. Each belief and action sends energy into the Universe until there is sufficient energy to manifest into the experience mirroring your belief.

5. ***Your actions speak volumes.*** Your actions must dictate that which you believe you can create. Negative actions create negative results. You can't believe one way and act the opposite. Your actions will always follow your beliefs. Your actions are your beliefs put into motion and through your actions you demonstrate the power to create your world. Your actions are a stronger form of energy you project into the Universe ultimately manifesting experiences mirroring your actions. Therefore, by your actions you are instructing God and the Universal to produce results which you believe and demonstrate through your actions. Whatever your belief is you automatically believe the opposite is true as well. If you believe cheating helps you get ahead then you also believe proper business ethics yield lesser results. Your actions and words will mirror these beliefs.

6. ***Discover which beliefs are not working for you.*** Chapter 12 provides a method called the "Five Whys" to help you search the depth of your beliefs to find the real truth. Discovering why you believe what you believe is absolutely vital to changing your world. Your world mirrors your every belief, thought and action. People have good intentions and desire changes in their lives but take no action, lamenting they face another day of the same reality. Don't continually tell everyone how you wish you had a better job, but sit at home watching television each night instead of reading a book or taking a course online. Believe the action will benefit you and then take the action. Both aspects are necessary and these are choices you can make.

All the Pieces to the Puzzle

7. ***Both sides of the creation equation must be complete to generate the reality you desire.*** In addition to the work you do, the amount of time you spend, and your belief in yourself, you must have faith in the process, and faith in God.

Furthermore, prepare to receive what you have created. Expect richness in your life. Expect to receive more than you imagined. Prepare for the arrival of your success.

Previously I provided examples in my life of living in anticipation of finding my wonderful woman for a relationship. I described the actions I took to ensure I was healthy mentally, physically and spiritually. The same anticipation was evident as I performed a job search. I expressed extreme confidence and faith the position I desired was about to materialize knowing I had generated the required energy and work.

Live life and proceed with the faith that the laws described in this book are valid at all times. Go forth with the belief that once you put energy in motion, it will return to you manifested in a form your beliefs and actions create.

Remember that the act of **releasing** is one of the most critical steps in the process. By pushing you interrupt the process of the Universe finding the best solution for you. By relaxing, remaining patient, and at ease you allow the Universe and your Higher Self to bring you the best fit for your desires. Conversely, if you are full of worry, doubt, stress and frustration, all of these emotions radiate energy blocking the manifestation of your desires.

8. ***Claim and proclaim what is yours.*** This is no time for meek behavior. As you modify your beliefs and evolve them into more positive forces driving your life you are then ready to claim and proclaim to the Universe that

214

what you desire is manifesting. The act of proclaiming reinforces your belief you have put in motion all the proper forces to accomplish your goal. To sit and do nothing, yet proclaim you deserve wealth or happiness will accomplish nothing. When you have done the work, the act of proclaiming is similar to putting the cherry on top of the cake with whipped cream. The process in not complete until the cherry is on top, and you acknowledge the experience cannot commence until you have proclaimed you are ready to receive your abundance.

Be careful of giving power to your doubts; even if you have done the work, you will prevent or delay the desired outcome if your doubt is the stronger belief.

Express thanks to God and those around you every day for your success and creations. Each person drawn into your world and each experience you happen to yourself is your gift to yourself and manifested by God and the Universe. Share your good fortune with those you meet, as giving freely with no ties attached will help others and reinforces your belief that more abundance will come to you.

Treat yourself and others with respect. If you maintain a self-destructive habit, thus treating yourself disrespectfully, you cannot expect those around you to treat you respectfully. First, if you want love in your life, you must learn to love yourself and, more importantly, treat yourself lovingly. You can not expect to draw someone to you to love you when you do not love yourself. For years we have been told once we love ourselves then the right person will come into our lives. Yet no one really knew why this cause and effect worked. The answer is that by respecting yourself you are stating you believe you only will allow people into your life who respect themselves and you. The process of creating occurs everywhere in your life. Second, if you want abundance, you must be able to appreciate its value, do the work to make it appear, and be open to receive it with God's help.

9. ***Look inside for guidance and direction.*** Our intuition constantly provides information to assist us. God and our Higher Self work hard to provide information to us daily. Due to our busy lives and countless distractions, we filter out most of the information sent to us. Consequently, meditation, prayer, dream work — using any opportunity to quiet the mind — will produce an opportunity for valuable information and messages to come to you to guide you on your journey.

10. ***Know it was you all along.*** Once you appreciate the full magnitude of your ability to create everything in your life, you will begin enjoying each experience. Most of all you will treasure them and learn to laugh at yourself as you see yourself moving through each experience. As events occur or interesting people appear in your life you will naturally examine what beliefs and actions generated this particular result. Like Sherlock Holmes, or a crime scene investigator, you will attack each experience with passion to understand the depth of your beliefs. You may laugh at yourself as you discover some strange, tightly held belief realizing the impact this one belief has created for you.

Investigating how you were drawn into a particular event or into someone else's life is even more fun. Being drawn into another person's life is even more magical. If in a dark moment you believe you do not have anything to offer others, simply step back and notice all of the people's lives you have touched, remembering that each person asked for you to come forth to help them discover the depth of their experience.

People say that what goes around comes around. This concept is universally true, but not because God punishes you by succumbing to the negative energy you put out into the world. Rather, you automatically create a reality, a world, where you bring people and events into your life mirroring your beliefs and actions.

You must believe you can have it all. You must believe in the universal truth that you create it all. You must believe there is something better for you than what you can see with your present limited perception.

You must not take "no" for an answer; in fact negative thoughts are not part of your thought process.

You **can** have it all.

So what's stopping you from starting?

CHAPTER 17

So What's Stopping You?

*"He has not learned the lesson of life who does not
every day surmount a fear."*

-- Ralph Waldo Emerson

*"There are only two mistakes one can make
along the road to truth;
not going all the way
and not starting."*

-- Buddha

S o what's stopping you? What is holding you back from creating the world you have so long desired?
You made it this far in the book, but still remain unsure? Do
you still have doubt in yourself, your ability, and faith in God?

You may have many reasons why you believe you won't succeed or ever achieve abundance in your life. You may have suffered some very unfortunate circumstances, had a difficult
childhood or even suffered physical, mental or emotional trauma.

You may think you are not worthy enough, or smart enough, or
good looking enough. You may have already tried other times and
failed.

You may believe your circumstances are different from everyone else, preventing you from ever obtaining some piece of abundance. You are correct. If you believe your circumstances are

different, then you create that reality. If you believe that is what holds you back, then you create that reality. In reality everyone's circumstances are unique, special and different to each of us. We all have our own mountains to climb, emotional scars to manage, physical and mental challenges, and unsuccessful or incomplete attempts at achievement. Yet we all have the power within, the power each of us is given to change the future. We all create today and all of our tomorrows.

I have heard just about every reason anyone might offer for not moving forward. I know, because I have faced many of these obstacles on my own journey to success.

Let's confront each of the common reasons keeping us in gridlock. When finished, you will have erased all doubt in your mind that you do, in fact, have the ability and potential to create the world in which you wish to live.

Procrastination: Each day we have a choice to use new beliefs and take new steps to achieve success. We also have the choice to do nothing new. Choosing the same old action yields the same old results.

Most people choose inaction and procrastination for one of two reasons: fear of the unknown or a belief that the desired outcome will not be great enough to compensate for the time and energy required.

We may think keeping the status quo means we have not made a choice. If we procrastinate, we are making a choice to delay any new results. In fact, we are sending a message to the Universe and God that we are happy with the status quo, with being unsuccessful, and God is more than happy to help continue to manifest the status quo in our lives with which we are not satisfied. The choice is ours.

Fear of the unknown: Fear is the second strongest emotion after love. Actually, love and fear are opposite emotions. Every action you take in life is done out of fear or love.

Fear is a powerful emotional force, paralyzing us, freezing us into inaction. We fear the unknown because our minds have trouble imagining what our reality would be like if we succeeded. In chapter 8, I explained how our fear that the "pie" of abundance is limited warps our thinking, our beliefs and our actions. Our inability to view the "pie" of abundance as expanding, believing that all we could comprehend was all that was obtainable, has limited what we believe we can achieve. The same holds true here. If you can't, and are not, willing to imagine what your reality could be if you were to succeed at your goal, you will continue to generate unsatisfactory results.

Most of us fear the unknown. That fear produces a reality with events that reinforce the fear and gives us plenty of reasons not to change.

Sometimes I meet people who want desperately to end a relationship and move on in the world. In this situation, they often think they can leave once they find someone new. Although this is quite convenient and easy, they must understand that their actions and beliefs create their realities. They fear being alone yet want out of the relationship. They also fear they will never find anyone new, and decide a bad relationship is better than no relationship at all. Examine the actions and beliefs occurring in this situation. Remaining in the relationship tells God that the present relationship is acceptable. Furthermore, the fear-based belief that they may not find a new relationship is continually manifested into reality. No one appears with whom a relationship might be possible.

The act of severing a relationship while holding the belief that you will find someone takes courage, but it is the energy of your belief that will ultimately manifest itself in a new relationship. I have put this to test in my personal life by finding a wonderful woman to marry. My power to create was also tested and proven in my career when I chose to leave a company prior to landing a new job, and I eventually found a new position that surpassed my goals. To expect God to help you move forward you must demonstrate to yourself and God and the Universe that you have faith something better awaits you. There is an old saying:

*"To grab on to something new,
you must first let go of what is in your hand."*

Successful people face their fear of the unknown by having faith in themselves and God. If you must be intimidated by fear, then use it to propel you forward by fearing what you might never accomplish if you never start.

Maybe you sit on the sofa and eat to make yourself feel good when you know you should be busy doing almost anything else. Any action moving toward accomplishing your life-long dream would be better than behavior inflicting long-term harm to your body and mind. Yet, you remain without taking action. You rationalize your behavior, comforting yourself by believing you deserve to watch TV and eat chocolate chip cookies. Your mind will come up with 100 reasons why that behavior is acceptable: "I worked hard today, I need a break, and a few cookies never hurt anyone." The list goes on.

Yet, what if "sitting" moved you further away from achieving your long-term desire? Your response may be fear-based: *Well, I probably would not have achieved it anyway. I am not one of the lucky ones. God's grace is for others, not for me.* Have you used any of these responses (or others I may not have mentioned) in the past? Which do you use to convince yourself your behavior is acceptable?

To more closely examine your responses, answer this question: **How would you feel if the opportunity came for you to achieve your life-long dream and you weren't ready?** How sad and deeply painful it would be if you were not prepared when your golden opportunity arrived...if you hadn't sharpened your skills, through education or training, kept your mind open and alert for new information and maintained a healthy body with exercise and good food. If you did do some or much of the work and did not achieve your goal, you might even be heartbroken. Yes, if you must, use the fear of not achieving your goal to help push you along the way. If you accomplish your goal, you never have to endure the pain at all.

Unfortunately, some of us have become too comfortable with pain. If you put a frog in boiling water (so the story goes), it will immediately jump out. However, if you put a frog in tepid water and slowly raise the heat of that water, the frog will remain in the pot. Have you become too comfortable with the pain? Do you understand the pain only gets stronger? You now have the ability to use fear to get you up off of the couch and accomplish all you desire. The happiness this brings you will be greater than you can imagine.

Do not let fear stop you. It is your choice. If you do, it is your own belief preventing you from success. Remember, if you believe you can and will succeed, put in the time and energy, have faith and live your life with expectation, then the manifestation of your goal is automatic.

A limited perception of the future: If you are unwilling to move forward, to get up off the couch and take action, it is often due to a limited perception of the potential results. You may rationalize your inaction by convincing yourself you would not have accomplished your goal anyway; therefore the effort involved is not worth the energy. If your goal is to lose weight, you will be required to eat better and exercise for months to gain the shape and health you desire. Many times our minds are unable to see the power and benefits of achieving our goal.

In Chapter 8 I explained that we limit our abundance and success because our minds can only comprehend specific amounts. Your mind will block out anything beyond what it can comprehend. If your mind only believes there is a potential to lose ten pounds but can not visualize there is a potential for you to lose twenty, thirty pounds or more then your success will stop right where you've expected it and you'll never lose more than ten pounds. Further, if your mind can not visualize and comprehend the magnitude of benefits of your new weight — possibly being in a new relationship or the power or renewed confidence — then you will not achieve your goal, or at best achieve it briefly before returning to old habits.

Our limited thinking prevents us from seeing the numerous intangible gains that come with reaching for a goal past what your mind can comprehend. This applies for the amount of wealth you attract, how well you play golf, or any other endeavor you attempt. If you eat properly and exercise and obtain your desired weight, you gain substantially more than just good health. Your body is stronger to assist in tackling those home projects or various hobbies you desire. Your mind is more alert and can focus better helping you more quickly conquer new projects requiring keen mental power.

There are many more examples of the potential for your "gain" to be substantially more than just your immediate result:

- Over fifteen years ago I earned a Black Belt in Tae Kwon Do. The perseverance required was exceptional as the training was not only extremely physically challenging but required extreme mental focus. Besides the obvious ability to defend myself, the power of my mind and body to work together, coupled with the increased sense of discipline were benefits I had not anticipated. I received an additional benefit as my sense of discipline and greater ability to focus my mind has helped propel me forward in my business career and other endeavors.

- You may learn to play an instrument like a guitar. To play at a reasonable level requires years of practice and dedication. You may dream of being skilled enough to play a variety of styles and entertain friends. Along the way you may well gain an appreciation for music and those who play other instruments. You may also discover the depth of the sounds and complexity of the music when listening to others performing.

- You may desire a close relationship with someone with whom you are very compatible. As your relationship grows you may find your connection to this special other person intensify beyond anything you had anticipated or imagined. You may find in this new relationship you are not judged, you give freely never expecting anything in return, and feel someone truly understands you. This kind of connection has the power to bring you closer to God and enliven your life with an inner awareness of yourself.

- You may accumulate a substantial amount of wealth. In achieving this wealth you may have accomplished many goals, including employing thousands of people and helping them enjoy greater wealth, as well as providing quality products and services. You may have given people an opportunity to develop to their full potential. Once you have accumulated significant wealth you turn your attention to donating large sums to various charities as well as donating your time. Sharing your time and wealth with others may bring you more happiness than you thought possible.

The selling experience gained while I was unemployed and doing any job I could to make ends meet has helped me negotiate deals, present to large audiences, and communicate better with my loved ones.

Often we do not make the effort to walk through the door of opportunity because our thinking limits what we believe is on the other side. Believe there are limitless possibilities and your results will always be beyond your expectations!

Positive results have a synergistic and geometric effect on your life: each time you grow and learn you carry that forward into everything new you experience. You then view and review each experience with new eyes. You learn more from each experience and you accomplish more in each experience. Just like each grade in school builds on the previous grade, so does your learning. Therefore, when you step through the door, that single step will carry you many more steps forward. If you fail to see the vastness of your potential success, then you miss tremendous opportunities. I now seek out those "doors of opportunities" because I have had the strength and perseverance to walk through them many times and have never been disappointed.

Fear of failure: Many people make no attempt to move forward, thinking, "But what if I try and fail?" or "What if I try and end up losing everything?" Remember, you create it all of it. When you believe you have the power to create your world, and that creative power cannot be turned on and off but something you do with every breath, you will embrace knowing you create EVERYTHING in your world.

Success is rarely, if ever, accomplished in one attempt. Have you ever watched an infant attempt to take his/her first steps? She will pull herself up against something, holding on tightly to the sofa or chair, only to fall back down again. Does the child give up after a few tries? Stop and strongly consider that if we all gave up after a few tries, none of us would be walking and running today! This is no small accomplishment for the baby. In her world learning to walk is similar to us to obtaining as large of goal we can imagine.

The infant is relentless in her attempts and does not quit. Instead the infant — even one so young — figures out what went wrong, makes adjustments and tries again. Nowhere in the infant's head is the idea of failure.

At no time does the child consider she will never walk, how she will be viewed if she cannot walk, and how she will view herself if she cannot walk.

None of these thoughts enter her mind. **Only adults have these thoughts when approaching new goals.** Successful people only focus and think about how to accomplish their goal.

When you do not acquire your goal on the first or second attempt, you must consider three possibilities:

1. There is more to learn about the task involved,
2. Your approached must be adjusted based on what did and did not work,
3. Your lack of success may be due to an underlying negative belief that outweighs all of your positive actions.

First, any new project requires research and education. Expecting to roll a strike the first time you bowl — especially if you've never had your hands on a bowling ball — is unrealistic. The same is true for most other skills in life. The biggest roadblocks are not taking the time to learn and perfect our craft and not believing in ourselves and God that anything is possible.

Second, successful people *always* take the time to examine what worked and what did not, make modifications and try again. When you change your perception to appreciate failure as a learning opportunity, then you will take what you need from the experience and move forward. With every new journey, every new hobby, any new venture you take there is a learning curve, and it's usually a steep one. We will not succeed each time; yet each time *is* a success, because now you know what does ***not*** work.

Third, use the approaches outlined in this book to help you examine your beliefs and intentions. If you worked diligently on a project, but in the back of your mind kept reminding yourself of how many times you failed in the past, you set yourself up for failure. Remember, ***the dominant belief rules your reality.*** You may achieve some success, but not total success as long as a negative belief dominates your thinking.

Every Sunday in the fall your favorite football team at some point during the game calls a running play, executes the play and losses yardage. Should your team walk off the field and quit because that play did not yield a gain? Of course, not! They try other plays. At half time the coaches discuss changes in tactics and small adjustments to the same running play. You must take the same approach as you work your way toward success. Determine what pieces of the process are working, and discard the pieces that are not. Change your thinking from the instant gratification of immediate results such as executing one play and scoring a touchdown. Instead, focus on achieving results through constant improvement. Modify your beliefs and actions appropriately.

Finally, the past does not equal the future. You may have failed in the past. However, you now are wiser having learned from your experiences. Furthermore, you have new insight, provided in this book, into your ability to create your reality. With all the information in hand, your past will not equal the future. Your future can and will be different if you let go of the past and move forward with your power to create.

Wanting **rather than** *doing*: Eliminate words such as "want" and "wish" from your vocabulary, such as "I *wish* I could find the right person for a wonderful relationship". Claiming and proclaiming what you believe is yours because you have worked hard, prepared, had faith and let the result come in any form allows your energy to manifest. Successful people talk in terms of already having what they are seeking to achieve. When you reinforce your actions by reminding yourself you "have" achieved this goal, the subconscious believes it to be true and quickens the manifestation of your goal. Hear yourself when you use the words "wish" and "want". You are actually declaring you do *not* possess your goal and are still seeking it. Therefore, God helps you achieve that which you believe and put in to action which is you stating you do not *have* that which you seek. This is not a word or mind game. Your words project your beliefs, and your beliefs create your world.

Focusing on the negative, rather than the positive: What you focus on becomes your reality. Many years ago when I was unemployed during the fall of the year, I kept saying my goal was to *no longer be unemployed* during the holidays. Being without work through the holiday season, I was afraid, would negatively affect my faith and self-esteem. The result: I was unemployed during the holidays. It wasn't long before I realized I was focusing on the negative. The fact that I was acknowledging the possibility of being unemployed during the holidays gave the idea greater power every time I mentioned it. I learned to state my goals as, "I will be employed by December" or "New employment is arriving now." Shortly afterward, I received a job offer.

Focusing on the positive directs your mind to focus on your next action toward employment. Compare this to focusing on not being employed during the holidays where your mind can focus on how you may feel still unemployed at that time. The difference is action compared to a negative emotion. Action produces results.

Negative approaches rule many people's thoughts as they face new tasks. Often our first thought is, "But what if I fail?" Isn't it fascinating the majority of people first think of failure? The floodgate opens to more thoughts which freeze us in terror. Yet, is there such a thing as failure? You — literally — only fail if you *believe* you do. Every — and I mean *every* — successful person has been unsuccessful in his attempts at some point in his life. He simply does not take "no" for an answer. His focus is on the positive, not the negative.

Focusing on the short-term: You must change your focus away from immediate, quick results. Allow the process to unfold at the right speed.

The first part of this book explains how we became a society that looks for immediate results. The short-term result had become the bottom line: the only thing that matters.

Each of us has learned well that today's bottom line is all that is important. Every action you take, every thought you have, is pushed through this filter: Does this action give me pain or pleasure *right now*?

We know that smoking will kill us in the long-term, but if it helps us feel good right now...today, this minute, this second...many of us are willing to put the cigarette in our mouths because the long-term is exactly that, it's a long time from now. If you knew that you would shorten your life one day for each cigarette you smoked; if you were shown a chart of your life span where each day you could see the remaining days in your life dropping each time you inhaled, you would react much differently.

Most people have difficulty relating to what is long-term. We can reach out and grab the short-term. We can taste it. We can feel it. We can see it with our own two eyes. Some people will rationalize their behavior by thinking that anything can happen tomorrow, next week, next year, or in ten or twenty years. Therefore, they figure they can treat their bodies in any manner they wish, as long as it feels good in the moment.

A short-sighted viewpoint permeates all aspects of our lives. Our political system is built with a short-term focus. Our politicians are up for election every two to six years. To be re-elected, these lawmakers must take concrete and immediate action on behalf of their constituents. Politicians, by the very nature of their jobs, operate in the short-term because of their need to preserve their jobs. If politicians were not concerned about being re-elected, if they could instead focus on the long-term consequences of each issue, imagine how they might vote! Imagine what positive progress might be possible!

Only big successes are acceptable: We look for the quick win. We want to hit home runs. We play the lottery to win the big one. We want to take big steps all at once. Baby steps are for babies.

While we are working hard to create the one big deal to make us rich, we overlook all the small steps we can take to help us create the world we desire. Every day we can hit "singles" to get us where we want to be. Home runs are sexy, popular and exciting. Singles are boring, yet in the long run, hitting singles day after day, is very productive. I always marveled at the player who had 3,000 or more hits, as well as those who have consecutive game hitting streaks. Being consistently productive every day helps the player and the team in the long run.

Companies employing this short-term strategy don't spend money reinvesting in the structure of the company, from updated accounting systems to research and development, because in the short-term it reduces cash flow.

Remember in an earlier chapter I stated we try to take shortcuts? I was not talking about working longer. Finding balance is critical, and you can and must make time for what is important in your life. It just takes some rearranging of priorities. I had to adjust my schedule by rising earlier each day to fit in an exercise program. I find that I have more energy and can think more clearly after starting my day with a work out. This helps me accomplish all I need to, and more efficiently. The key is to work toward your goal consistently and in small steps. Go for singles, not the home runs.

You can hit a single every day. Opportunities arise for you every day to hit a single. Who do you think created those opportunities? You did. We have a tendency to overlook opportunities when they present themselves. Our attention can be so riveted on the big step that we miss the chance to learn about ourselves, to gain the knowledge offered to us every day, to relish the small successes that propel us forward toward larger goals. When you open up your mind and watch yourself go through the same motions every day, getting the same unproductive results, you should wonder what is wrong with the picture. You create opportunities for you to obtain what you want one small step at a time.

The goal seems not worth the effort or will take too long: Many people do not want to make the effort required to reach their goals. Your habits and beliefs have been with you a long time. Some of us can leave our bad habits behind and quickly replace them with more helpful thoughts and habits. For others it takes much longer. Take heart and consider that your old beliefs got you to this point, and you are reading this because you are not happy with where you stand.

Once you examine your beliefs and actions and change just one, the results will reinforce your courage to change. When you free yourself from your old beliefs and let them evolve as you grow and learn, you open yourself up to all the possibilities and opportunities the Universe has to manifest for you.

As we have discussed in earlier chapters, many people do not have the patience to wait for their goals to come to fruition. Expecting long-held beliefs to change overnight and generate success the next day is unrealistic. At the same time, the only thing that holds you back from success is you. The quicker you can acknowledge and modify the key beliefs which have worn out their usefulness and, in fact, created some unfortunate experiences, the faster you will reach your goals. Your goal will be achieved when you truly are ready, and as you get better at this process, your results come more quickly.

You have the ability and power to create everything in your life. If you have read the prior chapters of this book, by now you know and understand you do. Start small. Do not try to reinvent yourself in one attempt. Start by looking at your current situation without attempting to change any part of it. I have provided the tools you can use to examine why the people, places and events in your life mirror your beliefs and actions. As you examine each experience and see how your beliefs created the entire experience, marvel in the power you have to create anything in your world. Too often people get frustrated and give up their efforts believing they will wait too long before reaching their goal. If you are a parent with a teenager who believes he is in love and wants to marry, I am sure you shudder at the thought. You have experienced being in love and know the kind of maturity and effort needed to make a relationship work. Your son, however, may resist your input, because he thinks he is ready. In the same way, goals are not made manifest on *your* timeline, nor initiated when *you* determine you are ready.

Most of us want an expedited process in order to reach our goal. Yet the key to learning more about who we are is through the experience. There is an old saying that "Success is not a destination, it is a journey." Time is our friend, allowing us to experience each and every aspect of an emotion, a relationship, a success.

Let's assume you decide one day that you want to be a professional football player, and God gives you the ability and the opportunity in the next moment. You then go and play in a professional football game and even score a touchdown. Will you have truly experienced being a professional football player? No, because you will not have experienced the countless hours practicing, lifting weights, in team and coaches' meetings, working through injuries, reveling in games won and times you played well and bemoaning games lost and the mistakes you made on the field. Each of these experiences on the path to achieving a major goal gave you an opportunity to prepare yourself for the special moment of success.

The work you've done and the pieces of the journey you've experienced along the way all contribute to the appreciation, gratitude, joy, abundance and elation at the fulfillment of your dream. Albert Einstein said "The only reason for time is so that everything doesn't happen at once." We need time to learn from our experiences, make adjustments, and try again to achieve success. That is the creation process, and we are creative beings. Time is on our side.

Isn't it interesting that it takes very little time to destroy anything we have created, yet the building process can take days, months or even years? A life, a marriage, a building, anything can be destroyed instantly by a wrong word spoken, action or even intended destruction. Conversely, building a home, a lasting and loving relationship, a career or being the best at a hobby can take months or years. God created the concept of time for this specific purpose. Only through time can we as humans experience and appreciate each nuance in the building process of everything in which we are involved. The strong depth, breath and power of love can only be understood and experienced over time. The skills to manage people or a business, to lead a company or a nation, can only be learned over time. At any moment we can begin creating a new reality. The process of time fits perfectly with our ability to create experiences. Time is needed for the creation and experience of each. Destruction comes quickly to allow us to move into a new creative process immediately.

Achieving a goal requires basic ingredients of time, energy, skill and strong beliefs. A cake cannot be made without each ingredient in the recipe. If you tried to make a cake without flour, the result would not be what you wanted. It is impossible to have a fulfilling relationship unless you are totally prepared to experience the relationship and participate in it fully. The Law of Attraction will not bring you the person to create with you the perfect relationship experience if you are not ready. This is exactly the reason why so many people end up in less-than-satisfactory relationships. They continually tell themselves they are ready for the perfect relationship, but are not demonstrating the traits of the person they desire. Only when you can demonstrate that which you desire, does the "right" person materialize in your life.

Marvel at how powerful you were in creating your most interesting experiences. Every time I have moved past an old belief and let it evolve into something more positive, more loving, more focused on growing, learning and coming closer to God, the outcome has been better than I could have I imagined. Not just some times. Not just once in a while. Every time. Every time I made the effort; (and there were times it took great courage and unwavering perseverance on my part). But each time the reward, the outcome, the achievement was greater than I had hoped for.

It is important to note that the only reason the process required great effort and perseverance on my part was my own stubbornness to change! As creature of habit, we strongly resist change. The few times I did not resist and plunged head long into the opportunity, willing to evolve, the results happened sooner than expected.

Not living in the moment: Living in the moment is not about having short-term thinking. Living in the moment is absorbing everything possible in each experience, using your senses, including your intuition, to be fully present in the moment. In order to fully appreciate all the experience has to offer it is important not to let your mind wander or be distracted by other things. Remember, you created the experience. The experience contains lessons to be learned, benefits to appreciate, and emotions to feel and explore. Don't take the chance of missing any of these key elements.

Living in the moment and experiencing each event to its fullest allows you the opportunity to gain as much information as possible about yourself, what you need to learn, and how you can achieve your desires. As adults we limit our possibilities, thereby limiting our options to improve, to achieve and to create success. Each day there are many, many situations created for us, by us, to help us along the path to our dreams. All we have to do is open our eyes, hearts and minds to them. They are there, every day, because we put those opportunities there, just for us. There is no such thing as a wasted day; or a wasted event. Each and every event or interaction with someone is a chance for you to obtain an important piece of information. You may have been searching for information on how to finish a project, deal with a personal issue, have a better relationship with your spouse or children or improve a skill important to your work. Every day an opportunity will present itself for you to receive the information, but you must be present and aware.

Young children are amazing at noticing everything going on around them. If you take them to the carnival they see the wonder of everything there. Adults have learned to filter out noises, people and experiences and let in only those that they wish to hear, see or experience. Filtering causes adults to miss so much of the carnival of life. Be childlike. Anticipate the excitement with your eyes, ears and mind wide open.

Insisting on validation as you move forward: Often I hear this refrain: "If I could just get some sign, some feedback, to know I am on the right course, then I would not lapse into my old ways." You spend your days looking for something — anything — to indicate that your efforts and energy are paying off. Yet, if you understand how automatic the creation process is, validation is not necessary. Creating always ends in manifestation. Always. The combination of two parts hydrogen and one part oxygen always yields water. No other outcome is possible. If your beliefs are in line, and your actions and thoughts are working together, your results are guaranteed.

Requiring validation is a demonstration of fear. Knowing you create your reality does not require validation. When you ask for validation, thereby fearing you are not closer to your goal, your fear actually moves you further from your goal.

Sometimes we are faced with many choices and there is no method to determine which direction to take. You can find all the answers by listening to your Higher Self. Your Higher Self can see what you cannot see. Your Higher Self can see the future, since time does not exist in its realm. The choices are clear to your Higher Self, though it will only act as your advisor. The choice remains with us, as we each have free will. Prayer and meditation are good ways to connect with your Higher Self. Any method can be employed that helps you disengage your conscious mind and listen to your soul. For years dreams have been my way of tuning in to my Higher Self and receiving insight and wisdom.

When you stop seeking external validation and look inside yourself, your Higher Self will provide guidance and wisdom.

Spending time looking back and wondering "What if?" You may be constantly looking back at your life wishing you could change what has happened. You believe if you could only go back in time you would manage a relationship differently, put more effort into the job to get a promotion that never manifested, or speak your mind to someone who hurt you. Remember that what you focus on becomes your reality. If you constantly focus on the past then you believe that is the only method for you to achieve success. Focusing on the past demonstrates your belief the future does not hold the success you hope to acquire. By looking back and wanting to change your past you acknowledge to God that the future cannot be better than your past and God helps you manifest what you believe.

Some years ago I interviewed with a search firm on behalf of a large company. The job seemed like a perfect fit, as I had years of experience not only in the position they sought, but also in the same industry. Unfortunately, the interview process never went beyond the search firm. The company hired the first person they interviewed! This upset me for several months. It's also worth noting no interviews came my way while I lamented the lost chance. During this period I spent a lot of time examining my actions and beliefs and lamenting an opportunity lost. Finally I determined not to look back and reminded myself that I needed to move past the loss. I had to trust that other opportunities would come along. Within one week I was referred to a representative of another search firm, who was excited because they had been looking for someone with just my experience. This provided me with another example of my stubbornness delaying my success.

Lacking patience and creating inconsistency: Doubt and lack of faith in yourself and God causes delays in achieving your goals. Some days you are excited and full of optimism working hard toward your goal. On other days you are filled with worry and have difficulty taking any appreciable action. The variability of your emotions and energy makes any forward movement difficult. The Universe is not able to compile enough of the same energy together to manifest into the physical reality of your desires.

Think about it in terms of building a house. You may be able to lay a solid foundation of block or cement and then you begin to build a frame. Each day you believe in yourself and take action demonstrated by nailing another two-by-four in your house. The two-by-fours attached to the foundation are beginning to define the floor plan. The first few days or weeks you are doing great. Your positive attitude, combined with your hard work and actions continue for a couple of months. Some days you are very productive in taking giant steps toward your goal. You are able to complete more of the frame for your future house.

Then something happens. Your patience begins to wear thin. You feel frustrated and question your strategy, motives and faith. Stress at work or with family causes further doubt. In a spiritual or metaphorical sense, parts of your house's frame begin to sag or fall. Consequently, you are further from your goal. You may have days when you are filled with mixed emotions. On those days you may continue to build the house, but some of the two-by-fours get attached at wrong angles or in the wrong places. Later, when you are able to regain a more positive attitude, you have to re-do the work. Retracing your steps, having to do the work twice, creates even more frustration and fear. You now have to exert more energy just to catch up with where you were, which creates the potential for even more negative thoughts and impatience.

This back and forth of positive and negative energy causes a delay in manifestation of your goal. It may prevent the manifestation of the goal altogether. Many of you continue this way throughout your lives. You are constantly building, tearing down, rebuilding. Giving up is understandable.

Successful people stay the course. They are confident in their ability to achieve and although they set a timeline for their success and achievement, they are not bound to it. Some inventions, some creations have taken years longer than their creators ever imagined. The one constant is their belief in achieving their goal. Believe as though you have succeeded. Believe that you already possess that which you seek and your mindset will change. Your thoughts, actions, and beliefs will adapt to the reality of the world you desire.

If you have trusted your intuition and know you are on the right path, the stronger your beliefs and the more successfully you can push away the doubts the quicker you will achieve your desired goal. Once you've arrived, you might sit back and be disgruntled it took so long. You might blame God or others for the slow progress and possible setbacks. Yet, when you see how your own beliefs and actions impeded your progress, you might understand why it took longer than originally planned. Your own doubts and fears caused the delay. Eliminate your fears and doubts and you achieve much more quickly.

We also often wonder why we have to wait so long to obtain that which we desire. If you look back on the many experiences in your life, you will see there is a direct pattern and connection to all that you have learned. We can't run a marathon every day of our life. As humans, taking a vacation is valuable, providing a way to rebuild our spiritual, emotional and physical stamina to prepare for the next leg of our journey. When you experience a section of time appearing as if nothing new is happening, do not despair. Use your time constructively to exercise, keep your mind alert and stay focused on your end result. At the same time, enjoy the rest, knowing your next stage will soon come upon you.

We also need time to heal from hurts and sorrows, and to consider what we have experienced in anticipation of what is to come in our lives. We need time to rest, contemplate and prepare for the next success. We could not appreciate, comprehend, nor understand our world, learn and grow if everything happened at once. Time is valuable. Patience and preparation are golden.

You don't prepare to receive and experience your desire: Two other fundamental concepts must be understood and acted on in order to obtain what we desire: *We must prepare to receive, and we must prepare to experience.*

If we do not take the necessary steps in preparation to receive and experience that which we have so long desired we will lose our opportunity. Maybe your life-long dream has been to travel the world, hiking mountain trails, deep sea fishing or diving. One day, you and the other members of your department are rewarded with a trip to Hawaii as a bonus for the countless hours you have devoted to complete a project for your company. Here is finally your golden opportunity to receive and experience something you have always dreamed about. Are you prepared to appreciate the depth of the reward and experience the travel to its fullest? If over the last years you have been reading all about the art of deep sea fishing attempting to understand what it is like to reel in a 100-pound fish, you will have made a good start at your preparation. If you have taken diving classes for certification or have read books on the proper techniques for hiking rocky terrain you will be prepared for the adventure. But what if you had spent your free time in the past few years watching TV? Would you be fully prepared to experience this adventure to its fullest? We all know you would not be ready, nor would you be able to experience the process to its depth.

If you are unprepared to experience the adventure to its fullest, you might very well miss the reason you created this situation. You may miss out on the opportunity for the spiritual, emotional and mental experience of a lifetime, all because you were not ready. Perhaps another department at work — not yours — receives the bonus, passing you by all together. When you are prepared, you send a message to the Universe you are ready to experience the event to its fullest.

When you have done the preparation, your experience is enhanced by everything you've learned along the way and all your senses running at peak performance. You'll breath in, exhilarated by the mountain air, your eyes will take in the colorful sea creatures, flora and fauna of your deep sea dive, you will enjoy the pull of the great fish on your line and smell the salty breeze of the ocean as you reel in the catch of a lifetime. How magnificent the experience would be! Your energy will touch everything around you, helping to provide the perfect experience for everyone and everything you encounter.

These concepts apply to all parts of our lives. When I was searching for someone to spend the rest of my life with, I made a list of all of the qualities and traits I wanted in a partner. I wanted her to be healthy emotionally and physically, projecting a positive and generous radiance toward life with an inner drive to improve herself, while having fun along the way. I knew that if this woman were to come into my life, I had to be that same type of person myself. Similar energy attracts, but I also needed to prepare for her arrival to experience her to the fullest. My goal was to be in shape mentally, emotionally and physically in order to experience all she would bring me and for me to be able to share all of myself with her.

My desire to find this woman got me up off the couch quickly! I exercised regularly, and took all of the steps I have outlined in this book with regard to my thoughts and actions. I spent time reading and continued my introspection. When I finally met my wife, we both knew from the first date that we had so much in common. We both had prepared for each other and yet were surprised with the power of our connection.

Whatever experience or opportunity you wish to have in your world you must prepare for its arrival and be ready to experience it to the maximum.

A lost desire for adventure: Many people want to immediately know the outcome of each situation without having to wait. Initially it sounds like fun to know in advance that my team will win every game or that I will always get the low score in my golf foursome.

If we knew the outcome of each event, even if we won each time, we would grow tired of the game. The exhilaration, fascination and excitement of the roller coaster ride is that you do not know the outcome. The experience of the game IS everything.

Remember, you create the experience for yourself in order to learn and grow and comprehend more than you ever did. Each experience provides some unique piece of information necessary for you to choose your next step. Approach each day ready to explore each new opportunity and you will find your life much richer for the experience. Strike up a conversation with the person riding with you in the elevator or sitting next to you on the train. When we take these actions, we often come away amazed at the experience. We often exclaim "What a small world we live in," reflecting how we discovered the person sitting next to us was just the person we needed to meet to move forward on our next project.

Resisting change: There is an old saying that there is nothing as permanent as change. Change is all around you. Your children grow up, your parent's age, the trees get taller and your car's parts wear out. Those are examples of changes close to home. In the broader world there are economic, political and scientific changes affecting your life. You must move with the flow and adapt to everything around you. No matter how much you attempt to stay the same, you change every day. Success will come to you faster if you accept change and grow with it.

If, however, you push only the change you desire, you cut off all of the other possibilities. A horse with blinders on misses all that is going on around it. Enjoy your place in the world.

Insisting justice should be served for transgressions against you or others: Everything you experience did not happen *to* you. The people, places and events you experienced were created from your beliefs. If you are in a relationship in which you are treated poorly, you drew that person to you because of your beliefs that you should be treated accordingly. You have the choice every day to leave that relationship, to refuse to tolerate or settle for a relationship in which you are treated disrespectfully.

Your beliefs created the experience and you attracted this person into your life to experience exactly that which you believe.

You may be disrespecting yourself by overeating or smoking. On a spiritual and Universal level you asked him to mirror what you do to yourself. Once you view the amazing learning opportunity and consequently grow from it, you can marvel how wonderful it was he came into your life to teach you to respect yourself. No forgiveness is necessary because you created the scenario.

You may see others gain success or abundance unethically or selfishly. Often people ask me why these people are able to pass by honest, hard-working people for a promotion. There are many reasons this occurs: First, as I stated in chapter 13, being "good" is not enough. Successful people demonstrate assertive and positive-minded behavior. Honesty is admirable, but not enough. Second, although these people may demonstrate and believe unethical or impolite behavior is appropriate, their dominate belief is they can achieve success. Hence, they experience upward movement in their career. Third, although they experience some abundance, their lives will be filled with unethical and selfish relationships and events. As I stated in chapter 9, you can not believe one way and act another. A person believing unethical or unkind behavior is just will demonstrate similar behavior in all areas of his life. Consequently, he will experience this same behavior returned to him in his relationships and events. Fourth, you perceive only one piece of the experience. Just because they have abundance does not mean their lives are complete or without challenges. There are countless examples of lottery winners mismanaging their money shortly afterward. The money won was not the prize; dealing with the large amount of money created many experiences for which they had not bargained. Lastly, remember that anyone who is directly affected by these people has chosen this experience as his reality. Anyone who works for an unethical boss has created the experience by attracting that boss into his life based on his beliefs.

You encounter an obstacle and believe God is working against you: When you seriously begin changing your beliefs and actions, you will soon encounter a challenge. Perhaps you decide to stop smoking and you have been doing wonderfully for two weeks.

At the same time you believed you could quit if all the events in your life were stress-free, but were uncertain how you would react in a stressful situation. Further, you believed your will was not strong enough to resist temptation to start again if you were around other smokers.

You are invited to a party at a friend's house and soon discover several people are smoking. To further complicate the situation, your last two days at work were extremely stressful. You may be thinking, "God, why would you put this tempting and stressful situation in front of me when you know I am trying to quit? This doesn't help, it makes it worse!" Actually, you created the experience for yourself by your beliefs and as a test. If you believed you could not resist temptation being around other smokers while under added stress, this event mirrors your fear-based belief. At the same time you have an opportunity to resist temptation.

What you choose to do in this situation will tell you how far you have progressed and how much further you have to go. The experience provides a measuring stick for your growth. In similar situations, stop and appreciate what you have done for yourself. Realize you have choices. You can either smoke the cigarette or do anything that will help you relax. Pass the test and then congratulate yourself on a job well done. And of course, remember, you created the situation to start with. Instead of asking God why he is tempting you, thank God that he helped manifest the experience you requested to test yourself! The circle is complete.

If you have read through this book, you know I have repeatedly stated that you create your world. It's not like you have a choice, and yet you do have a choice. Examine any situation today in your life. Each moment you are making a choice to move forward in your journey to learn; or to stay where you are. Make no mistake, taking action or not taking action is in fact a choice you make. What you generate through your actions — or lack thereof — is what the Universe delivers to you. If you choose inaction, the result you receive will continue to be inaction.

Have you every felt as if you were in limbo, waiting for something to change in your life? Take a closer look and most likely you have refused to take even one action in a new direction. There are times to wait patiently with expectation *after* you have implemented a process to succeed and taken the appropriate steps. However, expecting action to come from inaction is completely illogical. Expecting action from your declaration of inactivity you've projected to God is not possible.

You simply do not have a choice to create or to not create. Every thought, every idea, every word and every action produces your reality around you. Creating is the very essence of who we all are. You create your world automatically. If you understand the truth of this concept, you are well on your way to changing your world into one containing more abundance in all areas of your life.

Dr. Phil once said that life is like holding onto a rope. You either move up the rope or eventually you go down, but staying where you are only lasts for a short while.

It is time to move up the rope because there is nothing stopping you.

Now, it's all up to you.

CHAPTER 18

It's All Up to You

*"So often time it happens, we all live our life in chains,
and we never even know we have the key."*

-- The Eagles, "Already Gone"

Whatever happens to you in your life, it is all perfect. Everything that happens, everything you create and experience, whether it appears good or bad, provides you with the exact opportunity to learn about yourself with the potential to grow spiritually and emotionally.

When an event occurs we often immediately begin to wonder if the results of our actions would have been different had we chosen a different path. When viewed from a spiritual perspective, you were on course to learn a specific lesson at this point in time. If you didn't learn it on this path and from these choices, then another set of people, places and events would have materialized to create a similar experience. You will realize your choices do not matter with regard to the lessons you need to learn. You simply decide whether you learn from them now and move on, or get stuck in recreating them again and again and again.

There is one last magical approach which helps solidify your ability to obtain success. The best part is this method gives you power to put all this "creating" into motion, relax into it and have a lot of fun with it. Knowing this last step can provide you with greater self-esteem and appreciation for the power of all of us to create our realities.

Through this entire book I have explained how we create our worlds and attract people to us who can help us in some way through the experience they produce with us. We create the events and experiences shaping our lives. This whole process can become extremely intriguing and downright fun when we consider how the process is viewed from the other person's perspective.

In every situation in which you find yourself, I have asked you to step back and determine the possibilities of each experience. What could be the secret information being sent by this new person entering your life? What is the deep meaning behind this event you are experiencing? Why is this person in your life? The previous chapters are filled with approaches, ideas and tips on how to examine your world differently in order to better understand how you create the events in your life and draw people to you.

However, the whole process becomes even more mysterious and fascinating when you step back and discover why you became a part of the other person's life! What information are you providing them? What lesson are they learning from interacting with you? What is so important about you being in their life that you crossed paths? Out of six billion people in the world, consider how important you are to each person you meet that they required you, yes you, be part of their reality in order for them to experience exactly what they needed to learn to grow! Knowing your presence in someone else's life is no accident and you are there to help them can only give you a sense of greater self-confidence! Discover what message you bring to that person and you will also learn a great deal about yourself. Furthermore, applaud yourself for helping present an opportunity for someone near you to grow. And most of all, feel good about yourself for realizing you do make a difference in this world.

Have you ever been at a sporting event or airport and watched all of the hundreds and even thousands of people? Consider how there can be so many people in one place and you will never come in contact with 99.9% of them in your lifetime. Yet the hand-full in the stadium you do cross paths with have an amazing impact on your life. Some of the people you meet in your life may only appear for ten minutes, long enough to provide you with information. Some may wind up in your life for years.

When it came time for me to obtain assistance editing this book, I was unsure who to approach. Knowing I create my reality, I put the notion out into the Universe while I began learning more about the editing process. My wife, Michelle, had tried to not be overly involved in my writing process to prevent showing any bias in her evaluation. However, one day as I expressed to her my challenge, she had an intuition about a childhood friend with whom she periodically kept in contact. Michelle left the decision to me. Michelle had no knowledge of whether her friend Alma would agree to assist, but if felt right, especially since Alma was an English teacher!

Alma eagerly agreed and did a wonderful job editing. As we neared the end of the project Alma and I discussed the impact our experience had on each other. For me, I not only completed an important step in the book-writing process, but became a better writer in the process. Just as important, the process had a profound impact on Alma. She discovered she wanted to elevate her already unique writing and editing skills and this book provided the perfect venue. Further, although having proceeded down the path of spiritual and emotional enlightenment many years ago, Alma became more and more spiritually re-energized as she read each chapter. There is no doubt both of us will reap benefits — perhaps not even be aware of all the benefits — for years to come. Creating your reality can be a lot of fun!

Imagine the impact you are having on someone else's life. The beauty and wonderment of this is realizing how special you really are! You were drawn into someone else's world and reality to provide information to them. What a perfect arrangement, because the experience, no matter how one-sided it may appear, was designed for *both* of you. There are no accidents in life. As soon as I meet someone new or encounter a new situation I immediately begin asking myself "What am I bringing to this experience? What is it I bring to this equation?" With this thought process in mind, I remain in balance and enjoy solving the puzzle my Higher Self has helped create for me and for the other person(s) involved.

Remember earlier when I mentioned my work situation in which I was frustrated at work, knowing my boss was pushing me aside? Eventually I told God to fish or cut bait and I was laid off that day. This incident occurred many years ago when my wife and I were dating. She was also unemployed, having been laid off from a major corporation. We lived a half hour apart and I had a strong desire for us to live in the same part of town in which I was currently living, to give me an opportunity to remain in close proximity to my sons and parents.

Back then I was already clearly aware of how I created my reality and the impact of my choices, thoughts and beliefs. For a while, events appeared to dictate this was one time my reality was going to be other than I desired and visualized. Michelle accepted a job offer, but the company was located thirty two miles to the west of her home, which was already thirteen miles west of where I lived. If she moved east to my part of town she faced a forty five mile drive one way to work, equaling well over an hour commute each way. Obviously, this was not a viable option. Michelle's pay in this sales position — a new experience for her — was considerably lower than her previous job. She longed to work again for the same company that had laid her off eighteen months earlier.

Each day we discussed our options and considered our next steps. Michelle owned a nice home, large enough for both of us. While it seemed logical for me to move in with her, I was not excited about moving west, farther from my sons and aging parents. To further complicate things, I landed a job south of where I lived. Neither one of us was happy with the possibilities or options facing us. However, I stayed steadfast in my belief and determination this situation would turn out to our satisfaction. I visualized both of us living in a wonderful home in relatively close to my family and our jobs. I also believed in creating this experience. This was not just wishful thinking, as deep within me I believed this was our path. We did our "work" by searching each week in various neighborhoods for newly listed houses for sale. My intuition and dreams told me there were new events on the horizon we had not yet considered. I simply needed to be patient.

Michelle stayed in contact with her old employer, sending resumes, making phone calls to various companies and following leads. Two months after Michelle began her new job, she received a phone call from her former employer. She went in for an interview and received a job offer shortly afterward. Not only was the job better aligned with her talents and desires, but also the company paid more competitive wages than her current employer. Perhaps even more amazing was the fact that her office would be located six miles east of my home!

We found a wonderful house in the area and Michelle only had a fifteen minute drive to work! Since then, my family has become her extended family.

Because I trusted my intuition, I awoke each day with expectation and patience. Lastly, I continually examined my beliefs and actions to ensure they were in the highest good for me and my wife.

There are other items of note to the story and this is one: we are both animal lovers and we wanted to adopt puppies from a local shelter. I had looked into adoption several times before but worked too far from home to care for the puppies properly. With Michelle working so close, we were able to adopt two adorable puppies. She was able to come home at lunch time and check on them. In addition, living in close proximity to my sons, one of them was able to stop by during his college school day and check on the puppies. All this was possible because we had patience, did our work, laid our plans, and put our desires out to God and the Universe!

To this day, this is one of the most powerful stories I can provide explaining and demonstrating how we create our reality. I visualized my intended results, we focused on the process, taking the right actions to help fulfill our dream, and most of all I stayed confident, was patient and had faith all would work out to our satisfaction.

At first Michelle was slightly skeptical of the process. She knew we created our reality, but nothing this big had happened for her before. Once this wonderful event occurred, she understood the depth and magnitude of our choices and how we created the results, and, perhaps more importantly, what the results looked like. Today, she often tells the story before I can!

There is subscript to this story. I knew if I believed all I wrote here, I had to continue to "walk the walk". Although comfortable in my last job I desired a position with greater authority and input on company decisions and direction. I began to put that out to the Universe. I believed I had completed the necessary work (although the work and growth never ends!) and preparation in finance with my extensive experience to claim and expect a step upward in my career. Several months later some organization changes occurred creating an opportunity for me to leave on my own terms. I left with faith in my self-confidence and knowing I create my reality, in my highest good.

With that said I took the risk and became unemployed, though determined to find much more than a better paying job. I wanted to work for a company in which I personally had an interest, a company in which I would be part of the upper management team, and able to use my considerable business knowledge and experience to help move the company forward. I needed a talented and supportive boss who would recognize my depth of knowledge and offer me the chance to be creative and take on new responsibilities.

It is difficult to be unemployed for any duration. At times I know Michelle was concerned for our future, even though she was well employed. During this time I encouraged her to follow her dream to change jobs within the company. She had prepared for a change but then the process slowed and what she expected to happen in a few weeks stretched into several months.

Human nature provided us both with many opportunities to second-guess ourselves. Occasionally, when we wondered if we would need to sell our house if I did not land a job, I stood fast in my belief I had created and put forth all of the proper spiritual energy to succeed. I quickly pushed all doubt aside, confident that a unique job opportunity would appear. I had spent years "doing the necessary work" on my career and personal growth, plus had faith in our true nature to create our reality. Michelle and I spent time meditating daily, examining our beliefs and actions and encouraging each other to grow more spiritually, emotionally and mentally. Any feeling of "waiting" was our own impatience manifesting. I strongly encouraged her that we continue with our belief that we had done the proper work, believed in ourselves and expected new dramatic changes to come.

In the meantime, a company that had shown interest in me several months before, but then slowed its search, contacted me. Suddenly, the process started gaining momentum. Within three weeks I had three more interviews and was offered the job. The people, opportunity and even the pay were above my expectations. My wife also was given the green light on her transition into a new role, and without coincidence (there are no accidents); we started our new jobs the same day!

There was no accident to these results. I had stayed focused on my goal. One technique I used was to periodically hand write the full description of the job, company and responsibilities I required and desired. I often write out by hand my goals and update them periodically. This process helps me reinforce my beliefs and keeps me focused on my goal so as not to be distracted by other less promising opportunities.

My wife's dream has been to acquire land in the country, build our house and own horses. She had grown up on a large farm and rode horses daily. As I wrote down my goals regarding a company I would want to work for, I was originally looking for something near our home. At the same time I was aware the best places for us to find land available for purchase were approximately forty minutes from where we lived.

One month before I was offered the job, I again hand wrote my requirements. On this particular day as I wrote out the last sentence which described how far the new company would be from our home — my desire was five or six miles — my pen ran out of ink! I could not write out on paper that this new company would be within fifteen minutes of my current house. The company for which I would work was, in fact, thirty five minutes from our home, but closer to potential property where we could own horses!

My energy had already manifested the result, the job offer simply had not occurred yet. In the end, the pen ran out of ink because what I had manifested was not correct with what I was about to write. Once I received the job offer, I knew (again): it was me all along.

In the end, my wife and I knew we manifested a wonderful, positive experience, involving abundance, surrounded by positive thinking people, doing work matching our inner strengths and talents. We both came home each day wondrously stating how much we truly enjoyed our jobs. We did the work, examined our beliefs and modified them when it seemed appropriate while growing closer to God and who we wanted to be. We were willing to face our fears and push through with determination, perseverance and faith, prepared for and expected nothing but the greatest results in our highest good.

It can happen for you.
You happen it to yourself.
Look around you.
It happens every day.
What you see in your world is everything you believe.
The best part is you can change some or all of it.
Now, it's all up to you.
Because,
it is and will be you all along.
Because,
it was you, all along.

CPSIA information can be obtained at www.ICGtesting.com
Printed in the USA
BVOW070422051011

272866BV00002B/162/P